BOOKS of HOURS BOOKS of HOPE

Medieval Books of Hours and their Readers

HANNIBAL

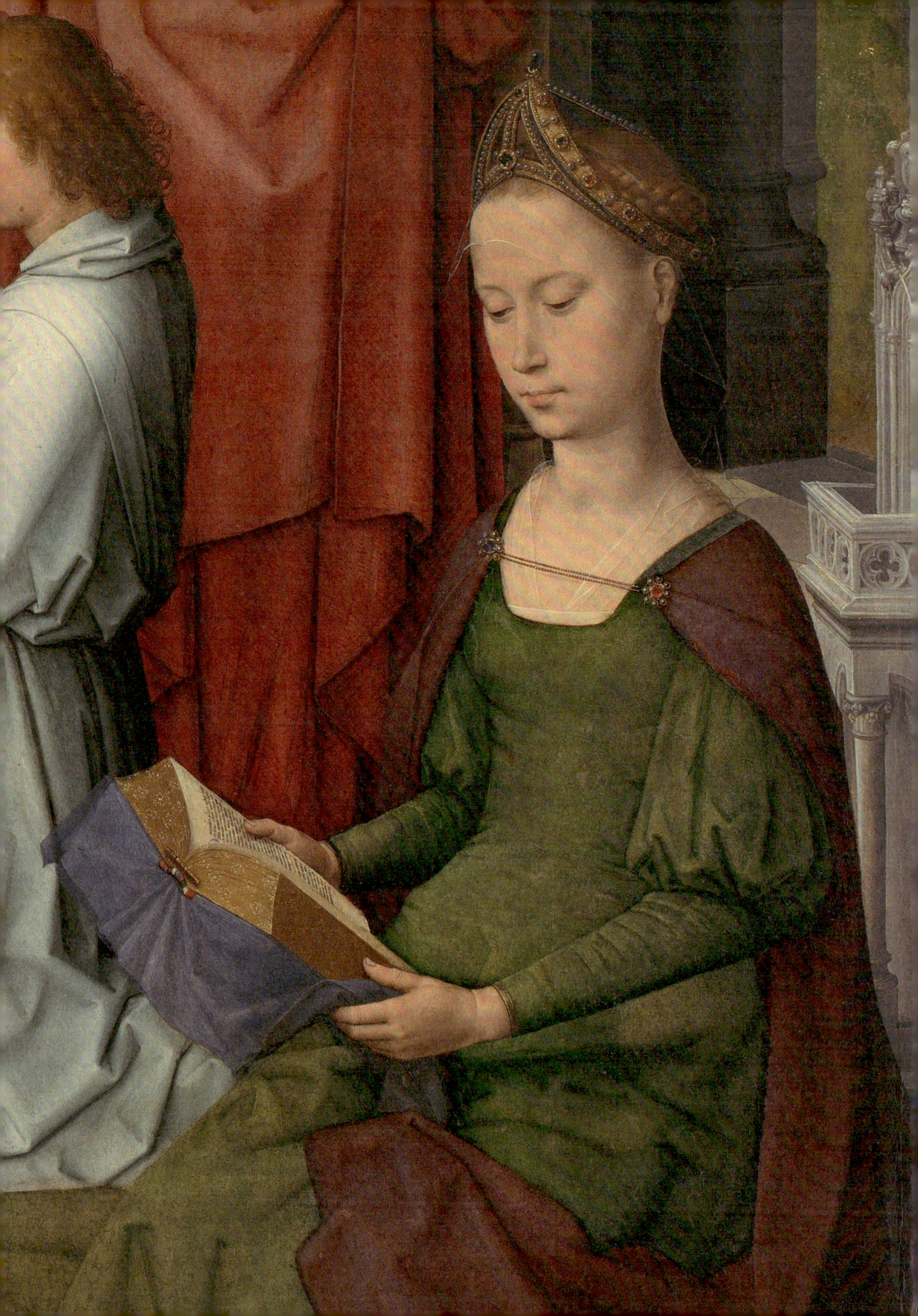

BOOKS *of* HOURS
BOOKS *of* HOPE

Medieval Books of Hours and their Readers

Edited by Evelien Hauwaerts,
with Emma De Nil & Caroline Van Cauwenberge

Preface

Dirk De fauw, Mayor of Bruges

Bruges is a city shaped by its readers. Books inspire, comfort and offer a sense of stability. They connect people across generations, passed down as treasured gifts to friends and family. The books we keep speak volumes about who we are, just as they always have. A flourishing reading culture is the hallmark of a vibrant society.

Books of Hours are a wonderful example of this: small, personal books, ranging from simple to luxurious, adorned with gold leaf and breathtaking miniatures. Moreover, they are the most thumbed-through treasures of the Middle Ages, cherished by their owners and valuable in every sense of the word. This publication will take you into the world of Books of Hours. Who read them? What themes were addressed? Why are they called that? And why do they keep appearing in Flemish portraits from the late Middle Ages? More than just spiritual guides, they were also a symbol of status and expressions of personal identity. Heritage will only come to life when we recognise the people and stories behind it.

The Public Library of Bruges is the city's foremost destination for book-lovers. It is also home to a renowned collection of medieval manuscripts, including treasures from the collections of the Jean van Caloen Foundation and the Flemish Government, attracting visitors from all over the world. In the world of illuminated books, the Public Library and Musea Brugge frequently cross paths. The collections complement each other beautifully, with the library's manuscripts regularly enriching Musea Brugge's exhibitions. With the support of a vast network of national and international experts, these manuscripts also play a prominent role in exhibitions, research and public engagement far beyond Bruges and Belgium. This publication is released in conjunction with the exhibition *Pride & Solace – Medieval Books of Hours and Their Readers* at the Groeningemuseum (4 April to 7 October 2025). The presentation designed by the team at the Public Library perfectly complements Musea Brugge's collections.

This elegantly designed publication celebrates medieval book culture and invites readers to reflect on the role of books in today's world. We extend our sincere thanks to all our partners for their dedication, and hope you find great pleasure in this book.

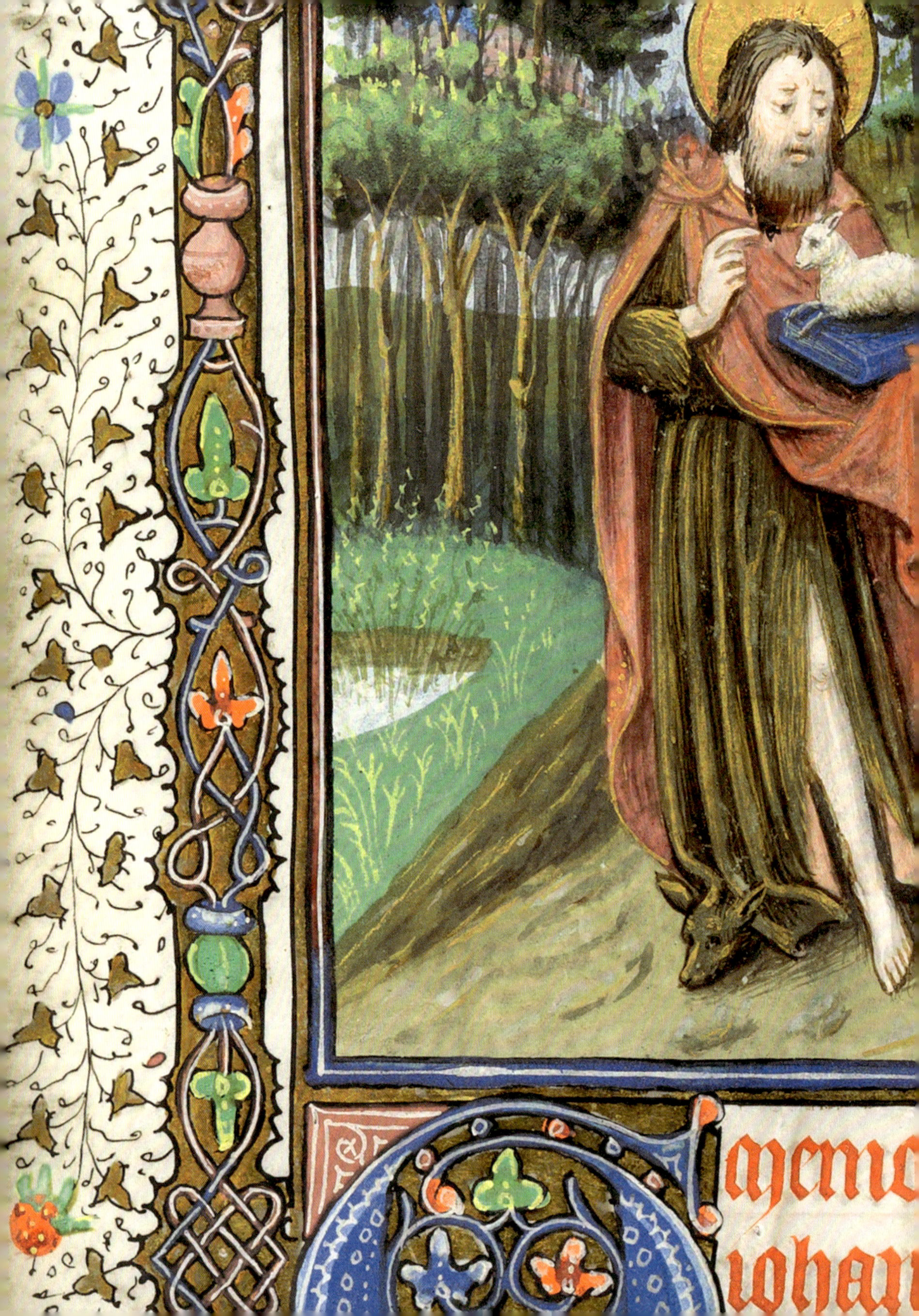

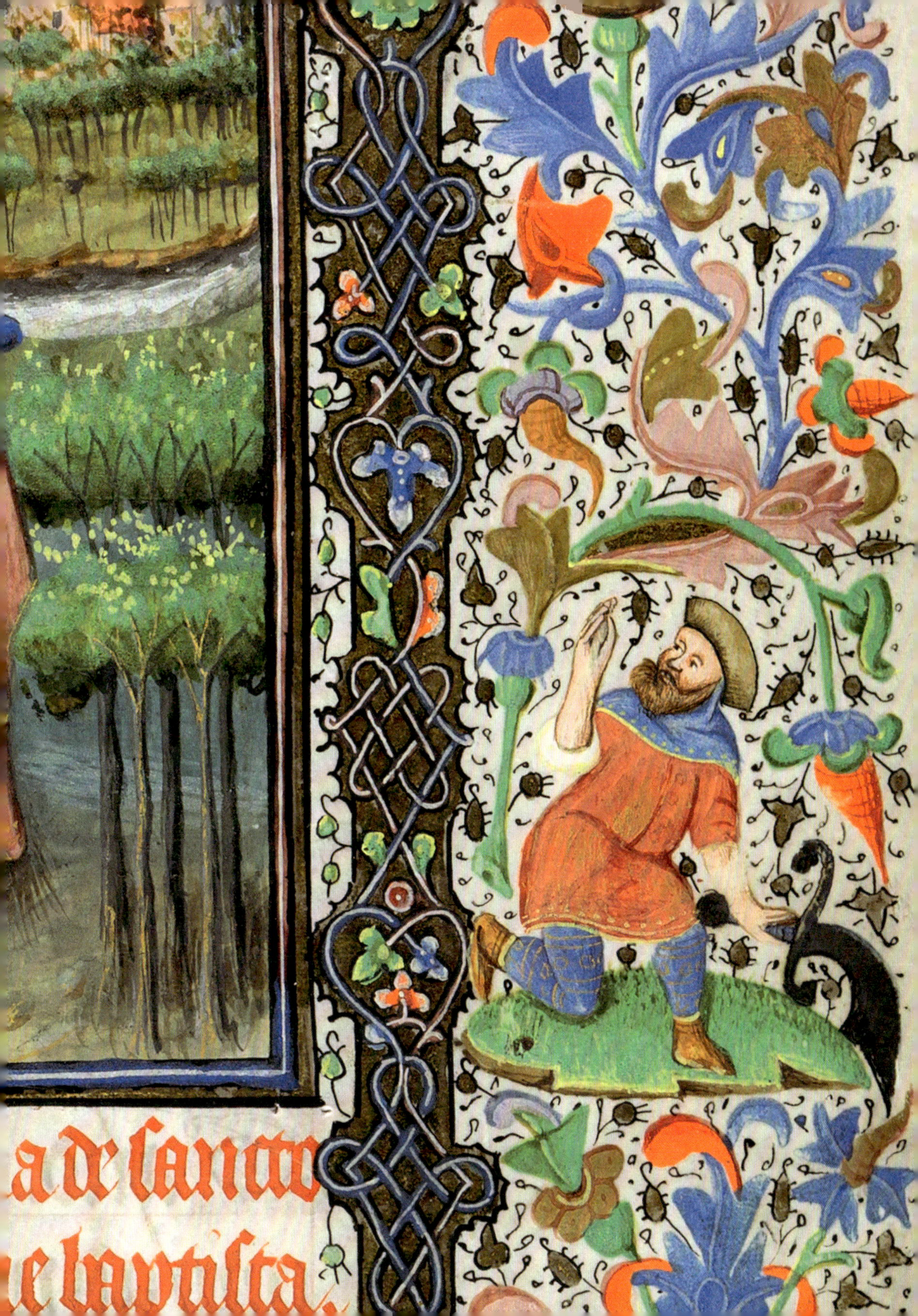
a de sancto
e baptista.

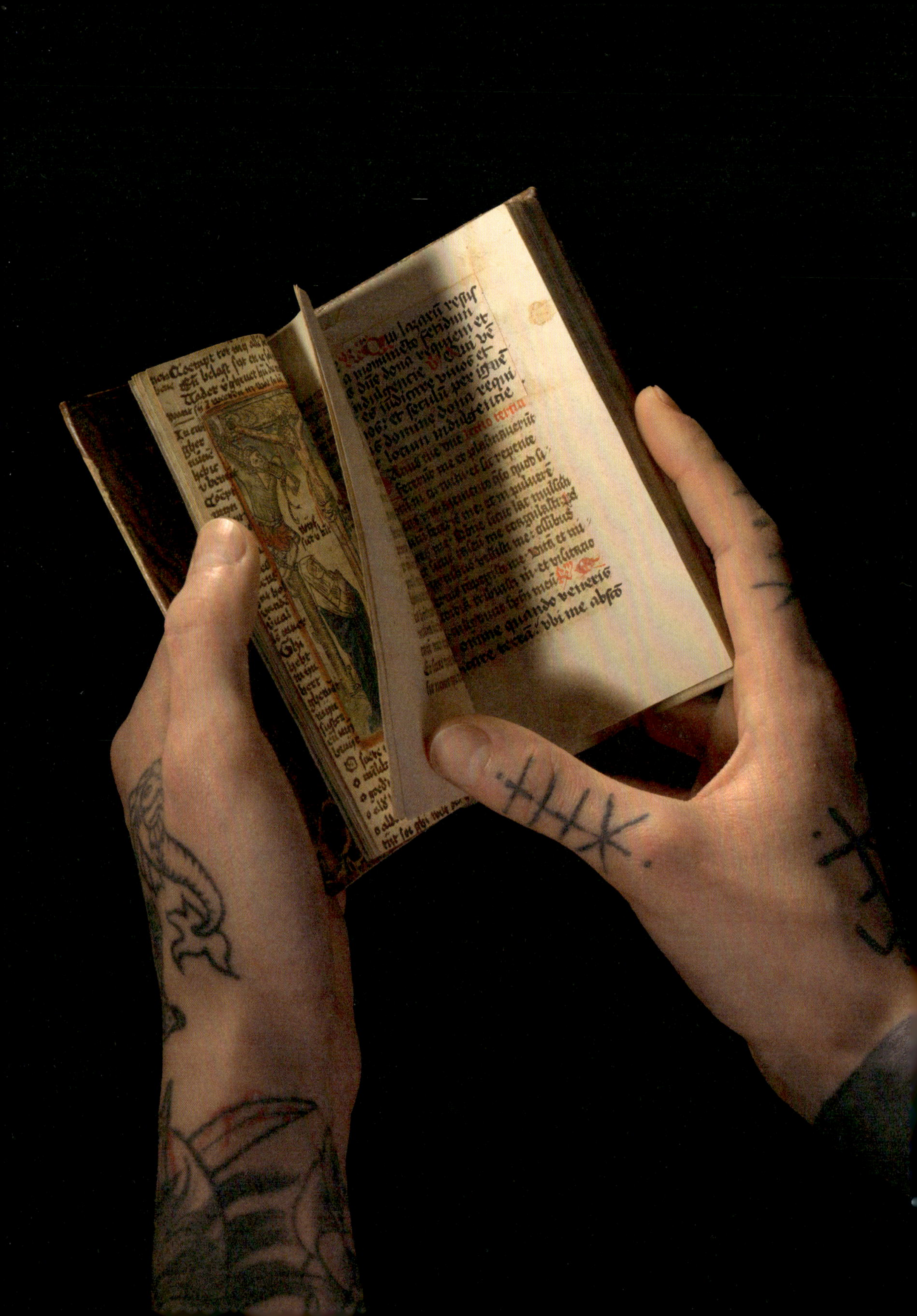

Introduction – IN THE HANDS OF THE READER

Evelien Hauwaerts

In an ideal world, medieval books would not be locked away in vaults or display cases. Of course, such precautions are essential today to protect them from theft and damage, but a book behind glass or stored in an acid-free box always feels somewhat sterile – the vital connection between book and reader is lost. A book belongs in a reader's hands. It truly comes to life when it becomes part of someone's personal story: a student shaping their future, a toddler discovering the magic of the alphabet, a holidaymaker losing themselves in a gripping murder mystery, or a believer seeking solace in God… Some books pass briefly through a person's life, whilst others serve as anchor points for generations.

fig. 1 Book of Hours, Southern Low Countries, late 15th century. Bruges, Public Library, Jean van Caloen Foundation Collection, Ms. 18, ff. 7v–8r.

This is especially true of medieval Books of Hours. These manuals of lay devotion were intensely used, cherished, adapted and handed down through the generations. No other book was as widespread or had such a profound influence in the Middle Ages. A Book of Hours was a companion, a talisman, a textbook, a time machine, and – for those who could afford a sumptuous copy – a source of aesthetic pleasure and pride. Many of the most opulent copies have survived and remain highly popular with collectors and historians today, usually for their artistic value or association with famous owners. The exquisite miniatures of *Les Très Riches Heures du duc de Berry*, for instance, are world-renowned.

This publication places the relationship between the Book of Hours and its users at the heart of the discussion, by focusing on content, meaning and use. Chapter 1 provides a concise overview of their textual components along with practical tips for identifying them. Chapters 2, 3 and 4 examine the people who produced, traded and used Books of Hours – with particular attention paid to the role of women as both creators and readers – and the spread of literacy beyond aristocratic and clerical circles. Chapters 5 and 6 delve into late-medieval mentalities. Chapter 5 explores why patrons chose to have themselves immortalised with their Book of Hours (by artists such as Hans Memling and Jan van Eyck), while Chapter 6 explains why late-medieval readers saw no contradiction in the presence of obscene and comic imagery in the margins of sacred texts. Finally, Chapters 7 and 8 look at the prac-

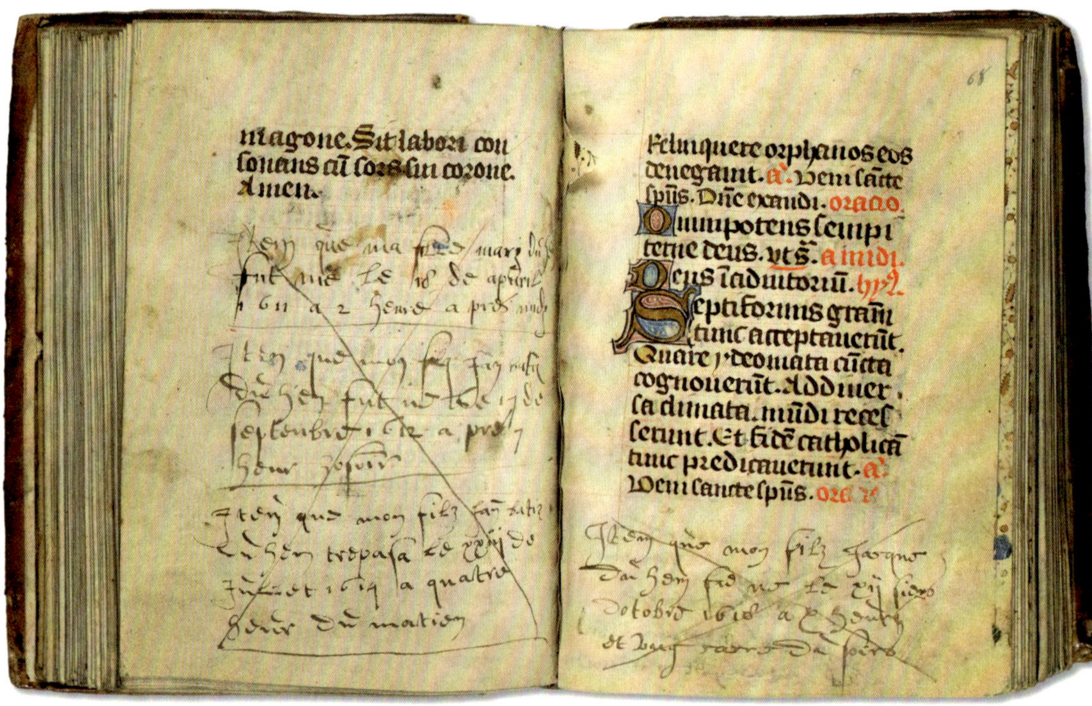

fig. 2 'My son Jean Baptiste du Hem was born on 17 Sept. 1612 … My son Jean Baptiste du Hem died on 23 July 1619',◆ alongside other dates, in Book of Hours, Troyes (?), c.1450–c.1501. Bruges, Public Library, Ms. 330, ff. 67v–68r.

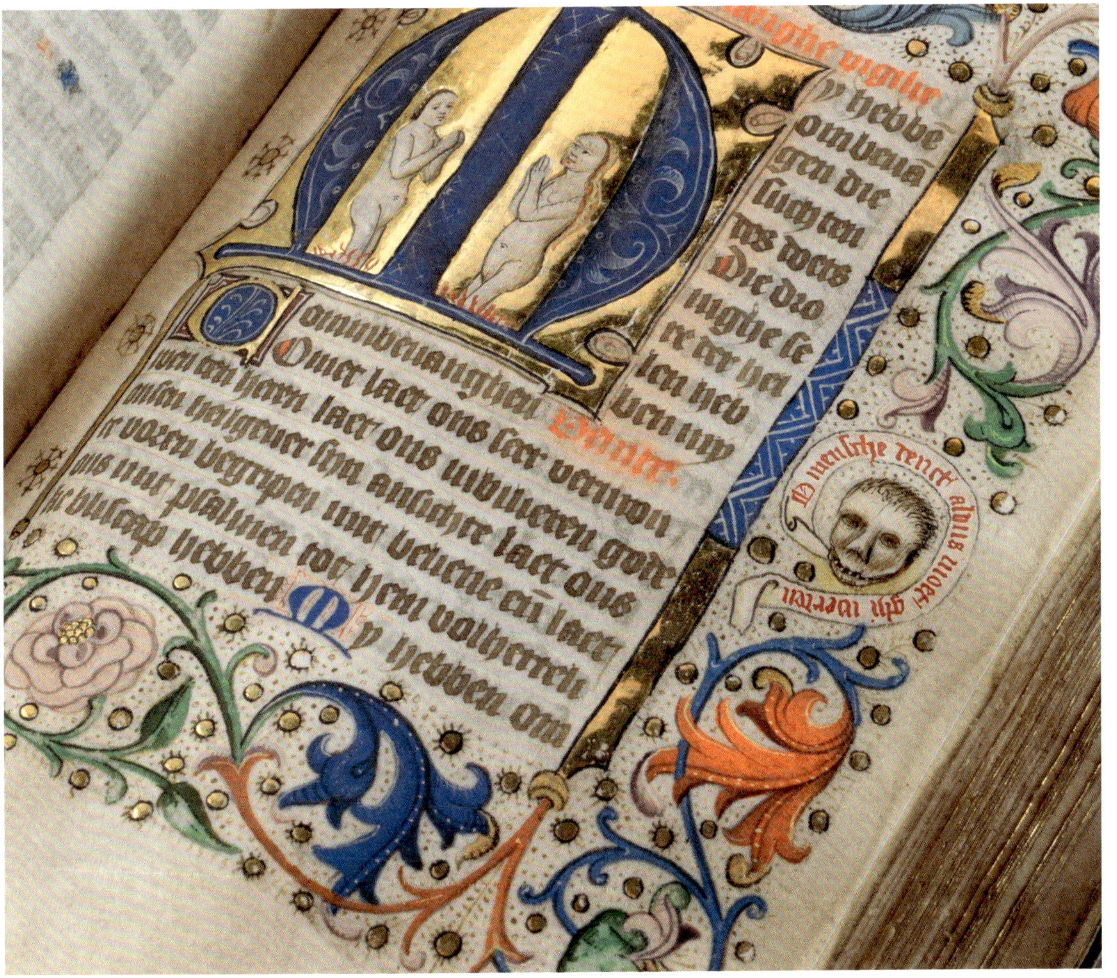

fig. 3 Office of the Dead with a depiction of a *Memento mori* skull and souls in purgatory: death is an important theme in Books of Hours. In Book of Hours (transl. Geert Grote), Zwolle, c.1465–c.1485. Bruges, Public Library, Ms. 673, f. 141r.

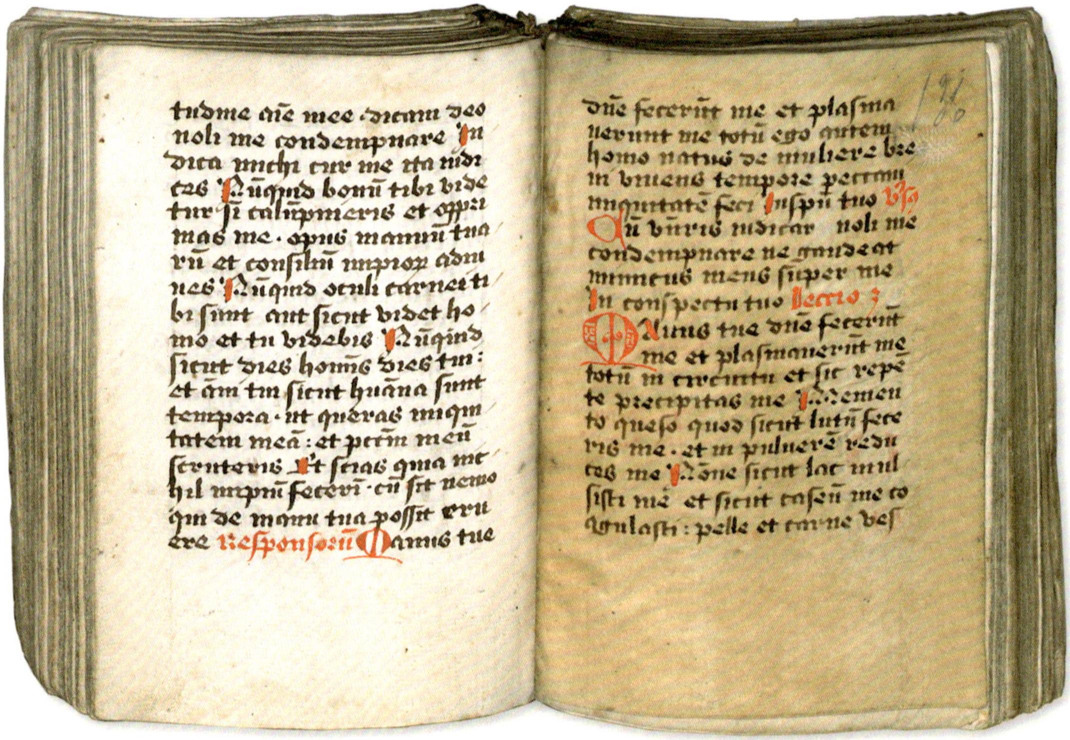

fig. 4 Left folio made of paper, right folio made of parchment, in Book of Hours, Limburg (Maaseik?), c.1510. Bruges, Public Library, Ms. 568, ff. 135v–136r.

tical tools that facilitated reading, such as spectacles and artificial lighting.

In this publication, we deliberately focus on modest and well-worn copies – books that served their owners faithfully for generations. Take, for example, Manuscript 330 (figs 2 and 40) from the Public Library of Bruges. This Book of Hours has never been selected for exhibition. It is worn to the core, covered in dried candle wax drips, fingerprints, smudges and stains. In the margins, four successive generations of owners have scribbled notes, some of which were later crossed out. This is not the type of Book of Hours a curator would typically showcase in a prestigious exhibition. And yet…

It is precisely this kind of book that reveals so much about medieval people – and in which we, as modern readers, can recognise ourselves. The notes in Manuscript 330, for instance, record the birth and death dates of family members as written by a grandfather, father and son (all named Philip du Hem), as well as by daughter-in-law Dorothea. Only three of the ten children recorded in this book survived infancy. When one reads that Dorothea had to record the death of her daughter Marie only eleven days after her birth, one cannot help but feel a profound sense of human connection across time and space. Or consider a prayer added to the back of Manuscript 328 in the Public Library, in which Saint Fiacre is implored for protection against tumours and cancers 'which doctors cannot cure'.[1] This added prayer not only reminds us that people in the Middle Ages also feared the spectre of cancer but also underscores how medicine was an integral part of their worldview. Through such notes and texts, we are repeatedly confronted with the universal themes that have preoccupied humankind for centuries: death, love, suffering and hope.

The more modest examples not only reveal insights about their users but also offer clues about their makers. Manuscript 568 (fig. 4) is a perfect example. It is a simple manuscript, with hastily executed script and minimal decoration. The text is written on paper, a more affordable alternative to parchment – clearly a book intended for buyers on a budget. The inner and outer leaves of each gathering, however, are made of parchment, albeit of very low quality. This clever use of a more durable material reinforced the book's structure without significantly increasing production costs. The maker was clearly aware that Books of Hours were used intensively and needed to be robust enough to withstand frequent handling.

The illustrations in this publication are largely drawn from Bruges collections, particularly those of the Public Library and Musea Brugge. Of the six hundred or so medieval books in the Public Library, around a tenth are Books of Hours, including significant holdings from the collections of the Jean van Caloen Foundation, the Flemish Community and the King Baudouin Foundation. Since the Bruges collection holds far more sumptuous Books of Hours than modest ones, we have, 'by necessity,' included illustrations of dazzling, richly illuminated examples in this publication. Fortunately, even these, in all their pristine beauty and splendour, can tell us a great deal about meaning and use. We even have a first-hand opinion from the medieval author Eustache Deschamps (1346–1406) who, in his satirical *Le miroir de mariage*, puts the following words into the mouth of a vain lady: 'I need a Book of Hours of Our Lady, as befits a woman of noble lineage: a work of fine craftsmanship, adorned with gold and azure, precious and elegant, carefully arranged and beautifully decorated, covered in the finest golden cloth. And when it is opened, two golden clasps shall hold it fast, so that all who see it may say and proclaim that

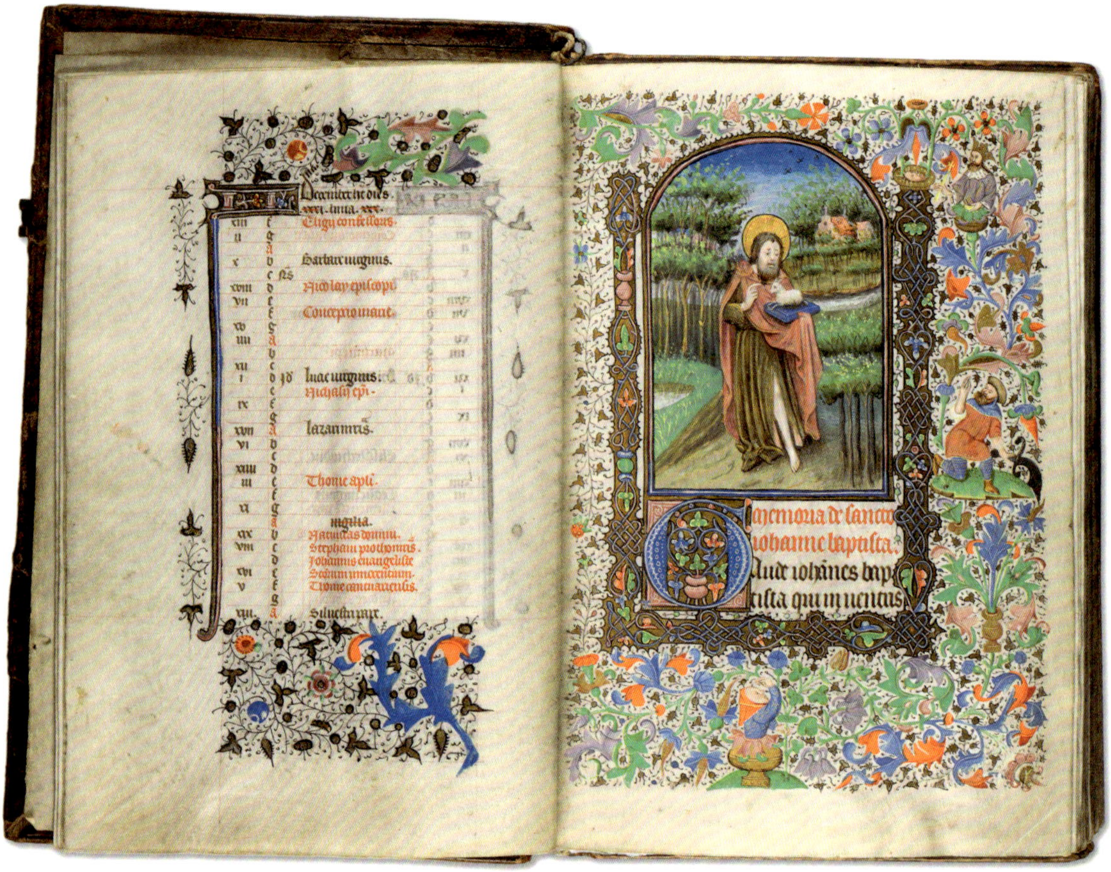

fig. 5 Pure elegance and luxury, in Book of Hours, Master(s) of the Gold Scrolls, Bruges, c.1440–c.1450. Bruges, Public Library, OCMW O.L.V. ter Potterie Collection, Ms. 5, ff. 6v–7r.

no finer Book of Hours can be found.'[2] For the influencers of the fifteenth century, a Book of Hours was not only a path to salvation but also a means of flaunting their wealth.

With this publication, we aim to paint a nuanced picture of the children, men and women who created, bought, read and cherished Books of Hours. The relationship between people and books is not just a matter of historical facts, but also of sensory experiences, stories and meaning. To bring this phenomenological connection to life, the epilogue takes us inside the mind of a monk and medievalist. He shares his experiences of daily prayer and the meaning he finds in texts once read by our ancestors. Through contemporary photography, we evoke the tactile experience and return the books to where they truly belong: in the hands of the reader.

1. Bruges, Public Library, Ms. 328, f. 107r: *'dont medecin ne peult guerir'*. Book of Hours, Northern France, 15th and 16th century.

2. *'Heures me fault de Nostre Dame / Si comme il appartient a fame / Venue de noble paraige / Qui soient de soutil ouvraige / D'or et d'azur, riches et cointes / Bien ordonnees et bien pointes / De fin drap d'or tresbien couvertes / Et quant elle seront ouvertes / Deux fermaulx d'or qui fermeront / Qu'adonques ceuls qui les verront / Puissent partout dire et compter / Qu'on ne puet plus belles porter.'* Dufournaud-Engel, *Le miroir de mariage d'Eustache Deschamps*. PhD dissertation, McGill University, Montréal, 1975, 43. Translation into English by the author.

◆ *'Item que mon filz Jan Batiz du Hem fut né le 17 de septembre 1612 (...) Item que mon filz Jan Batiz du Hem trépasa le 23 de juillet 1619'.*

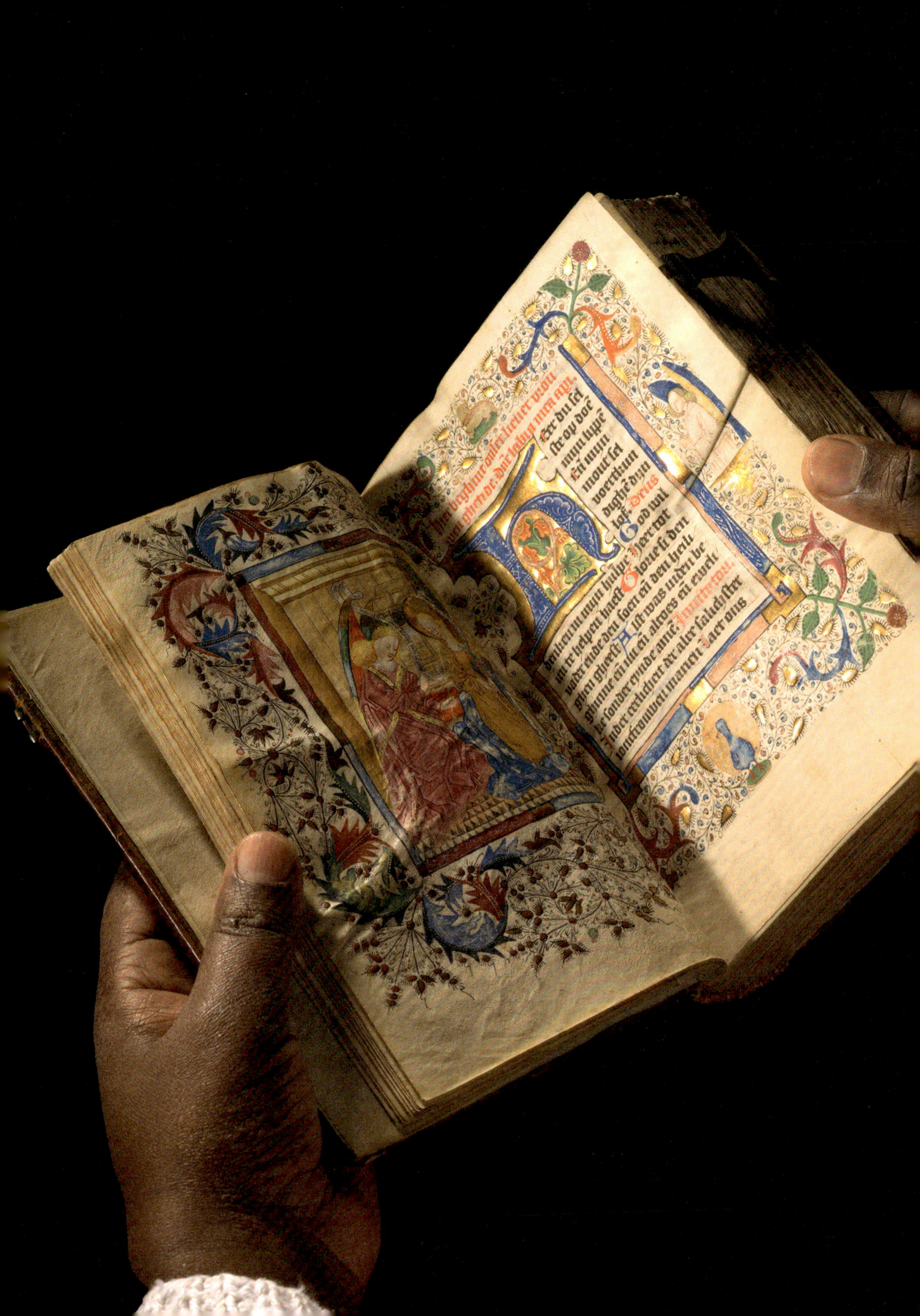

1. BOOKS OF HOURS: ORIGINS, USAGE, CONTENTS

In a Nutshell

A Book of Hours is a devotional manual designed for personal prayer, containing Offices (also called Hours) and other religious texts. Each Office is centred around a specific theme, such as the Virgin Mary or death, and consists of a carefully arranged selection of Psalms, hymns, biblical readings and prayers. These Offices are a simplified version of the Divine Office, adapted for laypeople, which monks, nuns and canons recited daily. The term 'Hours' refers to specific times of the day designated for prayer, following the daily structure of monastic devotion.

Evelien Hauwaerts

fig. 6 Book of Hours (transl. Geert Grote), Master of the Haarlem Bible (?), c.1460–c.1480. Bruges, Public Library, Ms. 674, ff. 13v–14r.

Origins

In monasteries and chapters, life was (and still is) structured around the Divine Office. This intricate liturgical programme involved a repertoire of texts and chants that changed daily. Knowing what to do at any given time required an array of books, including a breviary, a lectionary, an antiphonary and a homiliary.

The Divine Office was recited and sung at eight fixed times throughout the day, known as the canonical hours: Matins or Vigils at midnight, Lauds around 3 a.m., Prime around 6 a.m., Terce around 9 a.m., Sext at noon, None around 3 p.m., Vespers around 6 p.m. or at sunset, and Compline around 9 p.m. or before bedtime.

From the twelfth century onwards, additional prayers, hymns and shorter offices – such as the Little Hours of the Virgin, the Penitential Psalms and the Office of the Dead – were added to the regular Divine Office. This simplified form of liturgy laid the foundation for the later Books of Hours, designed for laypeople.

In the thirteenth century, spurred in part by the influence of the Dominicans and Franciscans, a broader religious interest developed among the laity. For this audience, books were compiled that included Psalms and the simplified Hours. Central to these volumes were the Hours and prayers dedicated to the Virgin Mary, revered as the primary intercessor between God and humankind. By the fifteenth century, the Book of Hours had become an exceptionally popular genre, often regarded as the 'bestseller' of the Middle Ages.[1]

When?

Prayer times for laypeople were considerably more flexible than those for monks and nuns: the nocturnal Matins and Lauds, for instance, were usually combined and recited at the break of dawn. To determine the approximate time, people in the late Middle Ages relied on the chimes of the bells in the towers of belfries, churches and monasteries, as well as the melodies of town trumpeters.[2]

The duration of each canonical hour varied. Morning and evening sessions lasted the longest: for example, praying Matins and Lauds of the Hours of the Virgin together took approximately thirty minutes, while Vespers and Compline in the evening were completed in around ten minutes each. The shorter daytime prayers, from Prime to None, were considerably shorter, requiring only about five minutes each, and could easily be fitted around other daily activities.[3]

Where?

Books of Hours were likely kept at home alongside other valuables, books or devotional objects (fig. 7). Those who could afford it could store and transport their Book of Hours in a small wooden box, along with other treasured items such as relics, rosaries and jewellery (fig. 8).[4]

There is little evidence indicating where Books of Hours were used within the home. It probably depended on personal circumstances. Wealthy families had their own chapel or separate rooms to choose from, while others may have chosen the cleanest, quietest space available. Sometimes, prayers explicitly instruct where the text should be recited, such as in bed upon waking.

Books of Hours were compact and portable, making them convenient to use in various locations. Laypeople carried them outside the home, especially to church, where they could pray at their own pace (before a crucifix or painting, for example), read specific prayers during quiet moments in the Mass (such as after the Eucharist), or follow special services such as the Mass of the Virgin or the Office of the Dead at funerals. Some prayers were even intended for outdoor recitation, such as in a cemetery.[5]

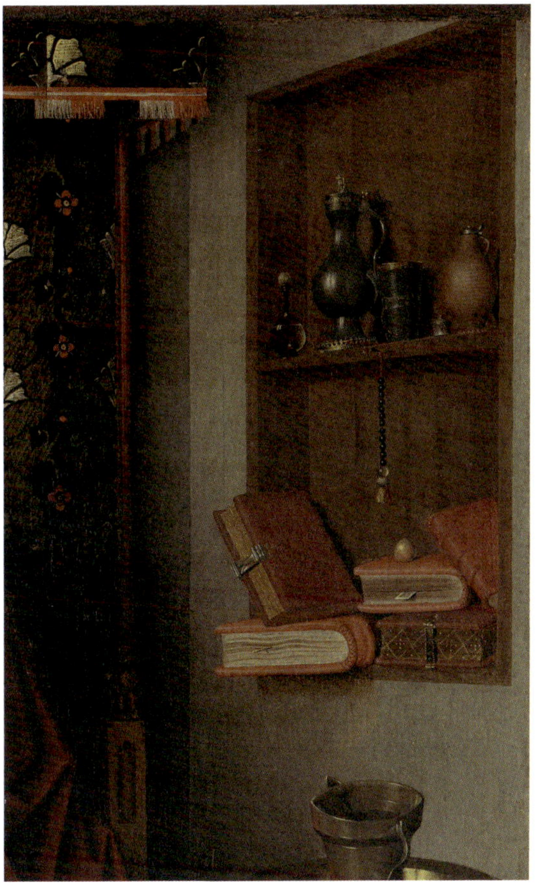

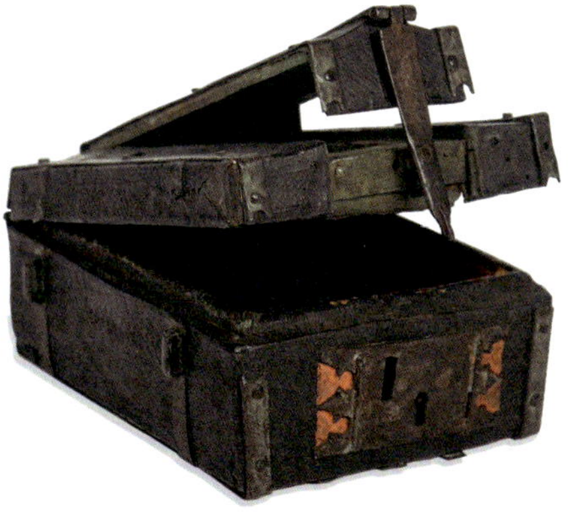

fig. 7 Interior with bookshelf. Follower of Jan van Eyck, *Virgin and Child* (detail), c.1450, oil on panel. Bruges, Musea Brugge, 2019.GRO0002.I.

fig. 8 Box for valuables, 15th century, iron, wood, leather, parchment, 9.3 x 15 x 18.5 cm. Loppem, Jean van Caloen Foundation, inv. 00195.

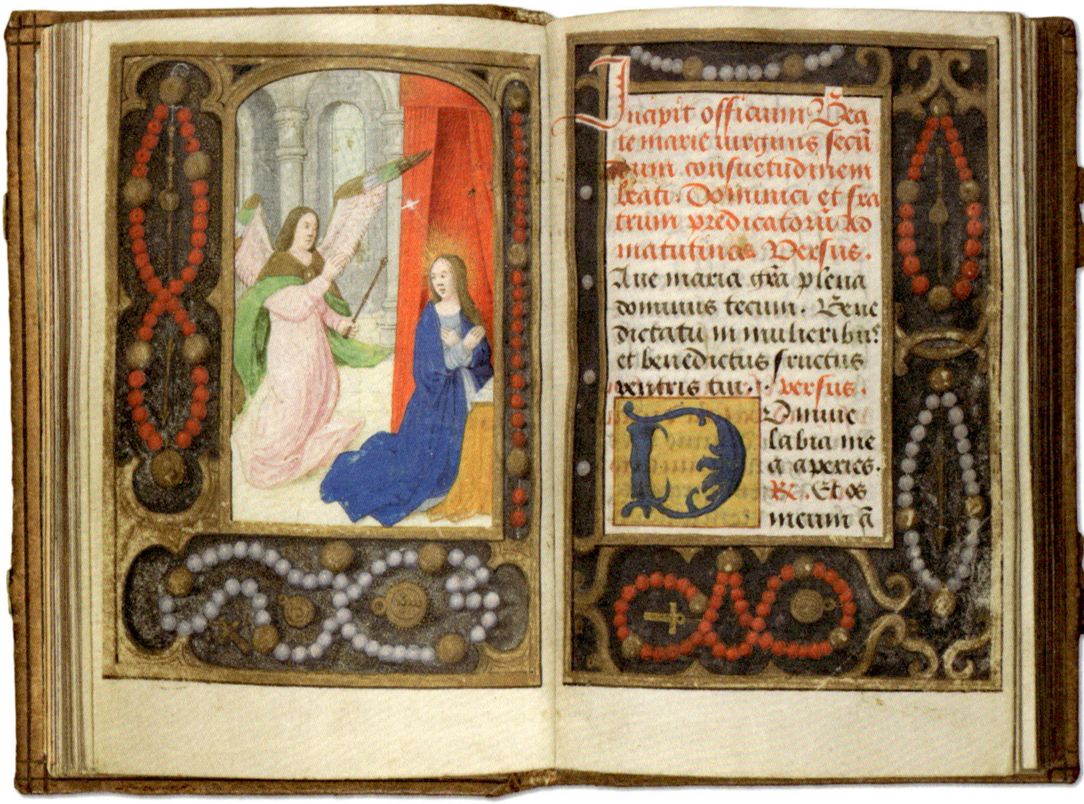

fig. 9 Trompe-l'oeil prayer beads in the margins, Book of Hours, Bruges, c.1500. Bruges, Public Library, Ms. 675, ff. 25v–26r.

How?

Some prayers contain specific instructions for the supplicant, directing them, for instance, to kneel (sometimes on bare knees), stand, sit, fold their hands, light a candle, or stand before a crucifix.[6] A Book of Hours was often used alongside other devotional objects, such as rosaries (see, for example, figs 9 and 82), miniatures or prints on the wall, stained-glass windows (see, for example, fig. 60), painted tiles, relics, inexpensive devotional figurines made of pipe clay or pewter (for example, fig. 10), ivory home altars (fig. 11) and paintings.

Even when read individually, a Book of Hours was deeply embedded in broader religious practices – at home, in the city, in church and within associations – fuelled by the growing lay piety of the late Middle Ages.[7] Outside the home, the Hours were often recited communally. Guilds and confraternities, for example, sometimes required members to read the Office of the Dead at a fellow member's funeral,[8] while from the late Middle Ages onwards, churches increasingly provided opportunities to experience collective recitations of the Marian Hours and other additional liturgies.[9] Even within the household a Book of Hours could be shared in group settings. Parents, for instance, used it to teach their children how to read, pray and commemorate the dead.[10]

Even in private, whether recited aloud or in silence, a Book of Hours evoked a world of collective oral performance and musicality. The dialogic structure of antiphons and responses, with its accompanying layout of rubric headings and varying font sizes, mirrors the liturgical practice of the choir responding to the verses of the soloist. Similarly, hymns, Psalms and litanies also echoed collective performances in abbeys and churches.[11] In this way, the Book of Hours connected private life to the world of the Church.[12] Through prayers for the deceased and the act of recording their own names to ensure future prayers on their behalf, readers connected with families and religious communities across generations – past, present and future.

Decoration

As with other medieval books, miniatures – and from the late fifteenth century, also woodcuts or engravings – in Books of Hours serve both decorative and structuring purposes.[13] In Books of Hours, however, the miniatures do not serve a narrative function, but primarily a devotional one. In fact, they are often entirely unrelated to the text.

Before reading, the supplicant could contemplate the image to prepare their heart and mind for prayer. The miniatures could also be used independently for meditation, separate from the texts: a depiction of the Crucifixion (fig. 12), for example, helped readers immerse themselves empathetically in the suffering and sacrifice of Christ and Mary.[14] Images could also enhance the impact of certain texts, as indicated by this instruction above a prayer: 'Pope Alexander VI grants a 10,000-year indulgence to anyone who reads this Ave Maria before an image of St Anne' (fig. 47).[15]

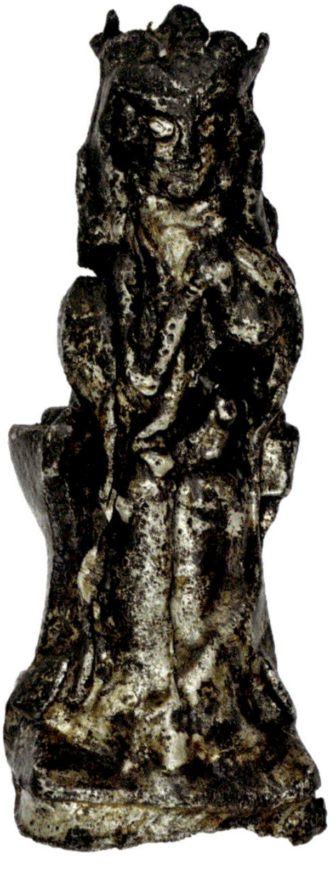

fig. 10 Virgin and Child enthroned, an inexpensive 'pocket saint' to carry or place in the home, Bruges (?), 14th century, pewter, 6 x 2.3 x 1.9 cm. Bruges, Raakvlak, col Beuck/1/1/A/345.

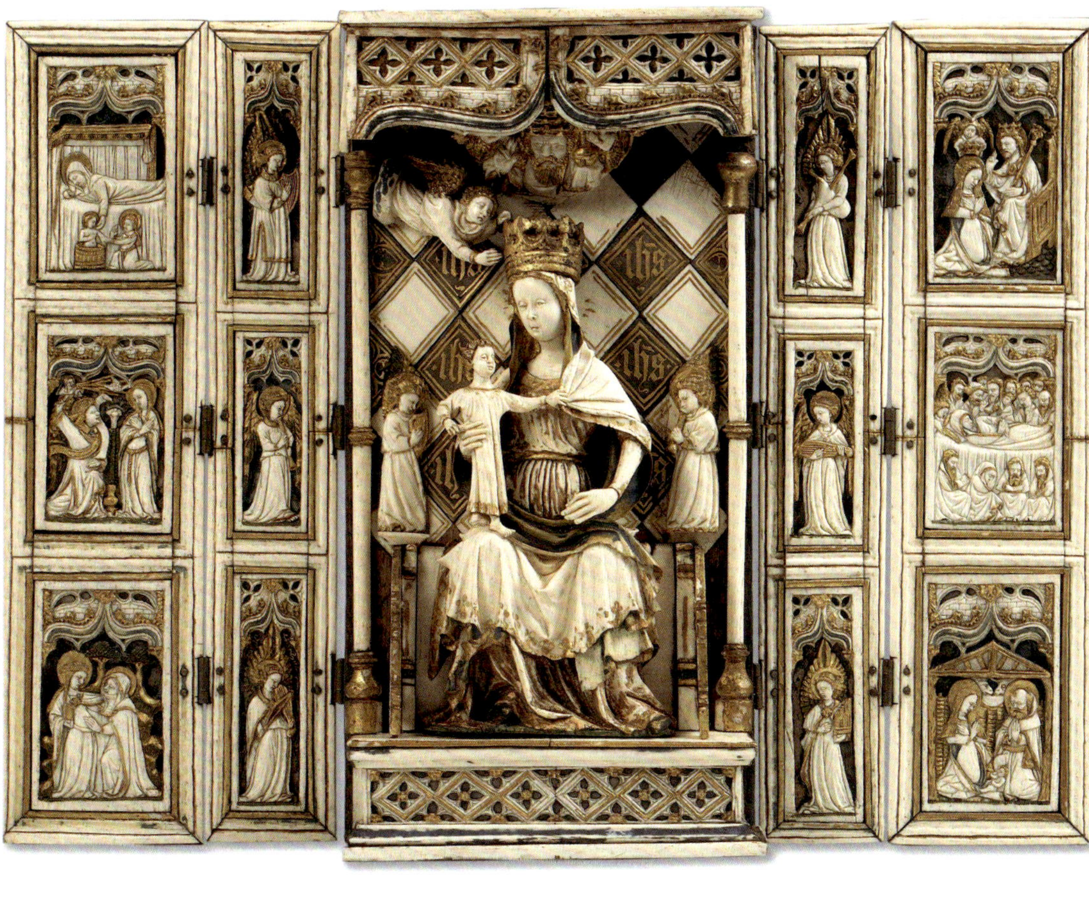

fig. 11 Portable polyptych with scenes from the life of the Virgin, Flanders (?), 1426–1499, ivory, 27.5 x 36 cm. Bruges, Musea Brugge, O.SJ0221.VIII.

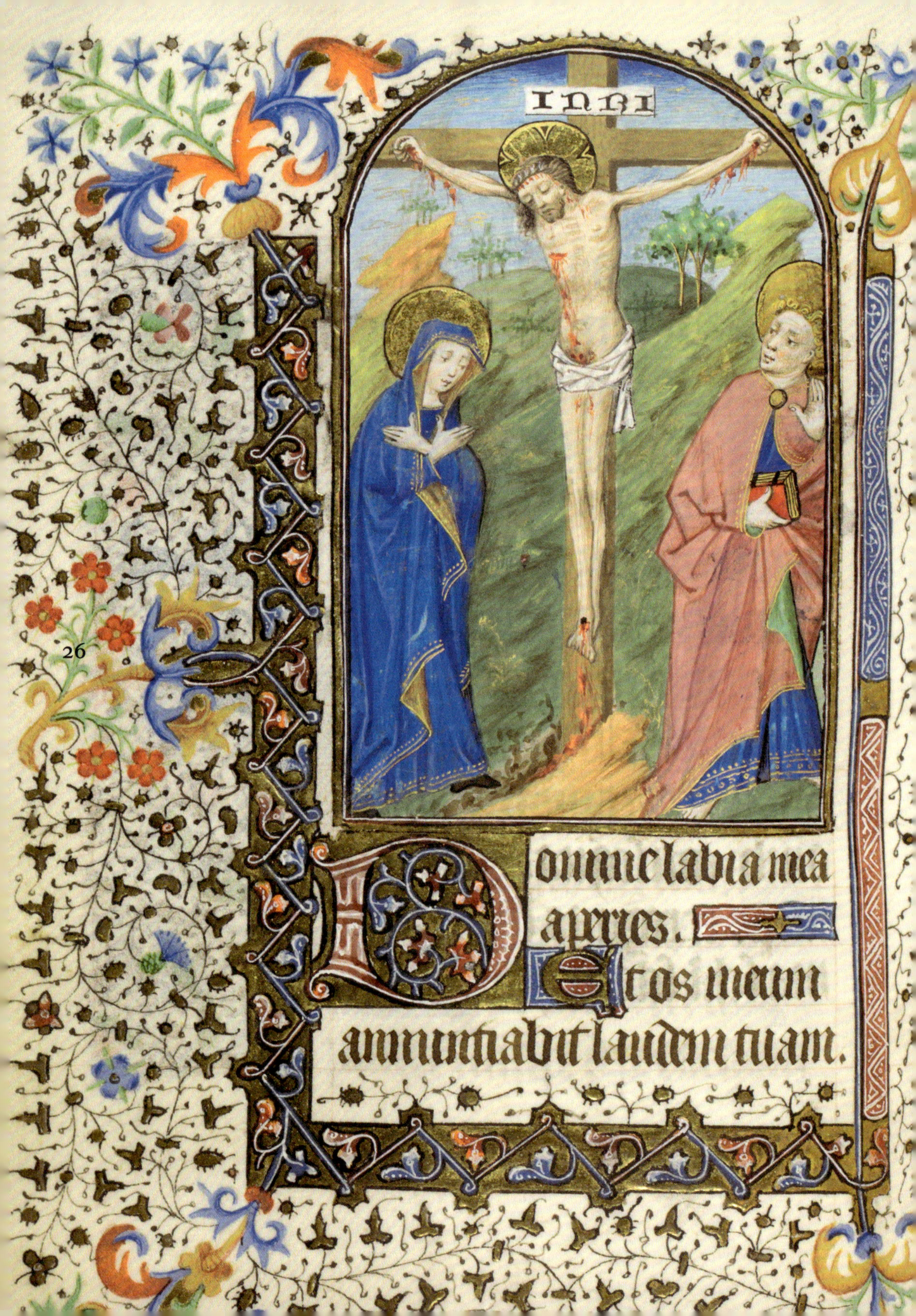
INRI
Domine labia mea
aperies.
Et os meum
annunciabit laudem tuam.

Main Texts

The content of Books of Hours can vary widely. The Hours of the Virgin, Penitential Psalms and the Office of the Dead usually form the core and are often supplemented by additional texts. Titles such as '*Incipiunt hore de sancta cruce*' can help identify a specific text component, though these are sometimes missing. Below is a basic description of the core texts, highlighting key points of recognition, such as the opening words (the incipit) and the most common themes in the miniatures or historiated initials.[16]

1. Liturgical Calendar

A Book of Hours typically opens with a calendar listing important ecclesiastical feast days honouring events from the Gospels (such as the Assumption of Mary) and saints' feast days. The days of the month are represented using kalends, nones and ides, a system derived from the ancient Roman calendar. The calendar is perpetual. Next to each day are the so-called golden number and the dominical letter, which are used to determine on which dates Easter and Sundays fall (e.g. figs 32 and 37).[17]

Miniatures: Activities typical of the month, such as grape harvesting in September, or zodiac signs (fig. 65).

fig. 12 *Crucifixion* at the beginning of the Hours of the Cross, in Book of Hours, Master of the Bedford Hours, Paris, c.1435. Bruges, Public Library, Jean van Caloen Foundation Collection, Ms. 12, f. 99v.

2. Gospels

From the fifteenth century onwards, Books of Hours often included four short passages from the Gospels. Together, these passages summarise the core of the Christian faith: John 1:1–14 (*In principio erat verbum*) on the mission of Christ; Luke 1:26–38 (*Missus est angelus Gabriel*) on the annunciation and the incarnation of Christ; Matthew 2:1–12 (*Cum ergo natus esset Jesus*) on the birth of Christ and the arrival of the Magi; and Mark 16:14–20 (*Recumbentibus illis undecim apparuit*), in which Christ sends forth his apostles and promises them power over demons, poison and disease. Sometimes the Passion narrative from John (18:1–19:42) was also included.

Miniatures: Portraits of the Evangelists or scenes from their lives. For the Passion: Christ as Man of Sorrows.

3. Hours of the Virgin

The Hours of the Virgin form the heart of most Books of Hours. They exist in both a short and a long version. Books of Hours, particularly the Hours of the Virgin, were especially popular among female readers.[18] This is evident in a prayer to Mary at the end of Matins: 'Pray for the people, advocate for the clergy, intercede for all women.'[19]

The texts consist of Psalms, hymns, prayers and Bible readings, interwoven with recurring interjections such as antiphons, versicles and responses. The canonical hours are typically indicated by a short title, such as '*ad laudes*'.

Incipit: As with all significant Hours, the Hours of the Virgin begin at Matins with a standard opening, from *Domine labia mea aperies* (Ps. 50:17, O Lord, open my lips) to the prayer *Gloria Patri* (Glory be to the Father). This is followed by the Hail Mary: *Ave Maria, gratia plena: Dominus tecum* (Hail Mary, full of grace, the Lord is with thee) and Psalm 94, *Venite exultemus Domino* (Come, let us rejoice in the Lord).

Miniatures: Scenes from the life of Mary (mainly: Annunciation, Visitation, Birth of Christ, Annunciation to the Shepherds, Adoration of the Magi, Presentation in the Temple, Massacre of the Innocents, Flight into Egypt); or scenes from the Passion (mainly: Agony in the Garden, Betrayal and Arrest, Christ before Pilate, Flagellation, Bearing of the Cross, Crucifixion, Deposition, Entombment).

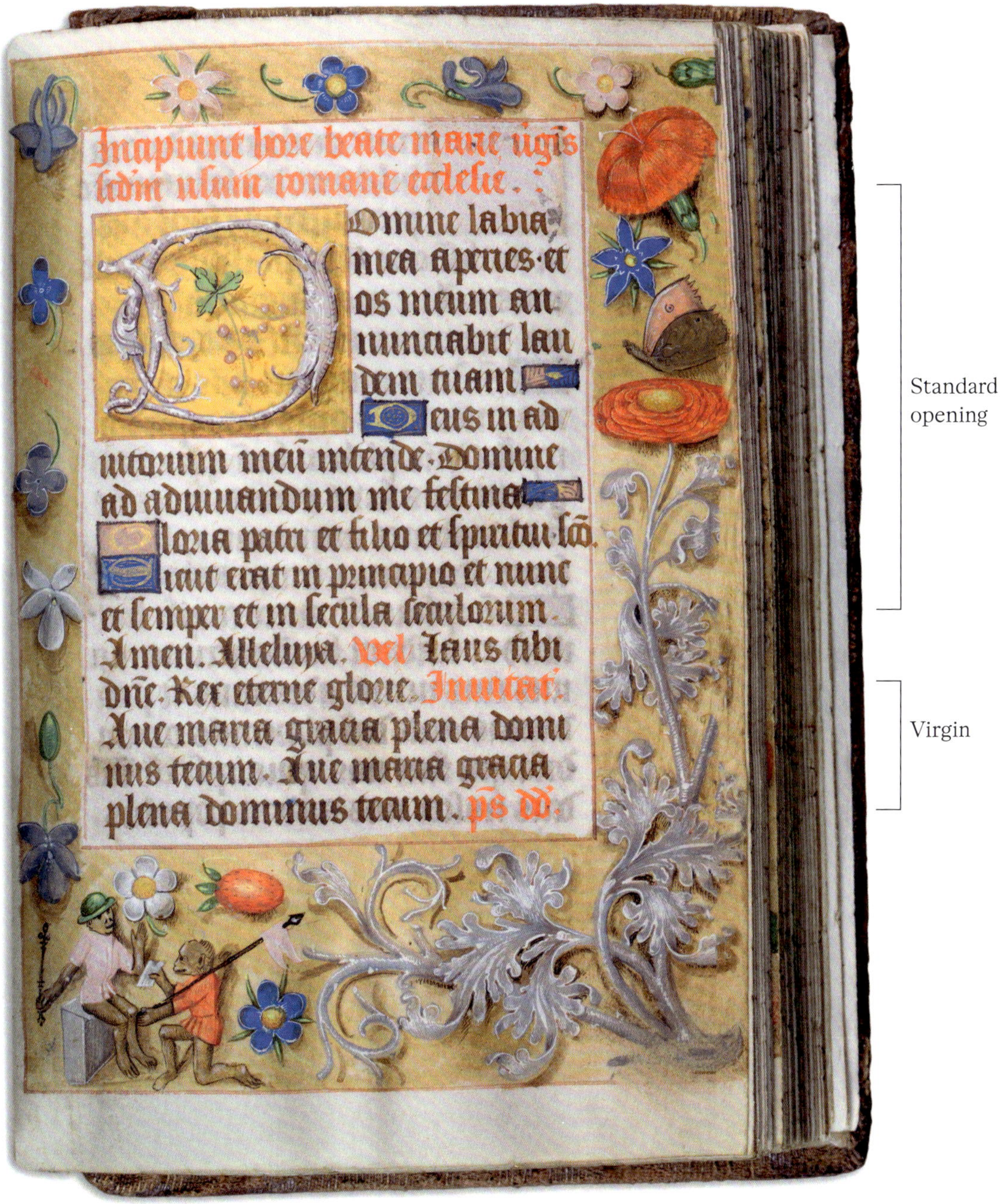

fig. 13 Beginning of the Hours of the Virgin in Book of Hours, Flanders, c.1475–c.1485. Bruges, Public Library, Ms. 324, f. 45r.

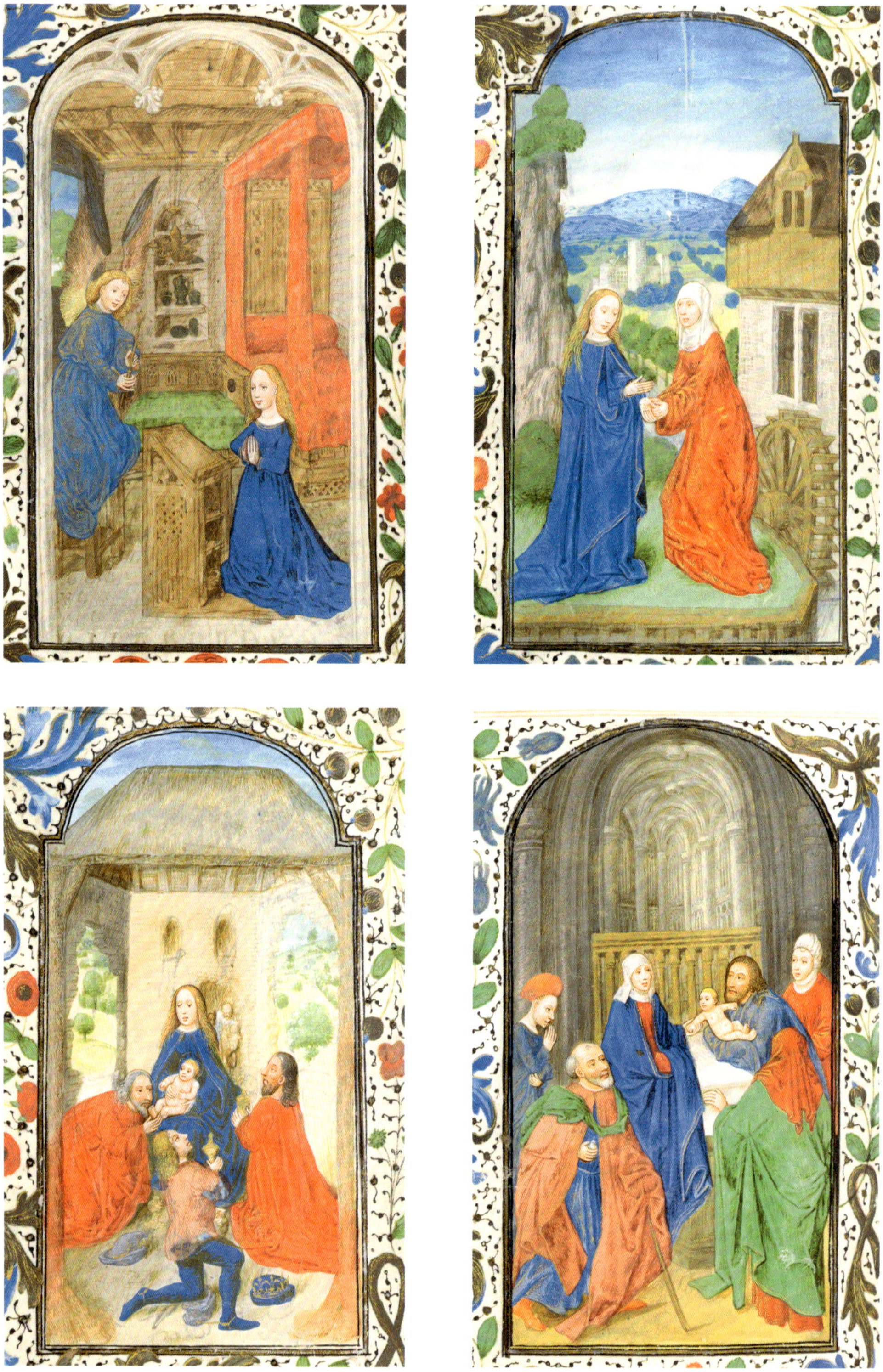

fig. 14 The infancy cycle at the beginning of the Hours of the Virgin, in Book of Hours, Master of the Flemish Boethius, Ghent and/or Bruges, c.1480. Bruges, Public Library, OCMW O.L.V. ter Potterie Collection, Ms. 4, ff. 41v, 49v, 59v, 64v, 69v, 73v, 77v, 84v.

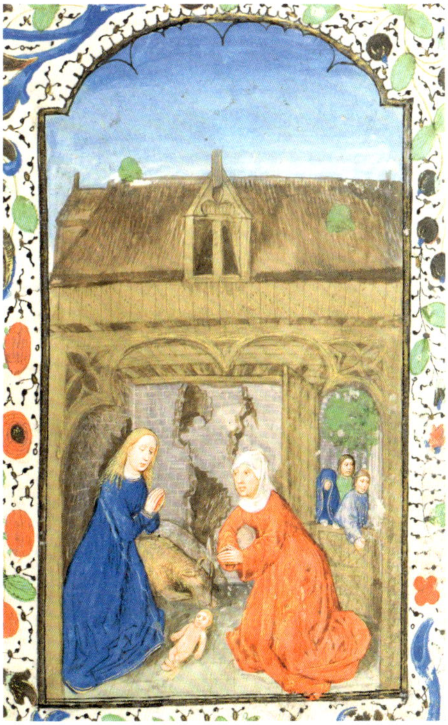
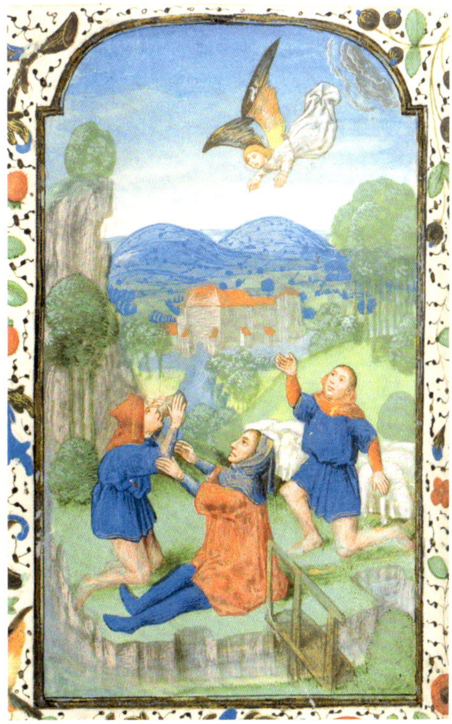
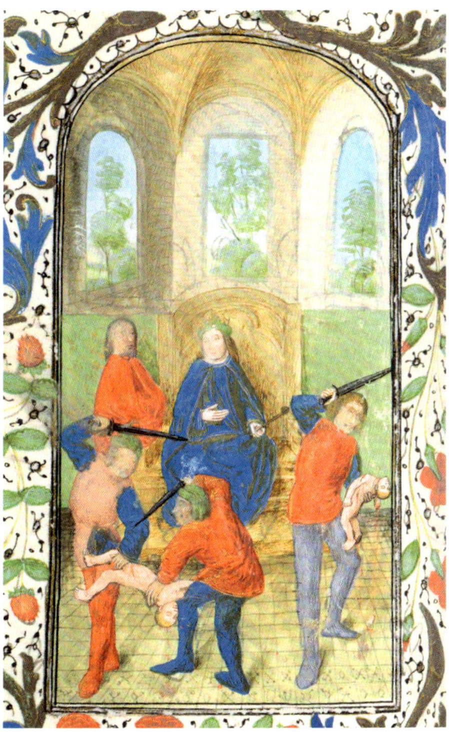
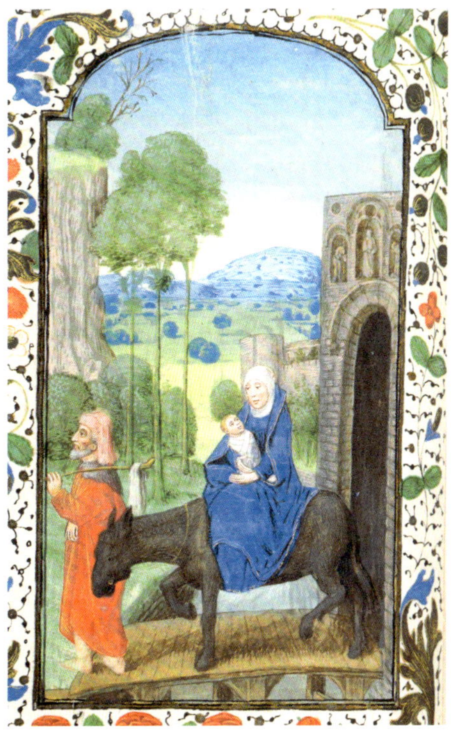

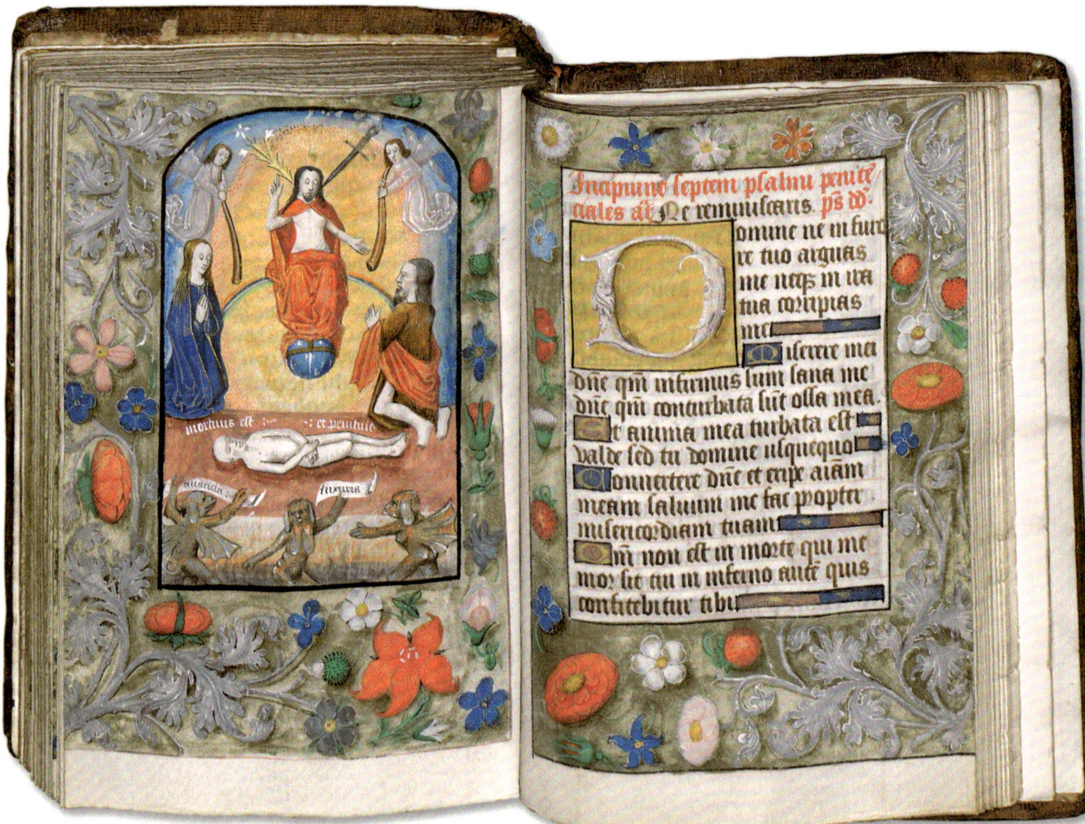

fig. 15 Penitential Psalms with *Last Judgement*, in Book of Hours, Flanders, c.1475–c.1485. Bruges, Public Library, Ms. 324, ff. 102v–103r.

4. Other Hours

Two popular sets of Hours are the Hours of the Cross, focusing on Christ's Passion, and the Hours of the Holy Spirit, covering the role of the Holy Spirit from the Incarnation to the Last Judgement. Neither contains Lauds. A more extensive variant of the Hours of the Cross is the Hours of the Passion, which does include Lauds.

Incipit: After the standard opening (see Hours of the Virgin above), the Hours of the Cross continue with the hymn *Patris sapientia, veritas divina* (The wisdom of the Father, and divine truth). In the Hours of the Holy Spirit, the opening is followed by the hymn *Nobis sancti Spiritus gratia sit data* (May the grace of the Holy Spirit be given to us).

Miniatures: Hours of the Cross and of the Passion: Crucifixion, or scenes from the Passion. Hours of the Holy Spirit: Pentecost, or other events involving the Holy Spirit.

5. Prayers for Mary: *Obsecro te* and *O intemerata*

These two heartfelt supplications to Mary appear in almost every Book of Hours. Chosen by God as an ordinary mortal, Mary was regarded as the most influential mediator between the faithful and God. *Obsecro te* begins with a list of Mary's attributes, followed by a description of her joyful role in the Incarnation and her sorrow at her son's Passion, concluding with a plea for forgiveness, hope, faith, chastity, humility and patience. *O intemerata* is shorter and also addresses the Apostle John alongside Mary.

Incipit: *Obsecro te*: *Obsecro te domina sancta Maria, mater Dei* (I beseech thee, Holy Lady Mary, Mother of God). *O intemerata*: *O Intemerata, et in aeternum benedicta ... Maria* (O immaculate and forever blessed... Mary).

Miniatures: *Obsecro te*: Mary and the Christ Child, Deposition from the Cross, Lamentation or Pietà. *O intemerata*: Lamentation or Pietà.

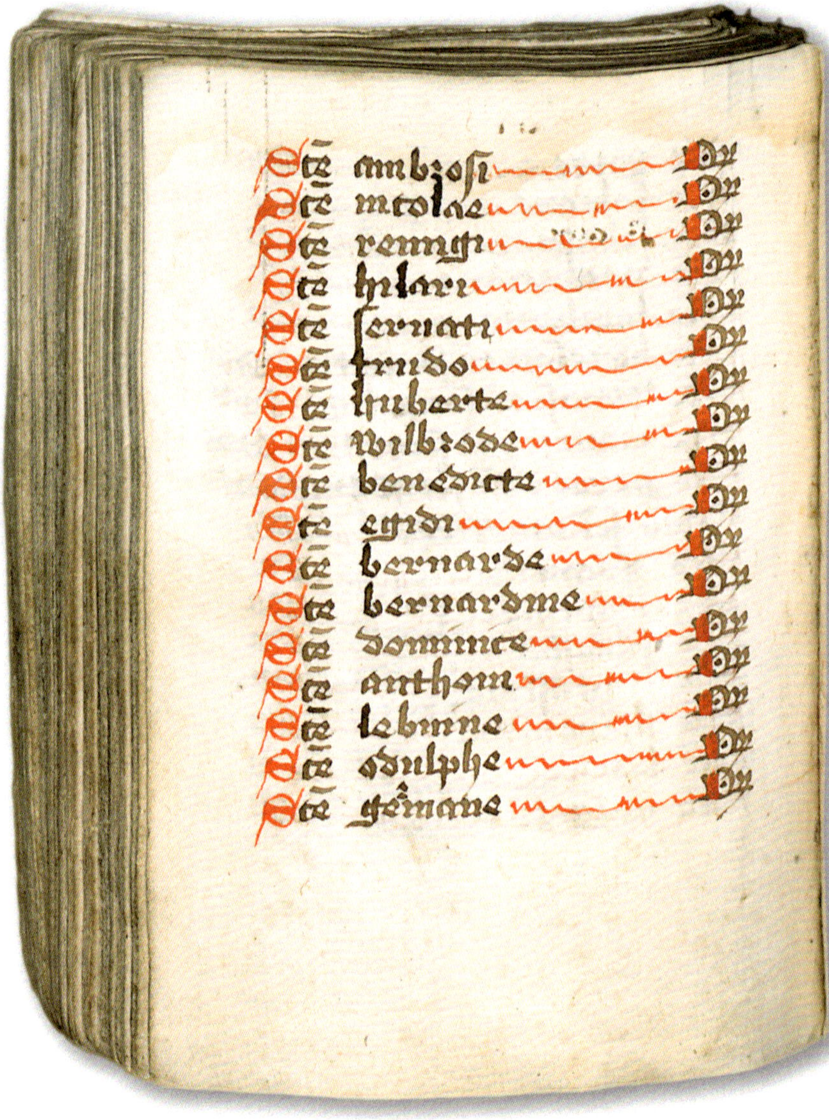

fig. 16 Male saints in the litanies, in Book of Hours, Limburg, c.1510. Bruges, Public Library, Ms. 568, f. 120v.

6. Penitential Psalms

The Penitential Psalms consist of seven Psalms focused on guilt, repentance, penance and forgiveness. They are central to the care of the soul after death. People read them for both deceased relatives and acquaintances, seeking forgiveness for their sins and thereby shortening their stay in purgatory, and for themselves, to avoid sins and lessen their own time in purgatory. These Psalms are often accompanied by depictions of the Last Judgement or King David pleading with God for forgiveness for his sins of adultery, murder and pride. According to tradition, David was the composer of the Psalms.

Incipit: *Domine ne in furore tuo arguas me: neque in ira tua corripias me* (Lord, do not rebuke me in your anger, nor chasten me in your wrath).

Miniatures: Last Judgement (fig. 15) or King David (fig. 97).

7. Litanies

The litanies are a rhythmic, incantatory list of saints' names, each followed by the phrase 'Pray for us.' After the *Kyrie eleison* and an invocation of Christ, God, and the Holy Spirit, a hierarchical sequence of saints follows. These usually include: Mary, angels, John the Baptist, patriarchs and prophets, apostles and evangelists, martyrs, bishops, confessors, church doctors, holy priests and monks, and holy virgins and widows. The litanies are easily recognisable by their layout, as typically only one name appears per line, followed by *Ora(te) pro nobis* or the abbreviation *or*, for instance, *Sancte Ambrosi, ora pro nobis*.

The litanies conclude with three series of short petitions, each beginning with *Ab*, *Per*, and *Ut*, respectively. These are also easy to identify from the layout as they feature a series of capital letters: *A*, *P* and *U*. Some examples include: *A subitanea et improvisa morte, libera nos* (From a sudden and unforeseen death, deliver us); *Per adventum tuum, libera nos Domine* (Through your coming, deliver us, Lord); *Ut omnibus benefactoribus nostris sempiterna bona retribuas, te rogamus audi nos* (That you would repay all our benefactors with eternal good, we beseech thee, hear us). These petitions may be followed by the *Agnus Dei* and other short texts.

Miniatures: All saints.

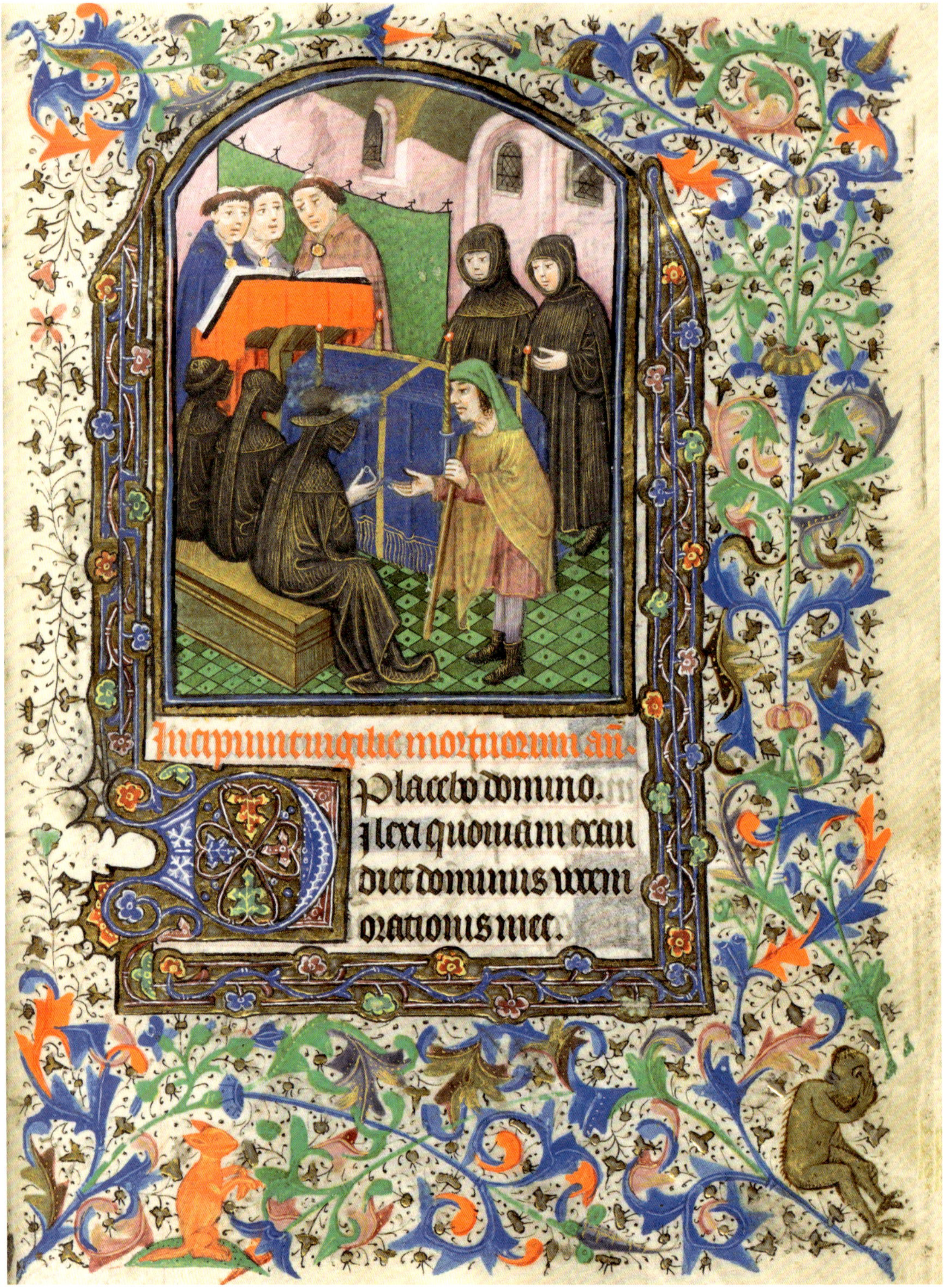

fig. 17 Office of the Dead, in Book of Hours, Master(s) of the Gold Scrolls, Bruges, c.1440–c.1450. Bruges, Public Library, OCMW O.L.V. ter Potterie Collection, Ms. 5, f. 98r.

8. Office of the Dead

The Office of the Dead is recited when someone has passed away. It is not an adaptation for laypeople but rather the formal liturgical text, as found in breviaries and antiphonals. The Office of the Dead consists of only three hours: Vespers, prayed the evening before the funeral; and Matins and Lauds, recited the morning of the funeral. Family members or acquaintances (such as guild brothers and sisters) of the deceased would pay monks and priests to recite the Office, in conjunction with the Requiem (the funeral Mass) and the liturgy at the time of burial. The text was also regularly prayed throughout the year to reduce the deceased's time in purgatory.

The texts draw heavily from the biblical Book of Job, which recounts a man enduring severe trials, and from Psalms. Vespers and Matins are sombre readings, with themes of adversity, death and the futility of life. In contrast, Lauds offers a glimmer of hope and redemption. The Office of the Dead includes Psalms that are deeply embedded in Western culture, such as the comforting Psalm 22, which has inspired artists such as Coolio, Duke Ellington and Pink Floyd: 'The Lord ruleth me: and I shall want nothing. He hath set me in a place of pasture. He hath brought me up, on the water of refreshment: He hath converted my soul. He hath led me on the paths of justice, for his own name's sake. For though I should walk in the midst of the shadow of death, I will fear no evils, for thou art with me.'[20] The closing line of the Office of the Dead also holds iconic status: *Requiem aeternam dona eis Domine, et lux perpetua luceat eis. Requiescant in pace. Amen* (Grant them eternal rest, Lord, and let perpetual light shine upon them. May they rest in peace. Amen.)

Incipit: [Antiphon] *Placebo Domino.* (I will please the Lord). [Ps. 114] *Dilexi, quoniam exaudiet Dominus: vocem orationis meae* (I have loved, because the Lord will hear the voice of my prayer.)

Miniatures: Scenes of deaths or funerals; or Death as a skeleton.

9. Suffrages

Suffrages are short prayers invoking a saint's help with specific needs – for example, Saint Sebastian was called upon for protection against the plague and other illnesses, Margaret of Antioch for a safe pregnancy and childbirth, and Apollonia for relief from toothache. Most Books of Hours contain a core group of the most venerated 'star players': the Holy Trinity, Mary, Michael, John the Baptist, the apostles, prominent male saints (e.g. Sebastian, Anthony, Christopher, Nicholas) and revered female saints (e.g. Mary Magdalene, Catherine of Alexandria, Barbara, Margaret of Antioch). This selection could be expanded to reflect regional preferences or the patron's personal devotion. The inclusion of Thomas Becket, the Archbishop of Canterbury assassinated in 1170, for instance, is characteristic of Books of Hours intended for England (for example, fig. 21). The opening words of each suffrage vary, but they are often recognisable by their distinctive titles or accompanying miniatures.

Miniatures: Saint with attributes, or a significant scene from their life (e.g. martyrdom).

10. Additional Texts

A Book of Hours could be expanded or personalised with additional texts. These additions might include extra cycles of Hours, such as those dedicated to John the Baptist or Catherine of Alexandria, or additional liturgical texts, such as the Mass of the Virgin. Shorter readings for specific moments in the church service, such as prayers for the elevation of the Host, and meditative texts structured around a numerical theme, such as the *Fifteen Joys of Mary* or the *Seven Last Words of Our Lord*, were also common.

The additional devotional prayers could range from prayers to Mary (e.g. *Salve Regina*) to supplications for one's guardian angel or protection against thunder. Some of these prayers were indulgence prayers through which the Church granted the faithful remission of punishment. Among the most popular indulgence prayers are the *Stabat Mater*, sometimes accompanied by a miniature of Mary at the Cross, and the *Salve Sancte Facies*, typically paired with an image of Christ (fig. 19). Indulgence prayers often have a rubric heading detailing the spiritual benefits granted.[21] In a South Holland Book of Hours, for instance, the *Verses of St Gregory* are accompanied by this instruction: 'Whoever devoutly reads the following prayer on their knees before [an image of] the Instruments of Christ's Passion, in a state of grace – that is, without mortal sin, or with the intention of repenting through confession and contrition when possible – earns by God's grace 90,000 years of indulgence, as granted by many popes.'[22] This instruction not only illustrates the medieval belief in an unfathomably long stay in purgatory but also highlights the pivotal devotional role of images in Books of Hours.

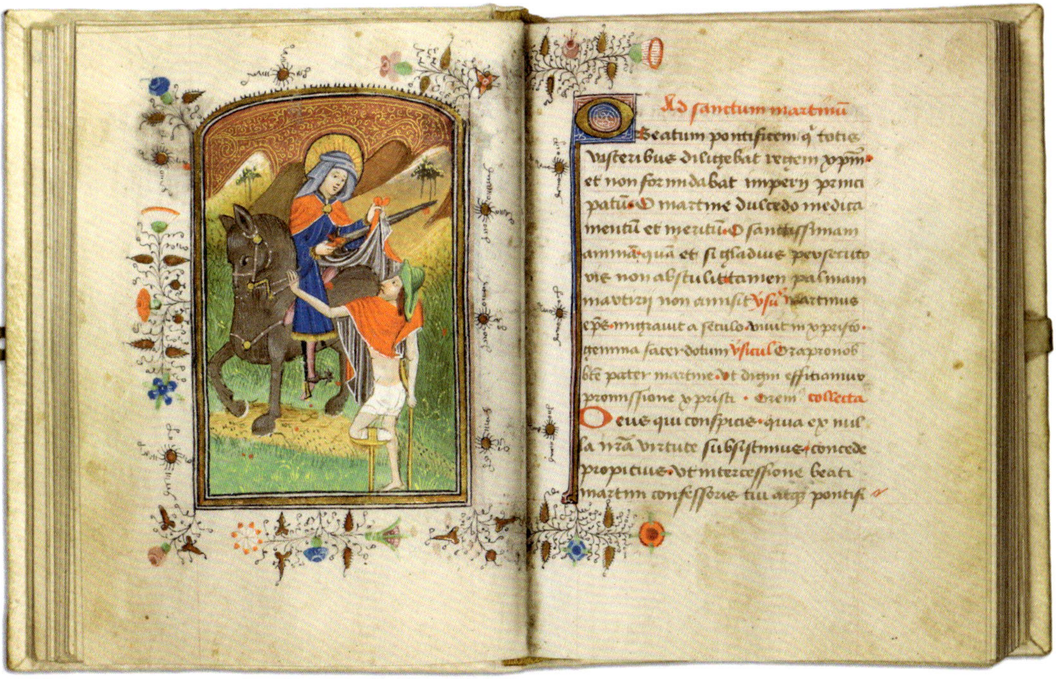

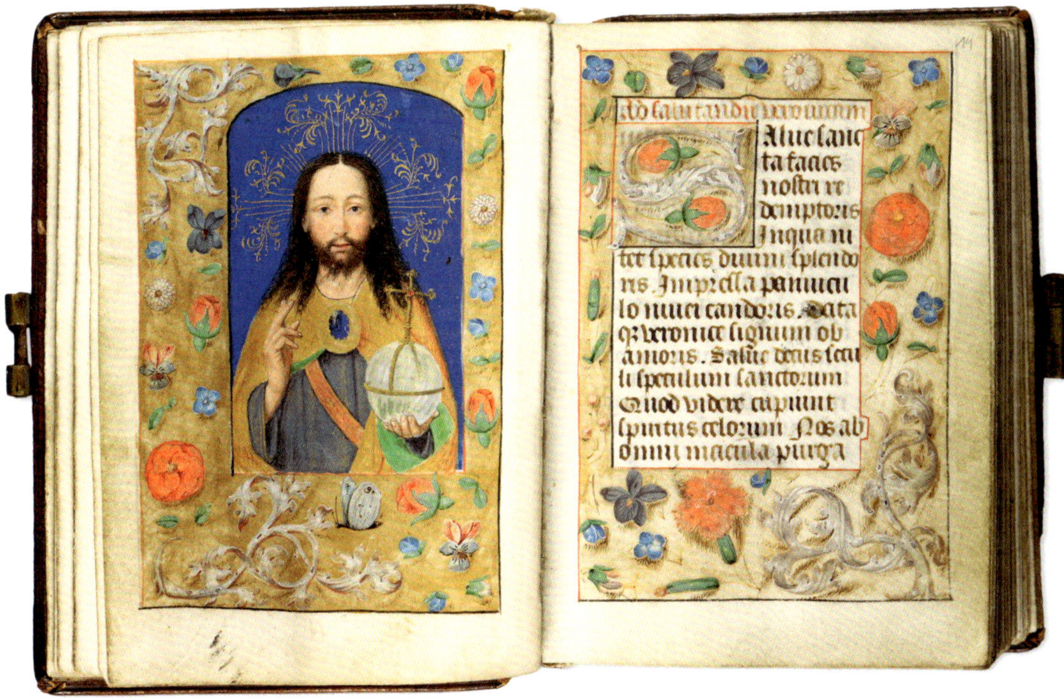

fig. 18 Suffrage for St Martin, in Book of Hours, Master(s) of the Gold Scrolls, Bruges, c.1430–c.1440. Bruges, Public Library, Ms. 742, ff. 46v-47r.

fig. 19 *Salvator Mundi* and the prayer *Salve sancta facies*, in Book of Hours, Ghent or Bruges, c.1490–c.1500. Bruges, Public Library, OCMW O.L.V. ter Potterie Collection, Ms. 3, ff. 13v–14r.

1. On the origins of the genre, see Duffy, *Marking the Hours*, 5–11.
2. They marked spiritual time, as in the popular children's song *Frère Jacques* ('*sonnez les matines*' means 'sound Matins'), and economic time, for example, the opening of the city gates or the end of the working day. See Le Goff, 'Temps de l'Église', 425–27. Time was calculated from the sun and stars, or the course of water and candles etc. See Landes, *L'heure qu'il est*, 88–107.
3. Timing based on tests carried out by the author.
4. Hindman, 'Gothic Traveling Coffers'.
5. See examples in Rudy, *Rubrics*, 256, 241, 283.
6. See examples in Rudy, *Rubrics*, 261–63, 256, 276, 279, 284.
7. For a recent study on the social dynamics around Books of Hours, see Zwart, *Religious Book Owners*. When we call the Book of Hours an instrument of private devotion, 'private' refers not so much to individual seclusion but rather to the possibility for the laity to take the initiative themselves in their experience of faith, rather than being entirely dependent on the professional clergy.
8. Duffy, *The Stripping*, 220.
9. Brown and Callewier, 'Religious Practices', 333.
10. Those who could afford it also owned other religious works, such as Bibles, sermons, exempla and lives of the saints. For concrete examples, see Zwart, *Religious Book Owners*, 133–63.
11. On the musical performance of Books of Hours, see Anderson, *Music and Performance*.
12. Whether it was a tool of assimilation or one of emancipation for laypeople in relation to the clergy remains a fascinating question. In the Low Countries, the translations of the Hours and Psalms by Geert Grote (1340–1384) were part of an emancipatory movement. See Dlabačová and Rijcklof, *De Moderne Devotie*.
13. On the production of Books of Hours, including their decoration, see Chapter 2.
14. On empathetic meditation and Passion iconography, see Marrow, *Passion Iconography*.
15. Book of Hours, South Holland, 15th century. Bruges, Public Library, Jean van Caloen Foundation Collection, Ms. 8, f. 138r.
16. For a more detailed discussion of content, see Wieck, *Time Sanctified*. On the miniatures in Books of Hours, see Wieck, *Painted Prayers*. The quotations follow the online edition and translation by Glenn Gunhouse of a Book of Hours printed in Antwerp in 1599, see https://medievalist.net/hourstxt/. The numbering of the Psalms follows that of the Vulgate.
17. The golden number (1–19) indicates the new moon according to a 19-year lunar cycle. For 1524, for example, the number is 5. Thus, in 1524, a new moon begins at each date marked with the number V. Following the same principle, each year has a letter for Sunday (A–G). In 1524, for example, Sundays fall on dates with the letter B in front of them.
18. See Chapter 3.
19. '*Ora pro populo, interveni pro clero, intercede pro devoto foemineo sexu.*'
20. '*Dominus regit me, et nihil mihi deerit: in loco pascuae ibi me collocavit. Super aquam refectionis educavit me: animam meam convertit. Deduxit me super semitas iustitiae: propter nomen suum. Nam et si ambulavero in medio umbrae mortis: non timebo mala, quoniam tu mecum es.*' Douay-Rheims translation.
21. On rubric titles and miniatures for indulgenced prayers, see Rudy, *Rubrics*.
22. South Holland, c.1510–c.1520. Bruges, Public Library, Ms. 327, f. 167r. Citation translated from Middle Dutch by the author.

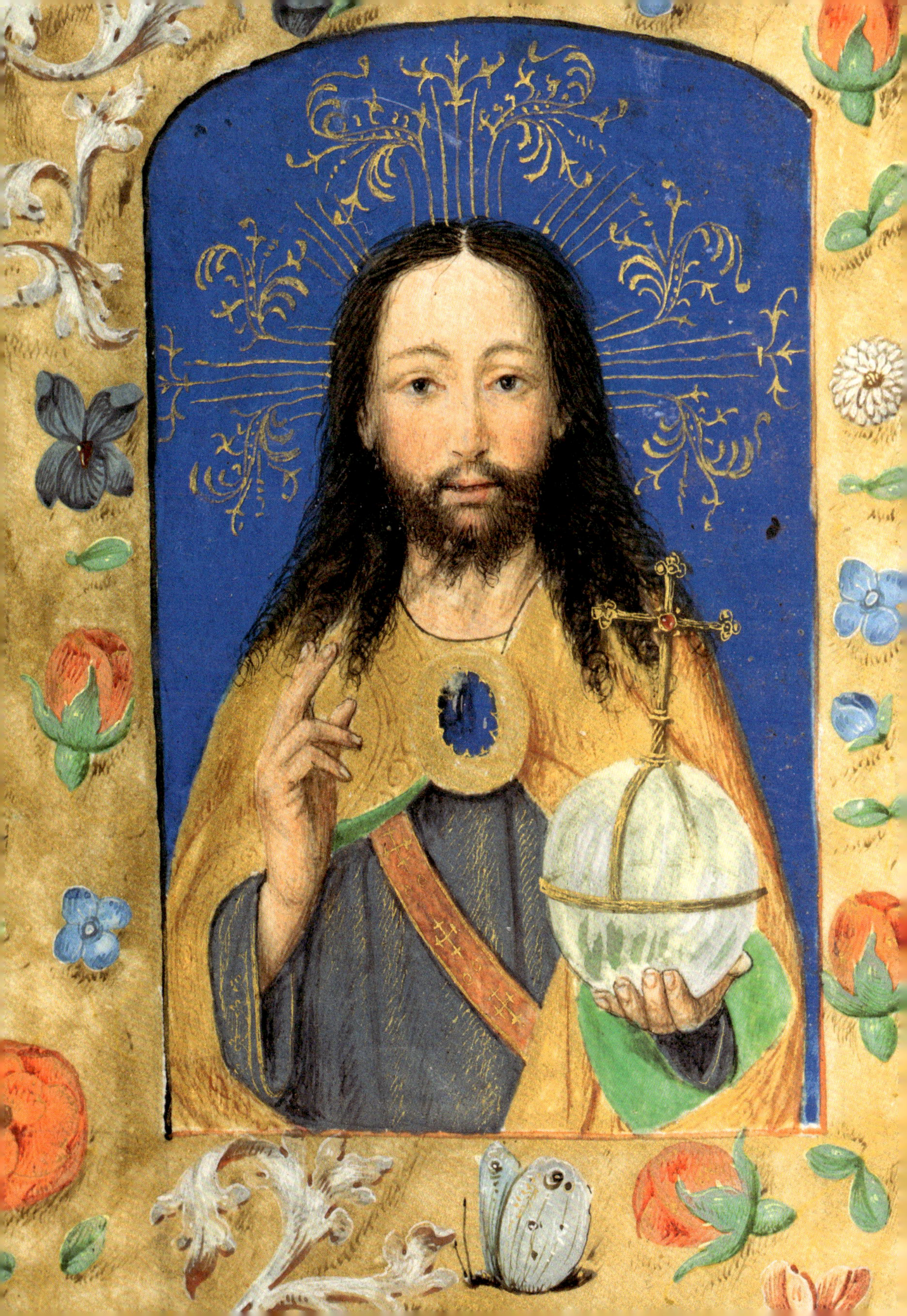

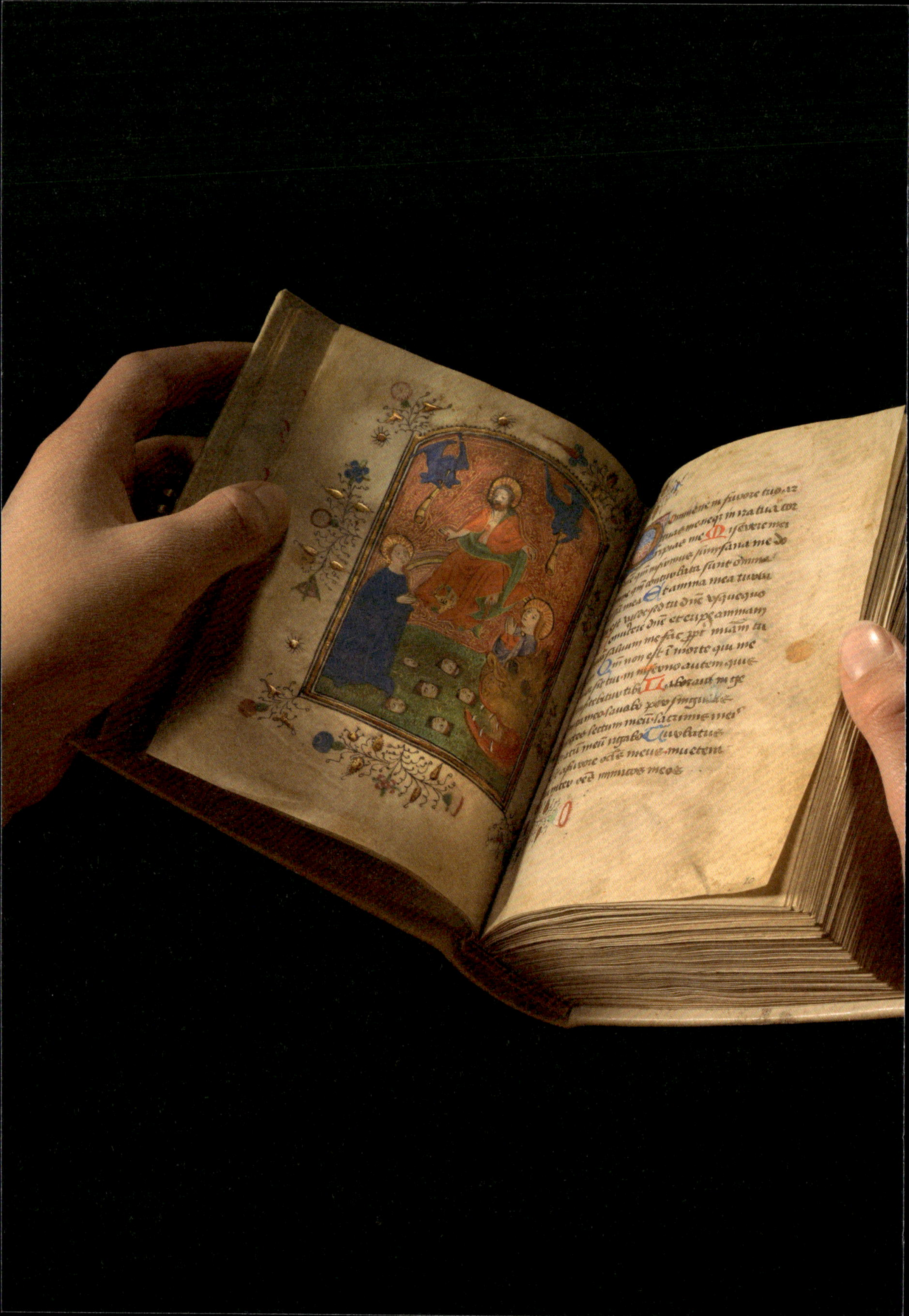

2. BIG BUSINESS: BOOKS OF HOURS AND THEIR MAKERS IN FIFTEENTH-CENTURY BRUGES

This chapter examines the men and women engaged in producing Books of Hours in fifteenth-century Bruges, highlighting their roles, networks and contributions to the thriving manuscript trade. Central to this study is the account book of the Guild of Book Producers and Merchants of St John the Evangelist, one of the few surviving primary sources on the Bruges book trade.[1] In 1457, Bruges's aldermen mandated that all book-related trades join this guild, transforming a loosely connected network into a recognised professional body.[2] The association remained distinct from Bruges's formal *ambachten* (trade guilds), however, focusing more on religious and social functions than strict craft regulation.[3] Its account book, though primarily a financial ledger recording annual dues, apprenticeships and funerary costs for deceased members, thus also offers invaluable insights into the lives and practices of those who created some of the most coveted books of the fifteenth century.

Caroline Van Cauwenberge

fig. 20 Book of Hours, Master(s) of the Gold Scrolls, Bruges, c.1430–c.1440. Bruges, Public Library, Ms. 742, ff. 19v–20r.

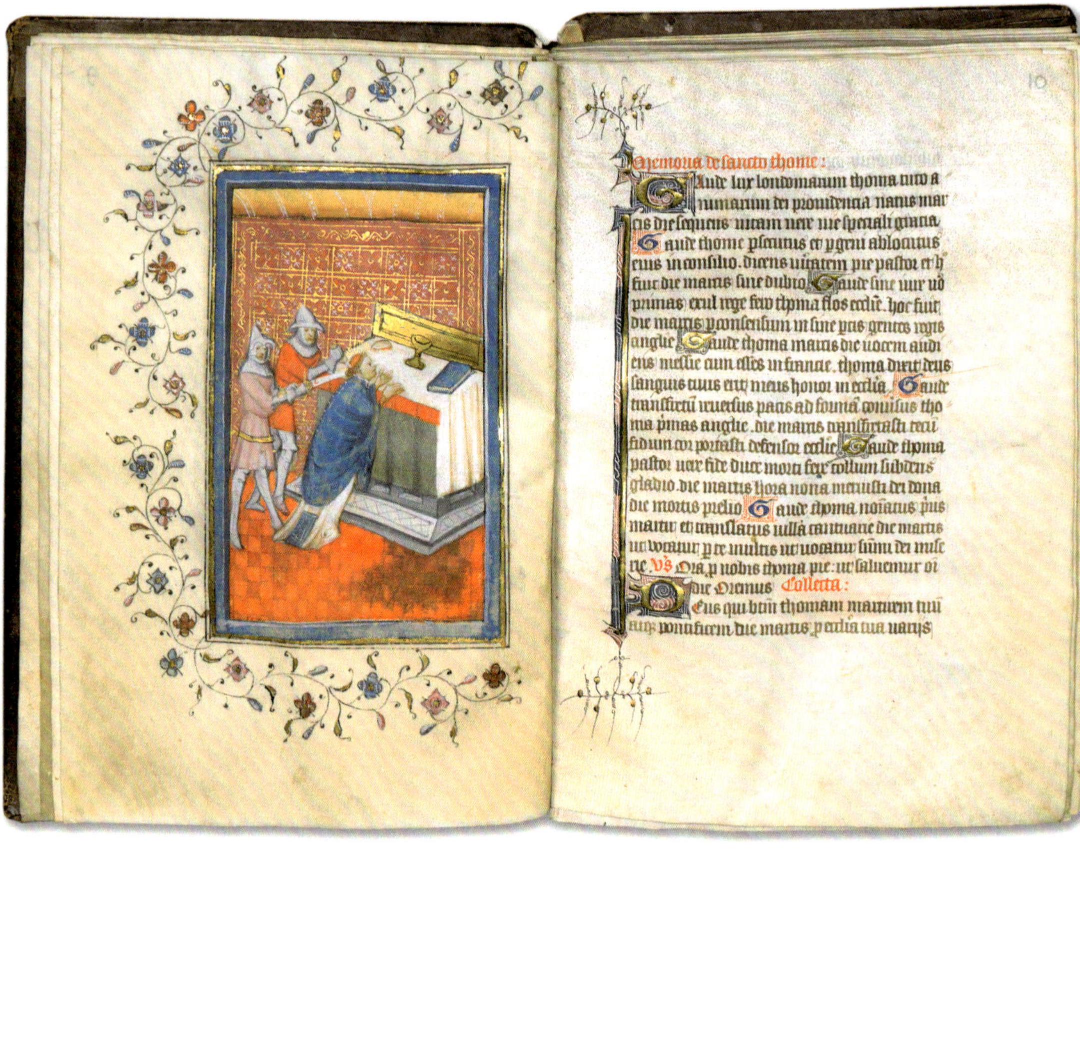

fig. 21 *Martyrdom of Thomas Becket* and a suffrage to the saint, *Bowet Book of Hours*, Bruges, c.1400–c.1420, Master of the Tall Figures (Beaufort Group). Bruges, Public Library, Ms. 736 (King Baudouin Foundation Collection), ff. 9v–10r.

Creativity and Commerce

The Guild of St John the Evangelist was unique in the Low Countries, as no other guilds exclusively for the book trade existed in the fifteenth century, even in major centres such as Ghent and Utrecht.[4] Yet, its emergence in Bruges is unsurprising, given the city's thriving commercial and artistic activities.

Home to the court of Philip the Good, Duke of Burgundy (1396–1467), Bruges flourished as a centre for luxury goods, including Books of Hours. Philip's bibliophilia inspired nobles and wealthy citizens to emulate his patronage, nurturing a vibrant manuscript culture.[5] Drawn by economic opportunity and growing demand, artists flocked to Bruges to join this 'creative environment', contributing to a specialised craft economy that adapted to the needs of the city's diverse clientele.[6]

Bruges's position as an international trade hub expanded its market for Books of Hours. A Portuguese royal agent's account lists luxury purchases such as Italian silks, Lille and Tournai tapestries, and Bruges-produced Books of Hours, underscoring the city's far-reaching networks.[7] A distinct line of Book of Hours production catered specifically to England, incorporating popular English saints such as Thomas Becket to appeal to this foreign audience (fig. 21).[8]

Once reserved for the elite, Books of Hours became increasingly accessible in the second half of the fifteenth century as Bruges's growing middle class gained purchasing power.[9] This rising affluence fuelled demand for more affordable Books of Hours, while luxurious versions continued to serve the well-to-do. At the same time, evolving devotional practices and increasing literacy further expanded the market, leading to a diverse production ranging from exquisitely illuminated ducal commissions to cheaper versions for a wider audience.

Efficiency and Adaptability

As demand for Books of Hours grew across social classes, producers developed faster, more cost-effective methods. By standardising common iconographies, such as the Crucifixion for the Hours of the Cross, and employing techniques such as tracing and stencilling, illuminators efficiently replicated compositions. Some, such as Willem Vrelant, turned to prints as models for details.[10] Decorative border motifs were frequently reused, or borders were traced from recto to verso, a method that prevented bleed-through on fine parchment while saving time. Tasks were also divided: skilled illuminators handled complex narrative scenes, while assistants worked on repetitive elements.[11] Rare examples of unfinished decoration offer insight into production stages and labour division. In some cases, borders were completed by one artist, with spaces left for the miniatures – likely intended for another illuminator but never finished (e.g. fig. 22).

A key innovation was the 'modular method' in which pre-prepared components – calendars, text quires, and single-leaf miniatures – were created separately and later assembled during binding. The standardised structure of Books of Hours suited this approach, allowing scribes to start new texts on fresh quires, forming discrete packets that combined into complete manuscripts. Full-page miniatures were painted on separate leaves and inserted to face specific text openings, simplifying both planning and assembly.[12] This method allowed illuminators and scribes to work on the same book simultaneously, accelerating production while offering clients greater flexibility to customise their books.

The impact of these techniques is evident in three Books of Hours by the Masters of the Gold Scrolls held in Bruges Public Library. Though all feature a Crucifixion scene based on the same model, their production methods vary. In Ms. 742 (fig. 23), the miniature was painted separately and inserted as a full-page illustration, exemplifying the modular method's efficiency. In contrast, Ms. 821 (fig. 24) has the scene painted directly onto the text page, a more traditional and time-consuming technique. Despite the more efficient assembly of Ms. 742, the quality of its Crucifixion miniature surpasses that of Ms. 821, demonstrating that this method did not compromise artistic standards. The differences in approach are also evident in the execution of the decorative borders and the script, which is simpler in Ms. 742 than in Ms. 821. The third manuscript, Ms. 5 from the Collection of Our Lady of the Pottery (fig. 25), is a more elaborate, refined version of Ms. 821. Together, these manuscripts illustrate how this group of Bruges artists balanced cost-efficiency with craftsmanship to meet the needs of a diverse clientele.[13]

Book entrepreneurs also explored printing as a means of increasing efficiency. Around 1475, Colard Mansion, in collaboration with William Caxton (d.1491), produced Bruges's only known incunable Book of Hours (fig. 26) intended for the English market.[14] Yet despite this experiment with mechanical production, Bruges remained a centre for handwritten manuscripts well into the sixteenth century, while its main competitor, Paris, fully embraced the new medium for the production of Books of Hours, spearheaded by prolific printers such as Germain Hardouin (fig. 27).

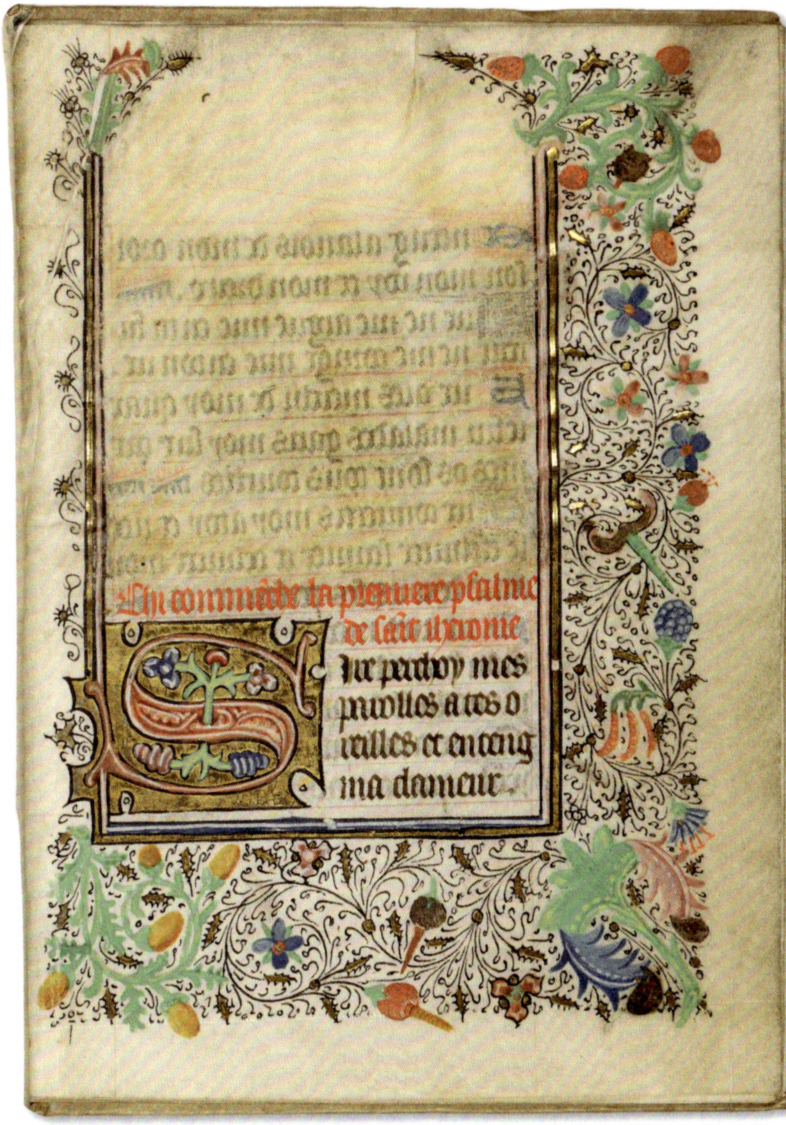

fig. 22 Unfinished decoration, in Book of Hours, Northern France (?), c.1460. Bruges, Public Library, Jean van Caloen Foundation Collection, Ms. 22, f. 1r.

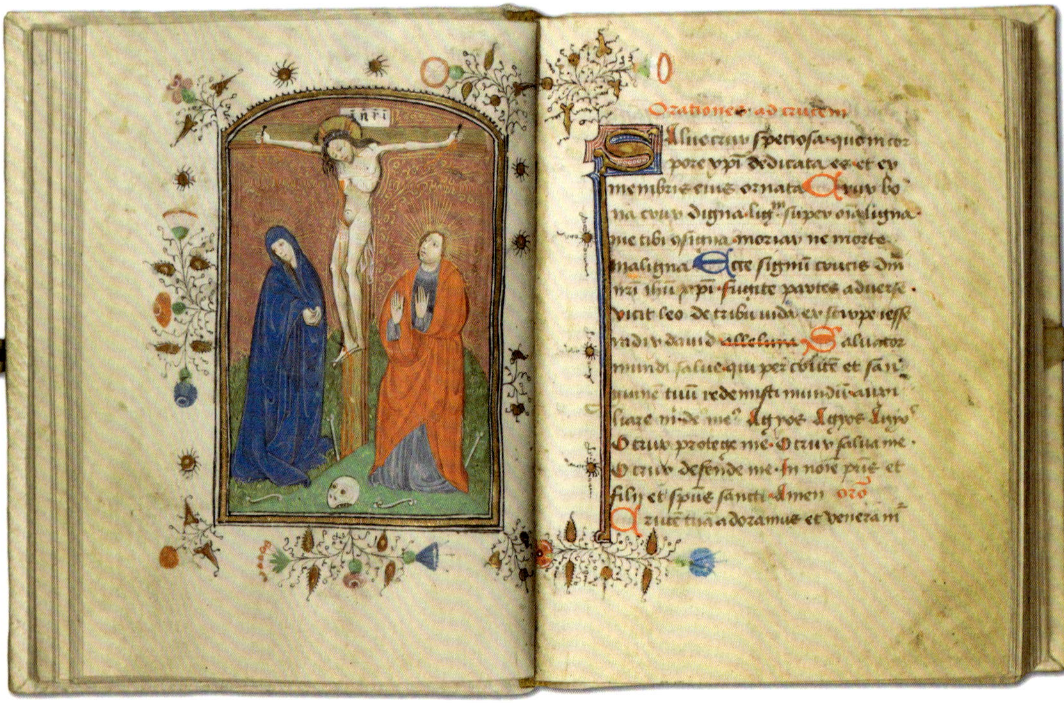

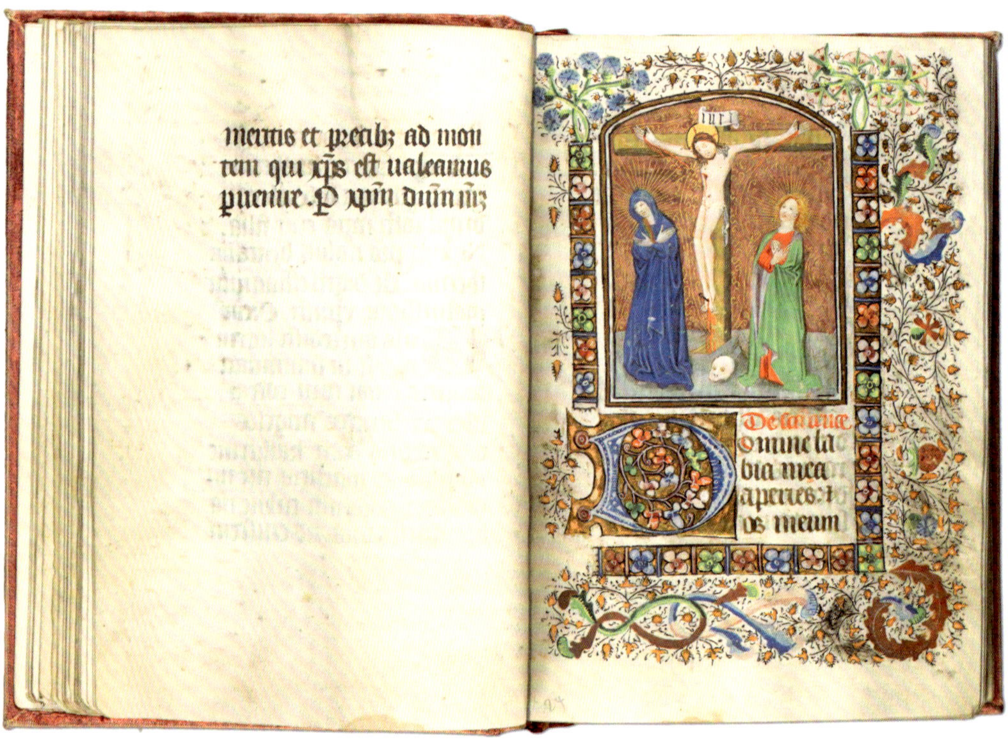

fig. 23 *Crucifixion*, in Book of Hours, Master(s) of the Gold Scrolls, Bruges, c.1430–c.1440. Bruges, Public Library, Ms. 742, ff. 33v–34r.

fig. 24 *Crucifixion*, in Book of Hours, Master(s) of the Gold Scrolls, Bruges, c.1430. Bruges, Public Library, Ms. 821 (Flemish Community Collection), ff. 23v–24r.

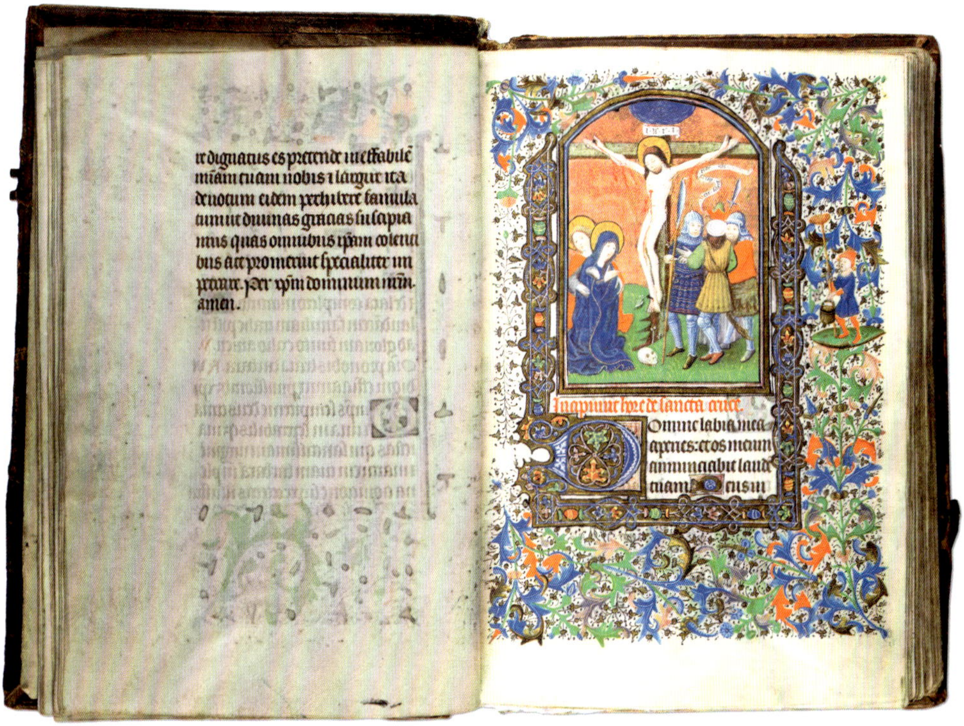

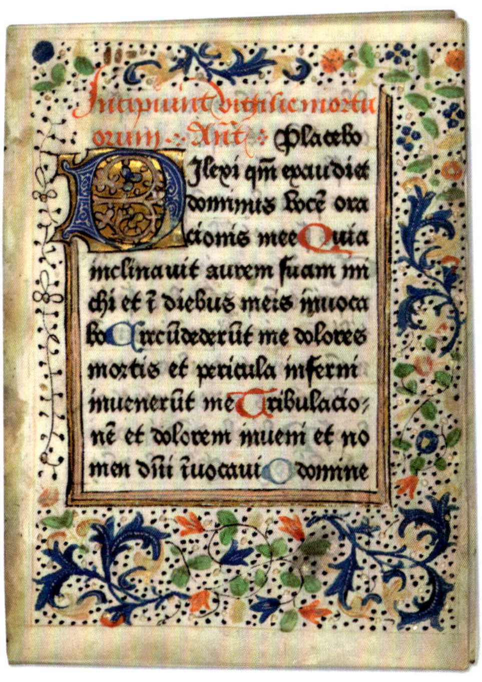

fig. 25 *Crucifixion*, in Book of Hours, Master(s) of the Gold Scrolls, Bruges, c.1440–c.1450. Bruges, Public Library, OCMW O.L.V. ter Potterie Collection, Ms. 5, ff. 15v–16r.

fig. 26 Book of Hours printed on parchment, with painted illumination, Bruges: Colard Mansion for William Caxton, c.1475. New York, Morgan Library & Museum, PBL 18386, f. 1r.

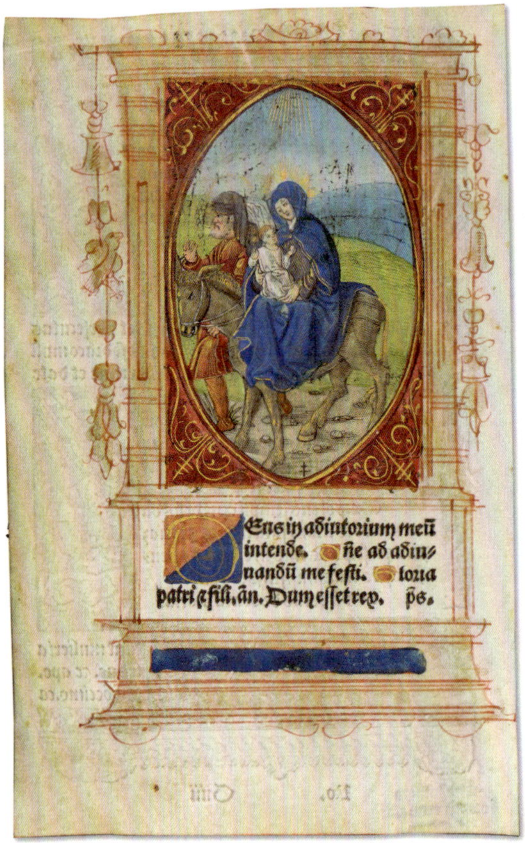

fig. 27 Book of Hours printed on parchment, with hand-coloured engraving, Paris: Germain Hardouin, c.1505. Bruges, Public Library, Jean van Caloen Foundation Collection, Ms. 26, f. 1v.

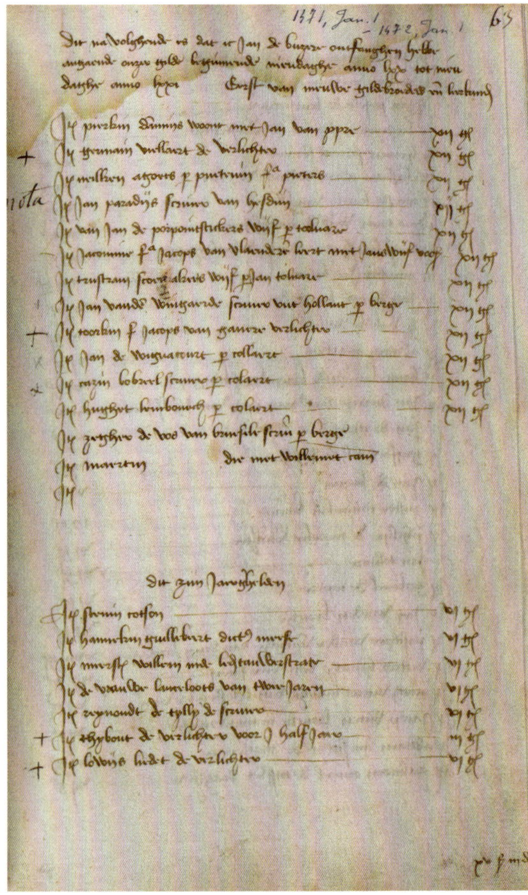

fig. 28 Register of the Guild of St John the Evangelist. Bruges, City Archives, Oud Archief, 384:76, f. 63r.

The People Behind the Pages

The production of Books of Hours in fifteenth-century Bruges involved many individuals, as detailed in the account book of the Guild of St John the Evangelist. After the 1457 ruling, all those engaged in book-related trades were required to join. While gaps in the records and accounting inconsistencies make it difficult to track precise membership over time, occasional notes on professions, origins and residences provide rare glimpses into this diverse network. A particularly revealing year is 1471, when the guild recorded 49 established members paying annual fees, 14 new admissions and 10 distinct professions – an unusual level of detail (fig. 28).

In the register, the term *scriver* or *boucscriver* refers to scribes – the most frequently mentioned profession in the 1471 records – with ten individuals listed. Of these, three are explicitly noted as coming from elsewhere, including '*Jan Paradijs, scriver van Hesdin*,' reflecting the draw of Bruges as a hub for skilled professionals. *Verlichters* and *verlichteges* (male and female illuminators) are also well-represented, with nine mentions. Celebrated masters such as Willem Vrelant, Philippe de Mazerolles and Loyset Liédet, renowned for their courtly commissions, appear alongside unknown illuminators such as a certain Thybout, who remains unidentified in terms of known surviving works. One name, Jan de Cat, is explicitly identified as a *boucbinder* (bookbinder), though others, including Anthonis van Gavere (fig. 29), are also listed.

While some clients worked directly with individual craftspeople or brought loose quires to a bookbinder, others relied on a *librarier* (stationer) to coordinate the work of these diverse artisans. Colard Mansion exemplified this role, working as a scribe, translator, printer and stationer.[15] A member of the guild since at least 1454, he remained active until 1484. The 1471 records highlight his status, noting that he paid the membership fees for three new members, probably his apprentices.

The register reveals the guild's role in fostering community through shared religious and social practices. At the guild's chapel in Eeckhout Abbey, members gathered for masses, feast days and funerals. The register lists 75 required attendance days annually, including Sundays and feast days, underscoring the significant time spent together.[16] These services provided mutual support, especially for deceased members, through prayers and funeral and burial arrangements. The centrality of these gatherings is reflected in the recorded expenses, which are largely dedicated to maintaining the altar and funding the ceremonies. It is therefore not surprising that members included religious figures from Eeckhout Abbey, such as 'Sir Alaert, priest at Eeckhout,' recorded in 1471.

Beyond Eeckhout Abbey, the guild's social life extended to nearby taverns and members' homes. Routine activities, such as account audits (the one recorded in 1471 by Jan de Clerc, for example), collecting dues or announcing a member's passing (both requiring an *ommegang* or pageant), often involved shared drinks.[17] Other gatherings, such as the annual *conincfeest* (king feast), when a king was chosen by lottery to rule the guild for a brief period, further highlight its camaraderie.[18] In 1475, this celebration took place at the tavern *Draexkin* (Little Dragon).[19]

While Eeckhout Abbey was the centre of the guild's religious life, St Donatian's Cathedral was central to its professional and commercial activities, with stalls built against the church and its *panden* (cloisters) where books were written, sold and bound as early as the fourteenth century.[20] By 1478, Colard Mansion was operating a shop there, having taken over a storefront previously run by bookseller Morissis de Haec.[21] Archival records from St Donatian's chapter further trace the rental of this workspace, revealing that after Mansion's departure, bookbinder Jan Gossin took over the lease.[22] This dense network of artisans and merchants near St Donatian's, combined with the guild's communal activities at Eeckhout Abbey, fostered interaction, and likely facilitated collaboration among the many individuals involved in book production in Bruges.

Mothers, Daughters and Masters

From the outset, women played a vital role in the Guild of St John the Evangelist, accounting for about a quarter of its membership between 1454 and 1500.[23] They contributed in various capacities: as apprentices, as collaborators working in family businesses and as independent professionals.

The 1471 entries highlight their diverse involvement. Several girls are listed as *leerkinderen* (apprentices), often through familial ties with male members, such as Jacomine, '*filia* [daughter of] *Jacops van Vlaenderen*'. Leading illuminators such as Willem Vrelant and Philippe de Mazerolles trained young women, demonstrating the industry's openness to female participation.[24] Women also trained other women. Jacomine, for instance, apprenticed with '*Jan de Porpointstickers wijf* [wife]' in 1471.

Among the 1471 members who paid their annual fees, 10 were women, paying a reduced rate of 3 groats compared to the men's 6 groats.[25] Most female guild members were wives or daughters actively contributing to the family business, such as '*Jane, Adriaen Karvoets wijf*'. Households functioned as both domestic spaces and as sites of production or trade, with all family members participating in the economic enterprise.[26] Widows, such as the '*wedewe Wallins*', frequently continued their husband's businesses, maintaining their presence in the book trade and ensuring economic stability for their families.

Some women, however, operated independently, notably the illuminator Kerstinekin (Christine) Yweins. She ran a successful workshop in the 1470s and 1480s, training both male and female apprentices and making notable financial

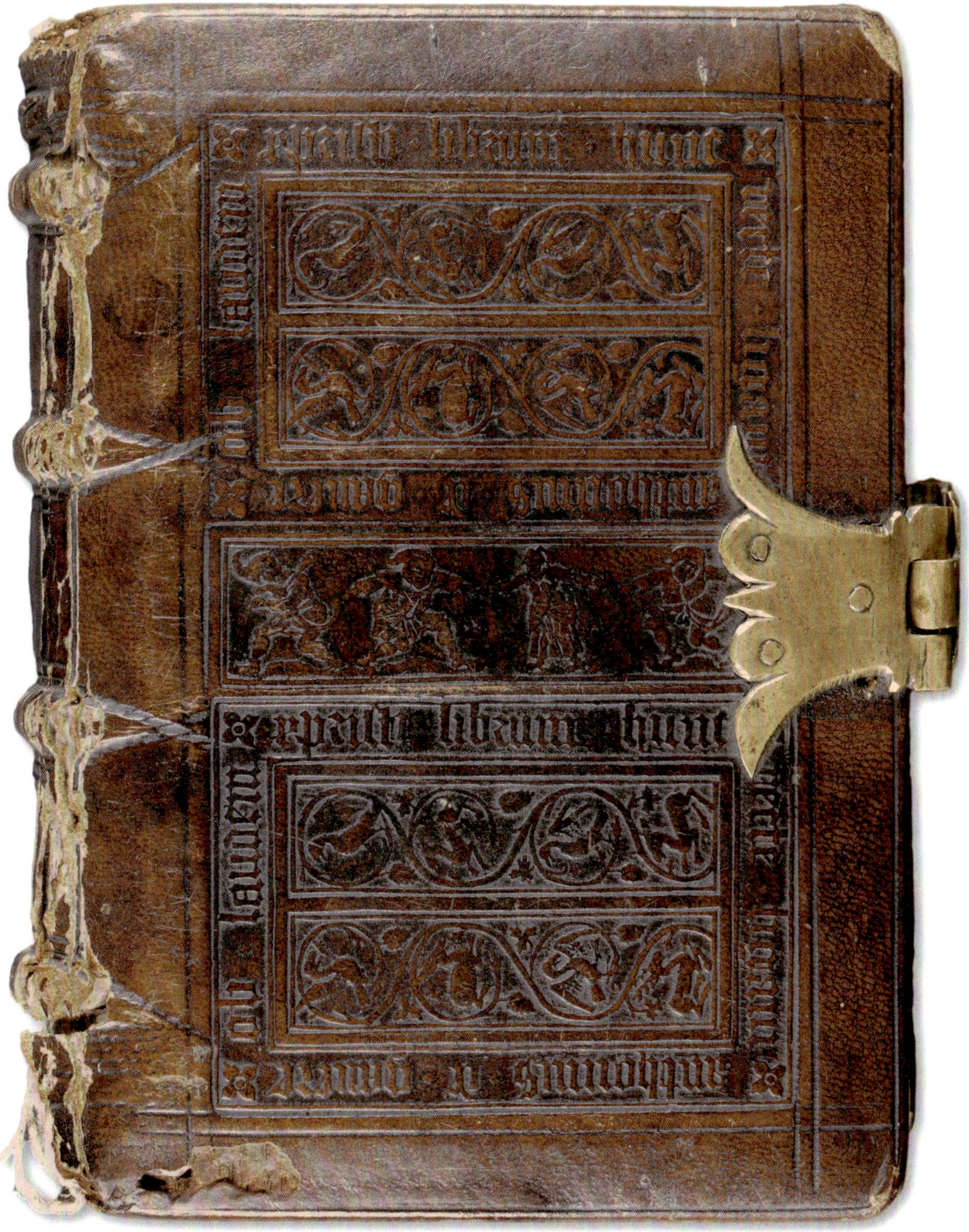

fig. 29 Cover with stamped inscription 'For the praise of Christ, I, Anthony of Gavere, have properly bound this book,'◆ Book of Hours, Bruges, c.1490–c.1500. Bruges, Public Library, OCMW O.L.V. ter Potterie Collection, Ms. 3.

contributions to the guild.[27] Her 1480 prepayment of 30 Flemish groats for her death mass – far exceeding the standard 4 groats – underscores her prominence and financial independence.[28]

Among the female members listed in the 1471 guild is '*Zuster* [Sister] *Tannekin Booms*', whose membership is notable since religious artisans were typically exempt from joining the guild. Her inclusion suggests she sought professional benefits, such as access to the guild's network.[29] Religious communities remained key players in commercial book production in the late Middle Ages. The Carmelite Convent of Sion in Bruges, for instance, hosted a collaborative workshop, with Cornelia van Wulfschkercke as its most well-known contributor. The nuns worked together, standardising motifs, reusing designs and adopting printed models to streamline production. In addition to liturgical manuscripts they produced Books of Hours, ranging from bespoke, lavish commissions to more affordable versions for a wider audience.[30] To market their work, they rented a stall at the Bruges luxury goods arcade, the Pand, to sell their crafts.[31]

Conclusion

The production of Books of Hours in fifteenth-century Bruges showcases the intricate interplay between creativity, commerce and community. The Guild of St John the Evangelist united artisans and tradespeople, fostering a network that drove innovation and collaboration. From streamlined production techniques to the vital roles of women and religious communities, the Bruges book trade exemplified adaptability and inclusivity in meeting the demands of a varied and expanding clientele.

1. The account book, held in Bruges's Stadsarchief (Oud Archief, 384: *Register van de Gilde van Librariërs*), begins on the 6th of May 1454 and continues almost uninterrupted until the French Revolution. Several authors have partially transcribed or published extracts from this source, including: Weale, 'Documents inédits', 253–329; Gilliodts-Van Severen, 'L'Oeuvre de Jean Brito', 1–515; Schouteet, 'Inventaris van het archief', 252–63.
2. The guild's formalisation stemmed partly from disputes with the painters' Guild of St Luke, which sought to regulate illuminators and control the production of standalone miniatures. See Vandewalle, 'Het librariërsgilde', 41.
3. Reynolds, 'Illuminators and the Painters' Guilds', 15.
4. Smeyers, *Vlaamse miniaturen*, 232.
5. Martens, 'Texts, Images and Sounds', 426–27.
6. Blockmans, 'The Creative Environment', 13.
7. Stabel, 'Production, Markets and Socio-Economic Structures II', 202.
8. Rogers, 'Patrons and Purchasers', 1165.
9. Stabel, 'Production, Markets and Socio-Economic Structures II', 240–41.
10. Bousmanne, *'Item a Guillaume'*, 141–48.
11. Alexander, *Medieval Illuminators*, 126.
12. The term 'modular method' was first introduced by Rudy, *Piety in Pieces*.
13. Cardon, 'The Illustrations and the Gold Scrolls Group'.
14. Hauwaerts, *et al.*, *Colard Mansion*, 70–71, cat. no. 26.
15. Adam, 'Printing Books in Bruges', 54.
16. Dewitte, 'Het Brugse St.-Jans en St.-Lucasgilde', 337.
17. Idem, 338.
18. Vernimme, *Het librariërsgilde*, 155.
19. Rek. 1475.
20. Dewitte, 'Boek- en bibliotheekwezen', 79.
21. Vandamme, 'Colard Mansion et le monde du livre', 179.
22. Bruges, Bisschoppelijk Archief, Acts of the Chapter of St Donatian, 8 October 1484; Idem, 11 October 1484.
23. Gil, 'Les femmes dans les métiers d'art'.
24. Idem, 248.
25. Idem, 242.
26. Stabel, 'Production, Markets and Socio-economic Structures II', 230–31.
27. Gil, 'Les femmes dans les métiers d'art', 247.
28. Rek. 1480, f. 107r.
29. Reynolds, 'Illuminators and the Painters' Guilds', 17.
30. Hauwaerts, 'Middeleeuwse vrouwen', 276.
31. As-Vijvers, 'Manuscript Production', 293.

◆ *'Ob laudem christi librum hunc recte ligavi Anthonius de Gavere'.*

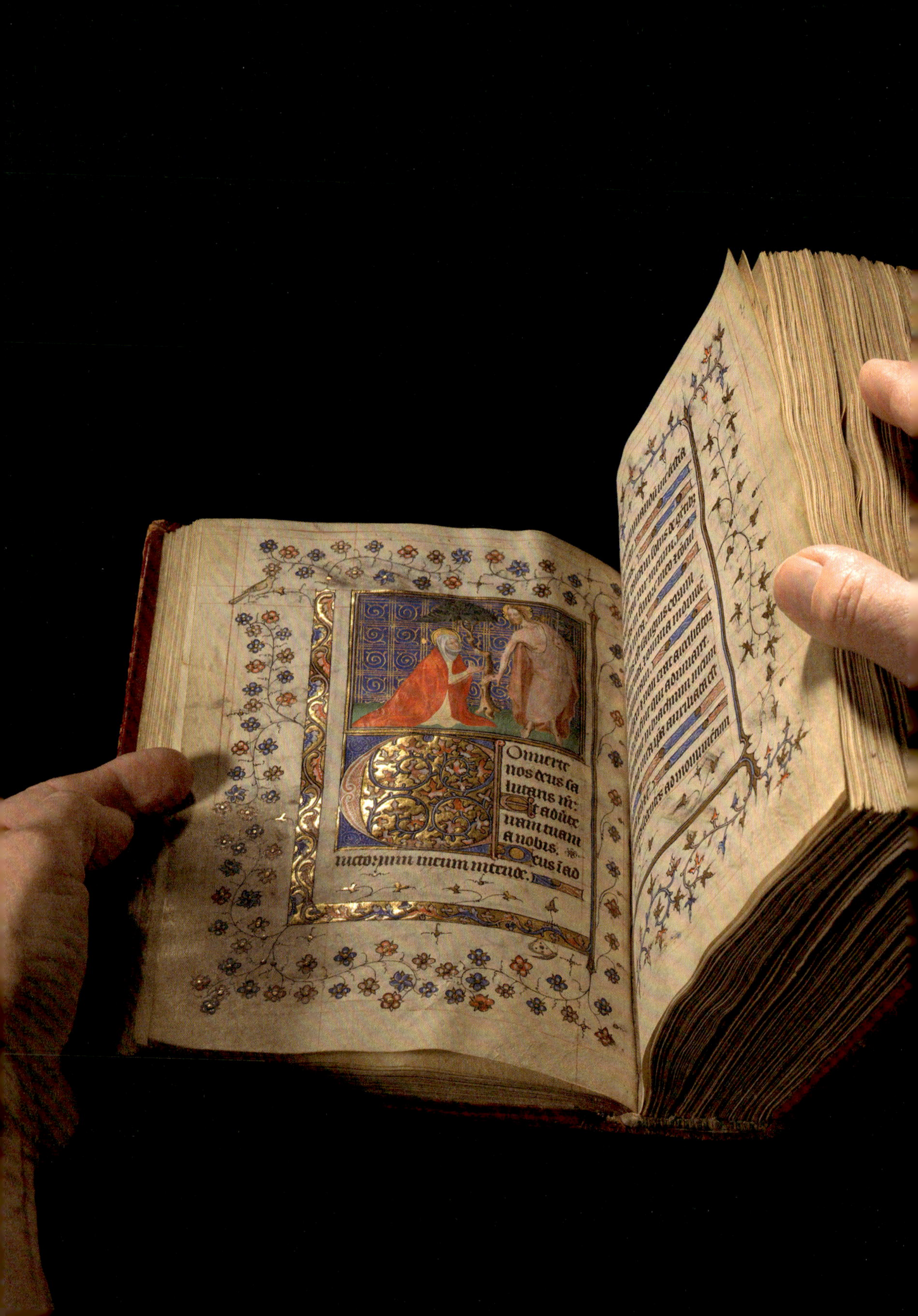

3. TRACES OF OWNERS AND READERS IN BOOKS OF HOURS

In the late Middle Ages, books were a valuable possession, and most people owned only a few – if any. A collection of thirty books was already considered a large and exceptional library. If someone owned just one single book, it was often a Book of Hours. It was not just monarchs and the aristocracy who could afford a Book of Hours, they were also to be found among various other social groups, such as (wives of) mayors, aldermen, judges, tax collectors, goldsmiths, clothmakers, surgeons, barbers, brewers, notaries, masons, painters, architects and tapestry merchants.[1]

From the late fifteenth century onwards, the increased production of modest Books of Hours and the rise in the availability of printed Books of Hours rendered them accessible even to those of more limited means. Unfortunately, little is known about the distribution of Books of Hours among the less affluent members of society as their lives are less well documented in today's archives than those of the higher social classes. Even though we might find their names inscribed in their books, we no longer have the means to learn more about their lives. On rare occasions, indirect evidence shows that poorer individuals did own Books of Hours. One such case is a legal record from 1500 concerning Avis Godfrey, a pauper woman in London who was accused of stealing a Book of Hours belonging to Elizabeth Sekett, a maidservant.[2]

Hanno Wijsman &
Evelien Hauwaerts

fig. 30 Book of Hours of Jacqueline of Bavaria, Paris, c.1410. Bruges, Public Library, Ms. 321, ff. 26v–27r.

What can Books of Hours reveal about the men and women who bought, read, treasured and gifted them? To uncover the history of a particular Book of Hours we can explore three key sources of information: the liturgical use of the texts in the manuscript, explicit evidence of ownership and signs of use.

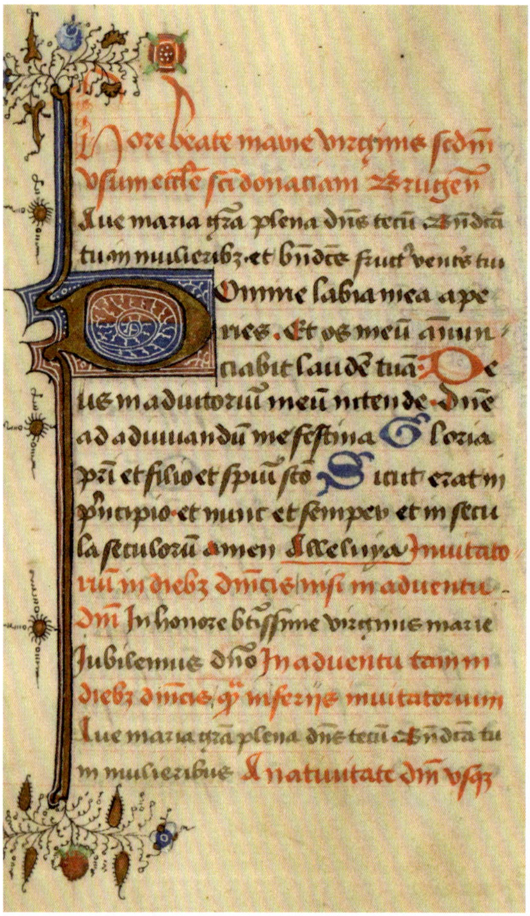

fig. 31 *'Hore beate Marie Virginis secundum usum ecclesie sancti Donatiani Brugensis'*, in Book of Hours, Master(s) of the Gold Scrolls, Bruges, c.1430–c.1440. Bruges, Public Library, Ms. 742, f. 77r.

Liturgical Use

First and foremost, it is crucial to analyse the contents of the Book of Hours in detail. The calendar, the hours, the litany and the prayers are not selected at random but are tailored to the commissioner or to a specific market. The most significant variable is the liturgical use, or *usum*, of the Hours of the Virgin. The use typically follows the traditions of a particular diocese, as each diocese had subtle variations in the verses and responses that the faithful were expected to recite.

In the fifteenth century, however, many Books of Hours also adhered to the universal Use of the Archbasilica of Saint John Lateran in Rome (Roman Use or *usum romanum*). This can easily be determined: in the Roman Use, the antiphon at Vespers of the Hours of the Virgin is *Dum esset*. If the text features a different antiphon, several other textual elements must be compared – primarily the antiphon and capitulum at Prime and None – to determine the specific use.[3] Many Books of Hours produced in Bruges were designed for export to England and follow the Sarum Use, a liturgy originally developed for the Diocese of Salisbury ('Sarum' in Latin) but widely adopted across the British Isles in the late Middle Ages. The texts vary not only by region but also by religious order (e.g. Dominican Use) or even by specific churches (such as St Donatian's in Bruges, see fig. 31). The presence of such a use may suggest that the intended reader had a personal connection to that particular church or order, for instance because their confessor belonged to it.

Textual variations can reveal not only a specific target audience but also the region of production; for example, the petition *Per quadragesimum et ieiunium tuum* appears exclusively in the litanies of Books of Hours from the Southern Low

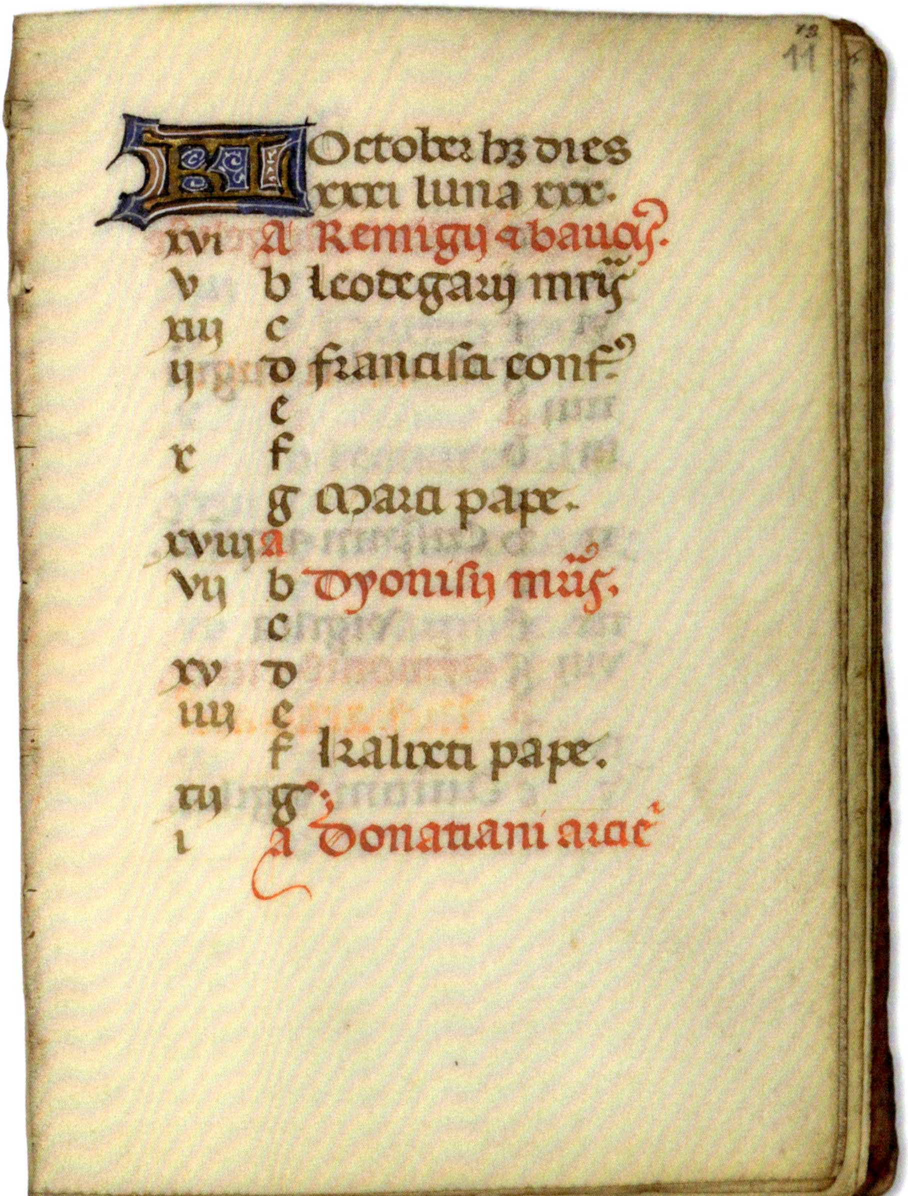

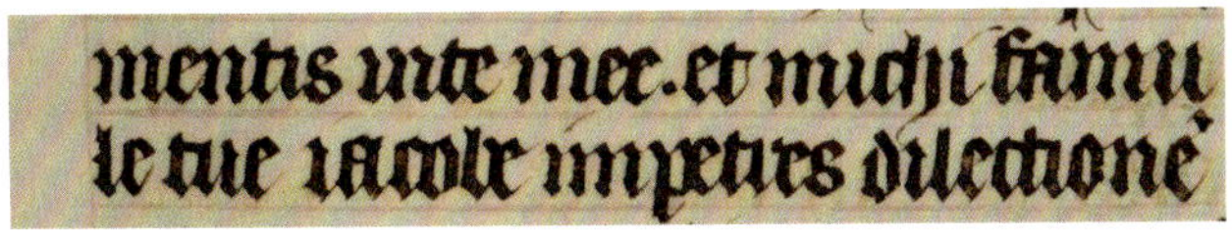

fig. 32 Saint Donatian of Bruges on 14 October (bottom line), in Book of Hours, Bruges, c.1460–c.1470. Bruges, Public Library, Jean van Caloen Foundation Collection, Ms. 14, f. 10r.

fig. 33 Female form and name *'famule tue iacobe'*, in Book of Hours of Jacqueline of Bavaria, Paris, c.1410. Bruges, Public Library, Ms. 321, f. 122v.

Countries.[4] In translated Books of Hours, or in Latin Books of Hours with vernacular rubric titles, the dialect used can also hint at a particular region.[5]

Beyond the Hours of the Virgin, the saints featured in the calendar and litany are especially useful for understanding the intended audience. Most calendars highlight feast days according to their significance: the principal feasts are written in red, sometimes in gold, while secondary feasts appear in black. As the veneration of saints differed by region and even by city, examining less widely recognised saints can offer valuable insights.

The Diocese of Tournai, for instance, which encompassed most of the County of Flanders, held particular devotion to Amandus in February, Eligius in June and Nicasius in December. Adelbert and Willibrord, both celebrated in November, were common to Holland, while the feasts of Cuthbert in March, and of Thomas Becket in December, were linked to England. Some saints can be even more closely associated with specific cities – for instance, Donatian (see fig. 32) and Basil were typical for Bruges, Bavo and Livinus for Ghent, Lambert for Liège and Mastidia for Troyes.[6] Unique saints in the suffrages and litanies may also suggest a particular region.[7]

While examining the saints can offer valuable insights, some caution is needed. The veneration of a particular saint in one city does not necessarily mean they were not honoured elsewhere – for example, Saint Genevieve (Genovefa) is strongly associated with Paris, yet she also appears in books produced in other parts of France and in the Southern Low Countries. Personal preferences could also influence the choice of saints. A patron might favour their namesake saint (such as Saint Catherine for a woman named Catherine, or Saint Peter for a man named Peter), a saint of particular significance to their family (such as Andrew for the Burgundian dukes), or saints linked to a specific religious tradition. A patron might, for example, be devoted to the Franciscan order without being a Franciscan friar themselves, in which case saints such as Francis, Clare and Bernardino might feature prominently in their Book of Hours.

Word choice and grammar in the texts can reveal clues about the owner's gender. In prayers, for example, nouns referring to the supplicant are sometimes in the feminine form. The Marian prayers *Obsecro te* and *O intemerata*, for instance, are written in the first-person singular since the supplicant addresses Mary directly. In several places, there are explicit references to the supplicant, such as *ego miserrimus peccator* (I, wretched sinner (male)) or *ego miserrima peccatrix* (I, wretched sinner (female)). In the latter case, the book was likely produced for a woman. The same can be inferred when there is a notable presence of female saints in the book. Unfortunately, these conclusions about gender do not work in reverse: there are many Books of Hours clearly made for a woman (based on ownership characteristics) but still written in masculine forms.

In rare cases, the name of the patron or intended recipient is included alongside such first-person references; for example, in an early fifteenth-century Book of Hours from Paris, we find *michi famule tue iacobe* (for me thy servant (female) Jacqueline) (see fig. 33). Based on the presence of this name and on other characteristics, it has been established that this book was likely made for Jacqueline of Bavaria (1401–1436), Countess of Holland, Zeeland and Hainaut (see also fig. 30).[8]

Marks of Ownership

Sometimes the owner explicitly marked a book as their own.[9] This could go as far as commissioning a miniature with their portrait, in which they are usually shown in prayer at the feet of Mary (see fig. 34) or another saint, such as a patron saint. More often, however, it took the form of a heraldic shield (see fig. 35) or an emblem (see fig. 36) in the margins.[10] Not everyone had a personal coat of arms, but it is a misconception that only rulers and the aristocracy bore them – citizens from various walks of life also displayed them. Identifying a coat of arms, however, can be challenging. The content of the manuscript can often provide a useful clue, as the liturgical use might point to a specific city, region or diocese, narrowing the search to families from that area. Coats of arms and emblems were more than just marks of ownership, they should truly be seen as personifications of the individual. Placing them next to an image of, or a prayer to, a saint, or even within a miniature of a saint, was a way of creating a personal connection, bringing the owner closer to the saint.

Handwritten ownership marks can sometimes reveal a wealth of information. Some books, for instance, contain a promise of a reward for the honest finder. As Books of Hours were often used outside the home, loss was certainly a real concern. In the late fifteenth century, Katheline Minne, the wife of the alderman Walrave Baelde of Ypres, wrote this in her Book of Hours: 'This book belongs to Katheline Minne. Whoever finds it and returns it will be rewarded with a golden penny. And if you don't know where she lives, ask at South Street, and they will show you the way, so go to the Gouden Hoofd.'[11] With such a generous reward, Katheline clearly valued her book highly.

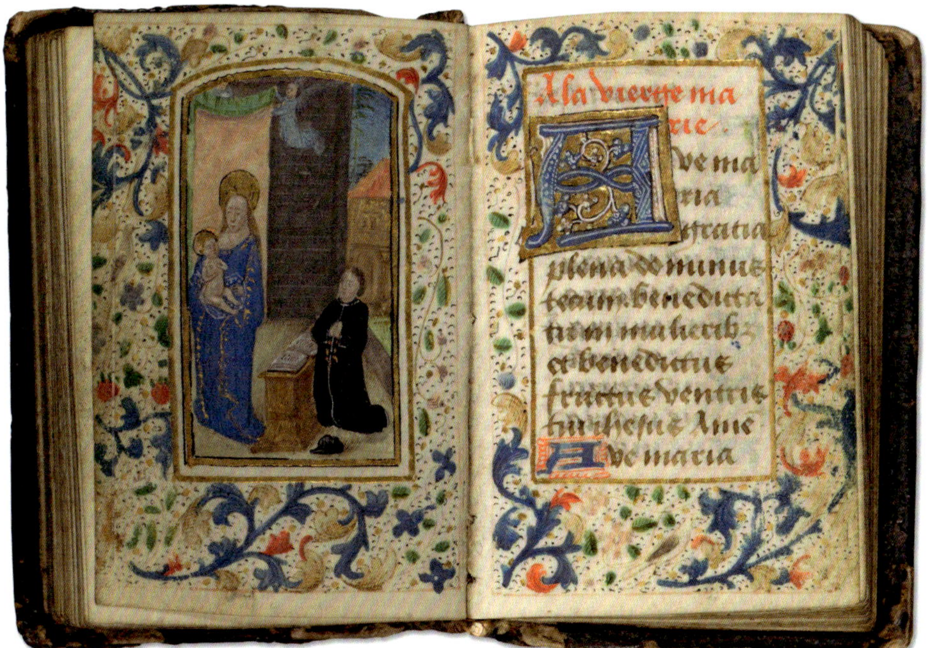

fig. 34 Portrait of an unidentified patron facing the *Ave Maria*, in Book of Hours, Cambrai (?), c.1470–c.1480. Bruges, Public Library, Jean van Caloen Foundation Collection, Ms. 15, ff. 67v–68r.

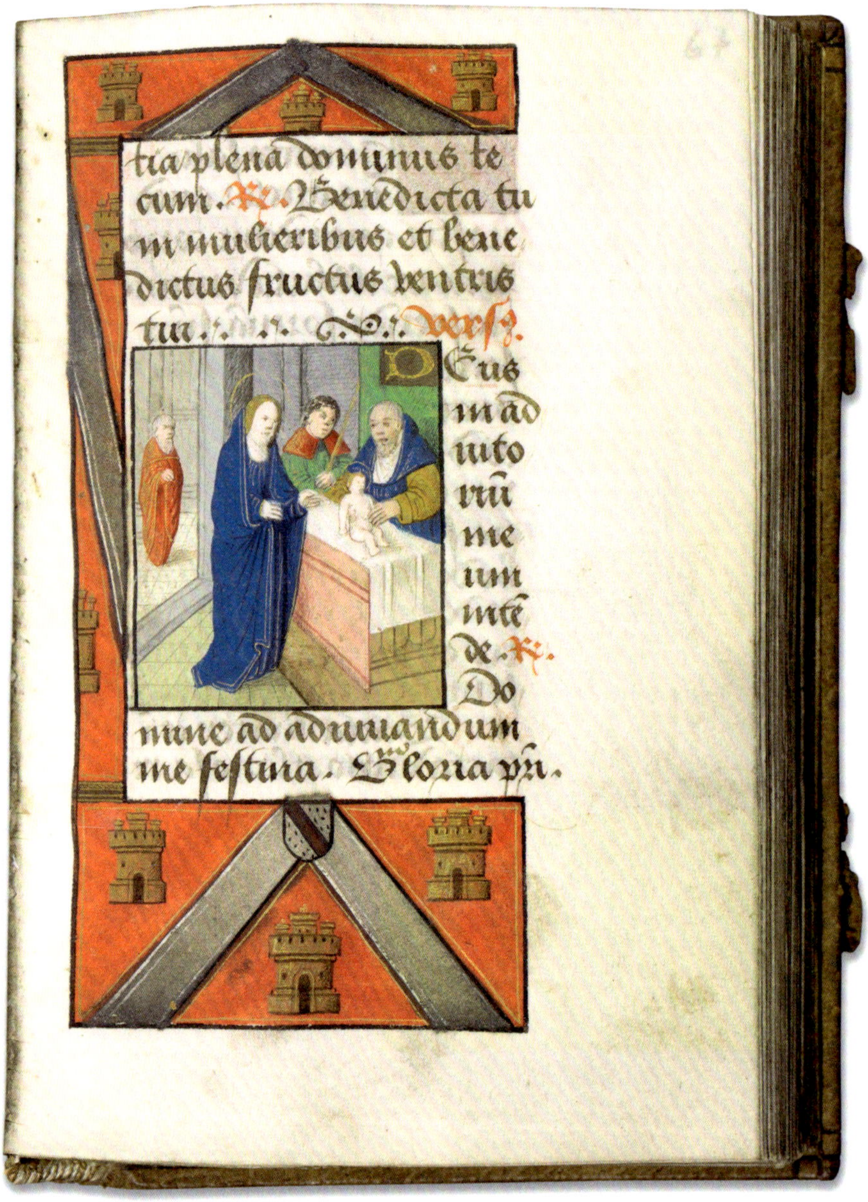

fig. 35 The coat of arms of the Bruges Metteneye family in the marginal decoration, in Book of Hours, Bruges, c.1500. Bruges, Public Library, Ms. 675, f. 67r.

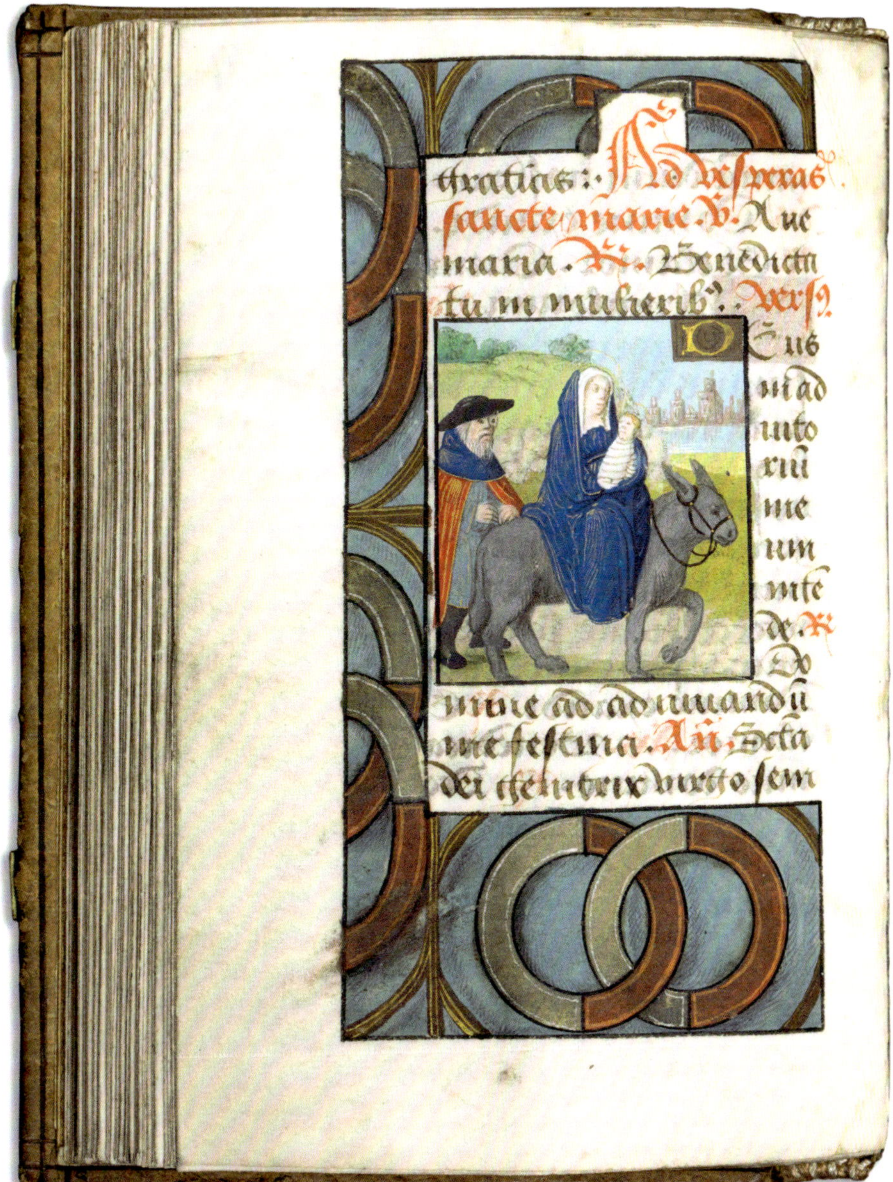

fig. 36 The emblem of the Bruges Metteneye family in the marginal decoration, in Book of Hours, Bruges, c.1500. Bruges, Public Library, Ms. 675, f. 71v.◆

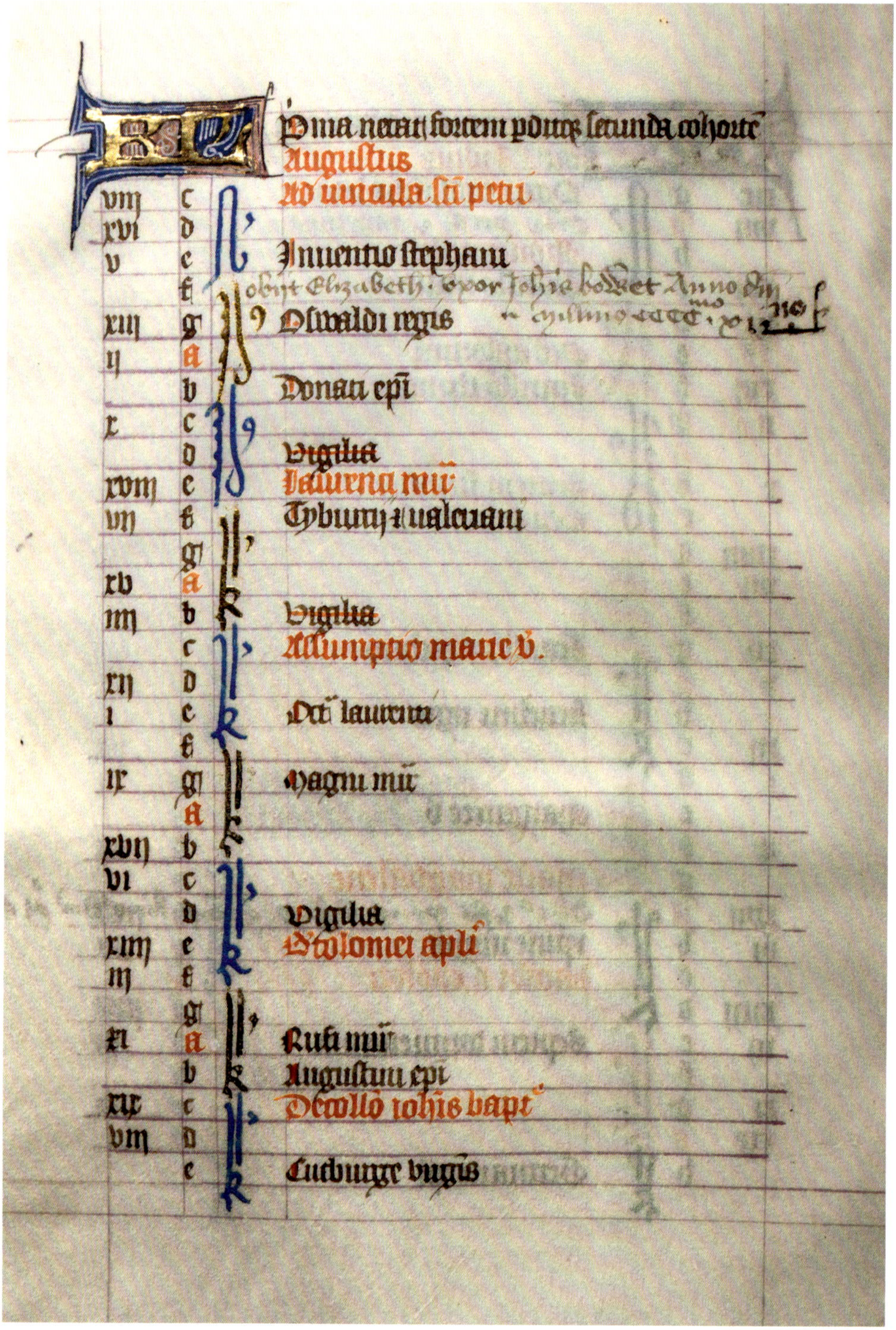

fig. 37 *Obiit* 'Elisabeth, wife of John Bowet, died in 1412',● in Book of Hours, Bruges, c.1400–c.1420, Master of the Tall Figures (Beaufort Group). Bruges, Public Library, Ms. 736 (King Baudouin Foundation Collection), f. 4v.

Signs of Use

In addition to textual features and explicit ownership marks, there are also various signs of use that shed light on how and by whom a Book of Hours was used. As a Book of Hours was such a personal object, it was often used to record family milestones: births, baptisms, marriages and deaths.[12] The dates of death and the names of the deceased were particularly important for the practice of remembrance. Armed with this information, descendants could pray the Office of the Dead and the Penitential Psalms for their deceased relatives, thereby shortening their time in purgatory. Thanks to their precious and durable nature, Books of Hours were the perfect place to preserve this kind of family history.[13] The books were passed down through the generations, with each new owner adding their own entries to the family chronicle.[14] Sometimes, events were noted as a list on a blank page, other times they were written in the margins (see fig. 2), or even added directly to the calendar on the corresponding day (see fig. 37). These entries can sometimes reveal the identity of the book's owner, even in the absence of other ownership marks.

A personal keepsake like a Book of Hours was particularly well-suited to customisation: a devotional print might be pasted in (fig. 38), a prayer added or a saint hastily noted in the calendar.[15] Thanks to the modular method of production, Books of Hours could easily be adapted when passed on or purchased second-hand.[16] The book could be disassembled and rebound with an extra leaf or even an additional quire; for instance, in a Book of Hours illuminated around 1430 by the Masters of the Gold Scrolls, a loose miniature of Saint Francis was sewn in around 1470 – almost half a century later (fig. 39). Some workshops even specialised in 'upcycling' old manuscripts to meet the high demand for Books of Hours.[17]

Conversely, certain parts were also removed or concealed, mostly due to censorship or changes in liturgy. In an ordinance of 1538, for example, King Henry VIII of England issued a decree that images of and prayers to the martyr Thomas Becket (e.g. fig. 21) be removed from all books. Personalisation sometimes also involved the removal or replacement of coats of arms and emblems belonging to previous owners. In this way, a Book of Hours would gradually evolve, whether for a single user or for successive owners. There are, of course, other signs of use, such as stains (e.g. from kissing a miniature), water damage (e.g. from outdoor use) and wax drips, which give a clear indication of how intensively the book was used, but reveal less information about the identity of the reader.

Ultimately, for historians and manuscript specialists, the Book of Hours is an object that requires a comprehensive, integrated approach to uncover its history fully. Few were written and illuminated in a simple, straightforward manner and left untouched thereafter. Almost always, modifications were made over time – to the binding, the leaves, the texts, the illustrations, the illumination and the ownership marks. As a result, Books of Hours often present complex yet captivating puzzles, offering valuable insights into devotion, family life, emotions and their evolution over time.

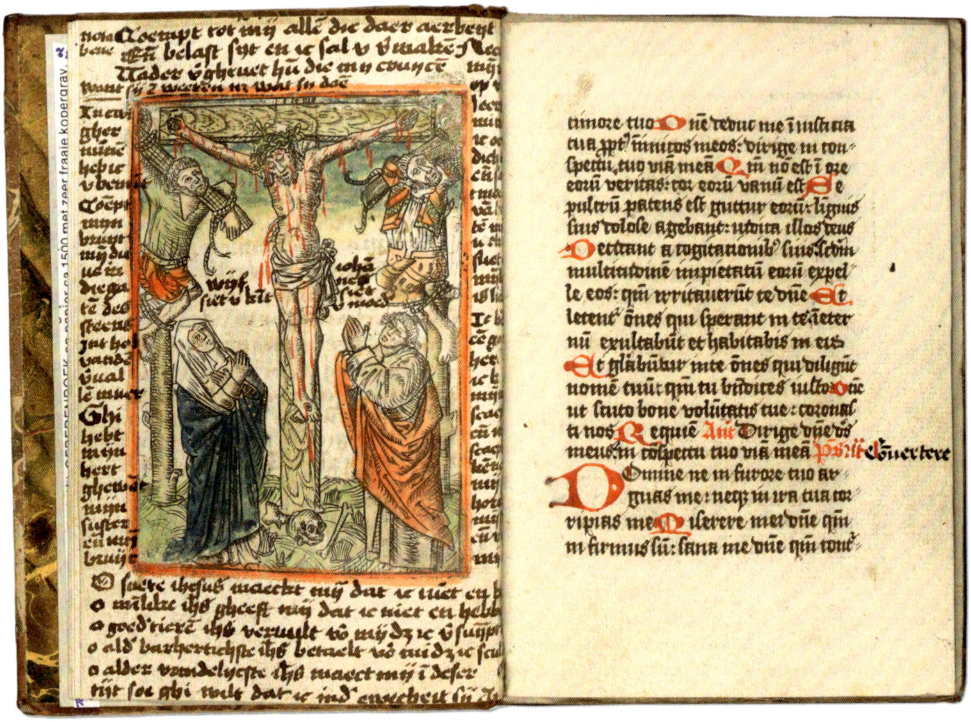

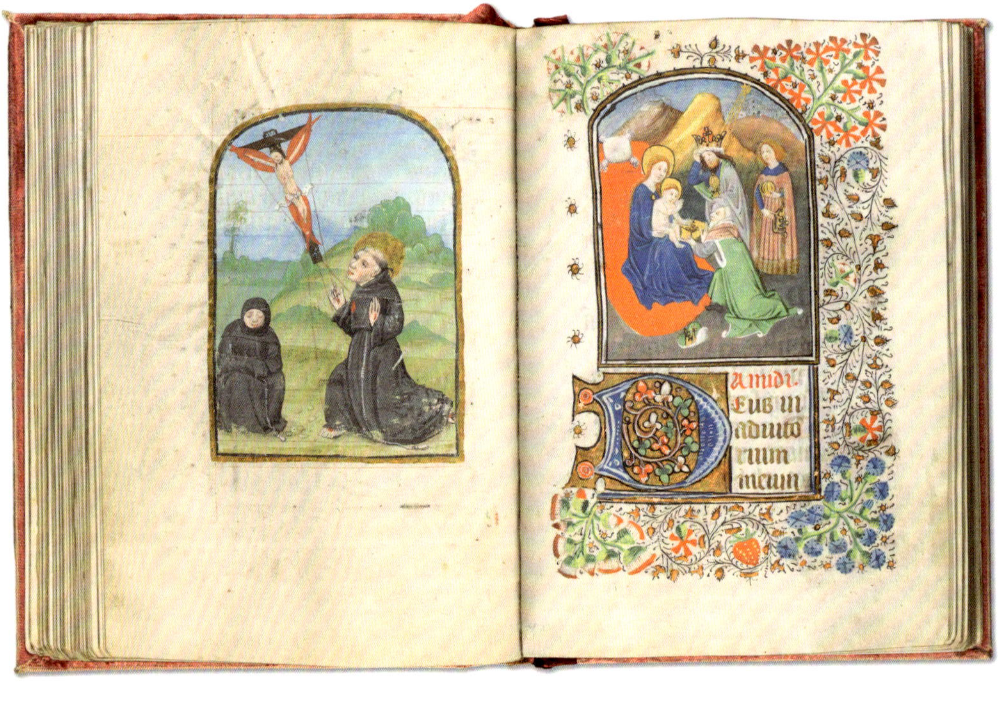

fig. 38 Inserted burin engraving and prayer added in the margins, in Book of Hours, Southern Low Countries, late 15th century. Bruges, Public Library, Jean van Caloen Foundation Collection, Ms. 18, ff. 4v–5r.

fig. 39 Inserted miniature of Saint Francis (c.1470), in Book of Hours, Bruges, c.1430. Bruges, Public Library, Ms. 821 (Flemish Community Collection), f. 66v.

1. On owners of Books of Hours in the Low Countries, see, for example, Zwart, *Religious Book Owners*, and Korteweg, '*Dit boeck hoert toe...*'.
2. Duffy, *Marking the Hours*, 4.
3. See De Hamel, *A History of Illuminated MSS*, 180, for a basic overview of uses based on the Madan method. The results of this method should be tested against more detailed profiles for each *usum*. For this, consult online checklists and overviews, such as those by Erik Drigsdahl (CHD Institute for Studies of Illuminated Manuscripts in Denmark) at http://manuscripts.org.uk/chd.dk/use/hv_chdtest.html. Use can also be identified through the Office of the Dead; see, for instance, Ottosen, *Responsories*, and the accompanying database at https://www.cantusplanus.de/databases/Ottosen/search.html.
4. Gregory Clark, in the online database *Beyond Use*: https://beyonduse.sewanee.edu/texts_list.php?texts=Per%20Petitions (accessed 20/12/24). On this research tool, see Hindman & Marrow (eds), *Books of Hours Reconsidered*, 213–33.
5. Stylistic features of the decoration and script also reveal much about the place and time of production. For instance, the coloured margins with seemingly scattered flowers and insects (e.g. fig. 19), characteristic of the so-called Ghent-Bruges style, are typical of production in Flanders after c.1480. For more on the Ghent-Bruges style see, for example, Kren and McKendrick, *Illuminating*, 199–202.
6. Two useful online tools for identification based on saints are: *Zeitrechnung des Deutschen Mittelalters und der Neuzeit* by H. Grotefend (multiple editions, also available online: https://bilder.manuscripta-mediaevalia.de/gaeste/grotefend/grotefend.htm), and Denis Muzerelle, *Calendoscope* (an online tool for medieval saint calendars and feast days): https://calendoscope.irht.cnrs.fr/.
7. As a comparison point for the suffrages, this online edition of a Book of Hours from 1599 is useful: https://medievalist.net/hourstxt/home.htm.
8. Smeyers, 'Een getijden- en gebedenboek van Jacoba van Beieren'.
9. The Bibale database collects information on owners and their books, as well as ownership characteristics: https://bibale.irht.cnrs.fr/.
10. A useful database for emblems and devices is *Devise, emblématique et héraldique à la fin du Moyen Âge*: https://devise.saprat.fr/.
11. '*Deise bock beoort toe katheline minnis diese wint ende werden brinct hij zal ebben eene goudin penninc voor zine loon ende weit ghij niet waerze wecht woont vraghter in de zutstrate omme men zalze jou wizen zoe went biden goude gouden hoofde*', Boston, Public Library, q. Med. 160, f. 113v; the Gouden Hoofd was an inn. See Zwart, *Religious Book Owners*, 62.
12. See Wijsman, *Handschriften voor het hertogdom*, 152–57. Owners also recorded other useful information, such as remedies for ailments (e.g. 'A medicine for the migraine', in Bruges, Public Library, Ms. 736 Coll. KBS, f. ii r.).
13. On medieval books as secure time capsules for important information, see Treharne, *Perceptions*, 63–64.
14. For instance, in Bruges, Public Library, Ms. 330 (fig. 2), family records spanning four successive generations between 1568 and 1662 are noted.
15. On the customisation of Books of Hours, see Chapter 2 and Rudy, *Piety in Pieces*.
16. See Chapter 2.
17. Rudy, *Piety in Pieces*, 243.

◆ This emblematic motif (two interlocking annulets, parti per pale, silver and gules) can also be found on the draped cloth over the prie-dieu in the portrait of Margareta Metteneye (c.1525–c.1530) by a follower of Lancelot Blondeel (Bruges, Musea Brugge, 1994.GRO0016.I).

● '*Obiit Elizabeth uxor Johannis Bowet, anno domini 1412*'.

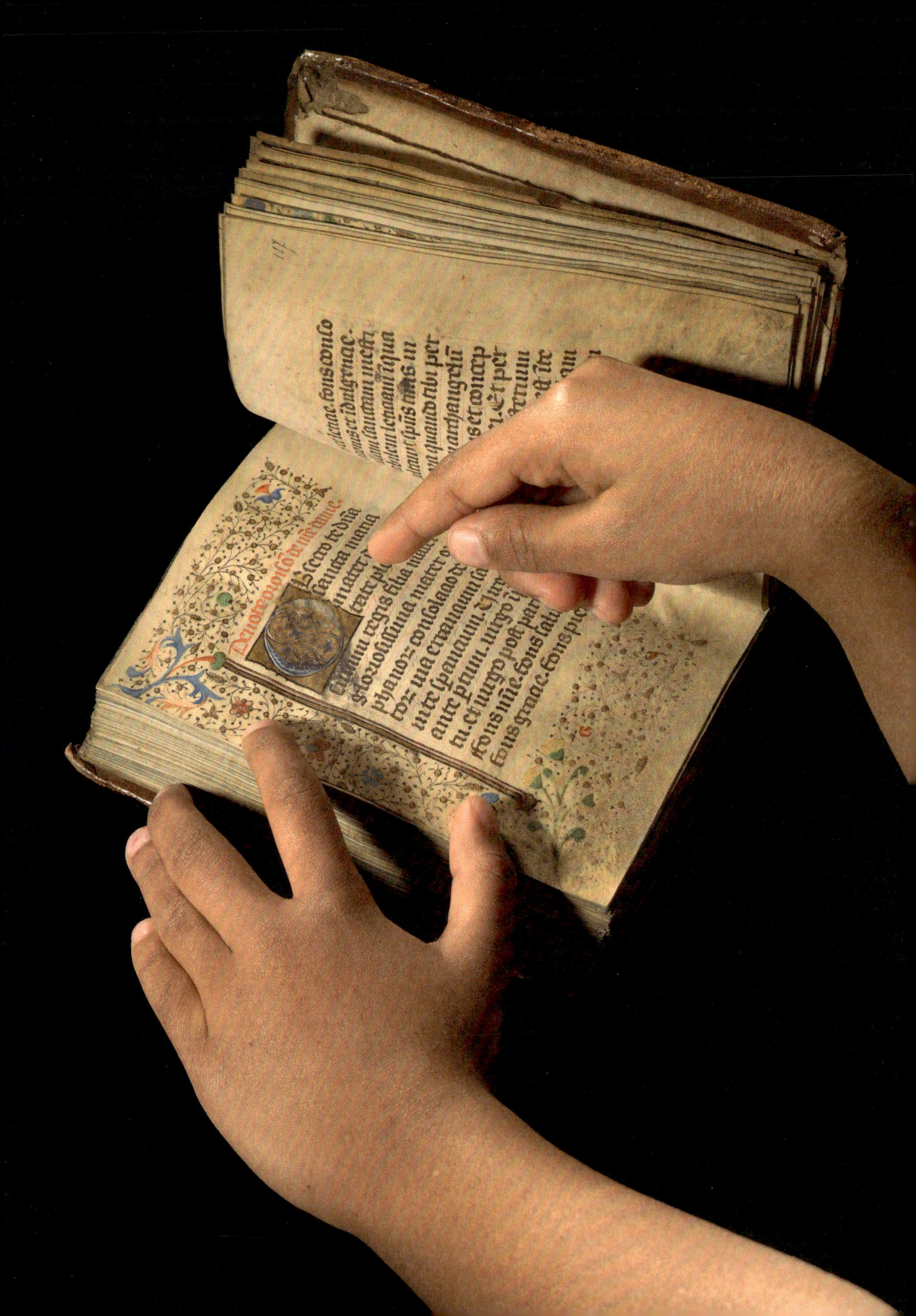

4. SCHOOLING AND LITERACY IN THE LATE-MEDIEVAL LOW COUNTRIES

Jeroen Deploige

He is intently weighing coins. In front of him lie four precious rings encircling a rolled piece of paper, an open purse filled with pearls, and a crystal goblet inlaid with a precious metal. She has an open Book of Hours before her: on the right-hand page, a full-page miniature depicting the Virgin Mary dressed in red and holding the Christ Child in her arms is clearly visible. The woman's gaze, however, is primarily fixed on the man's actions. Both are wearing distinguished yet somewhat outdated bourgeois attire, reminiscent of the Burgundian period. On the shelves behind the couple are a parchment roll, several folded and inscribed sheets of paper, a stack of accounts and approximately five books.

The Money Changer and His Wife, painted in Antwerp around 1514, is one of the most renowned works by the Brabantine artist Quinten Metsys (fig. 41). Rather than a portrait, it is a moralising work rich with subtle messages, contrasting greed and transience with devotion. As a result, the painting has prompted extensive iconological analyses and hypotheses regarding the circumstances of its creation.[1] What interests us here, however, is the natural presence of paper and parchment, books and private reading, and familiarity with calculations, all set within an unmistakably bourgeois environment.

fig. 40 Book of Hours, Troyes (?), c.1450–c.1501. Bruges, Public Library, Ms. 330, ff. 126v–127r.

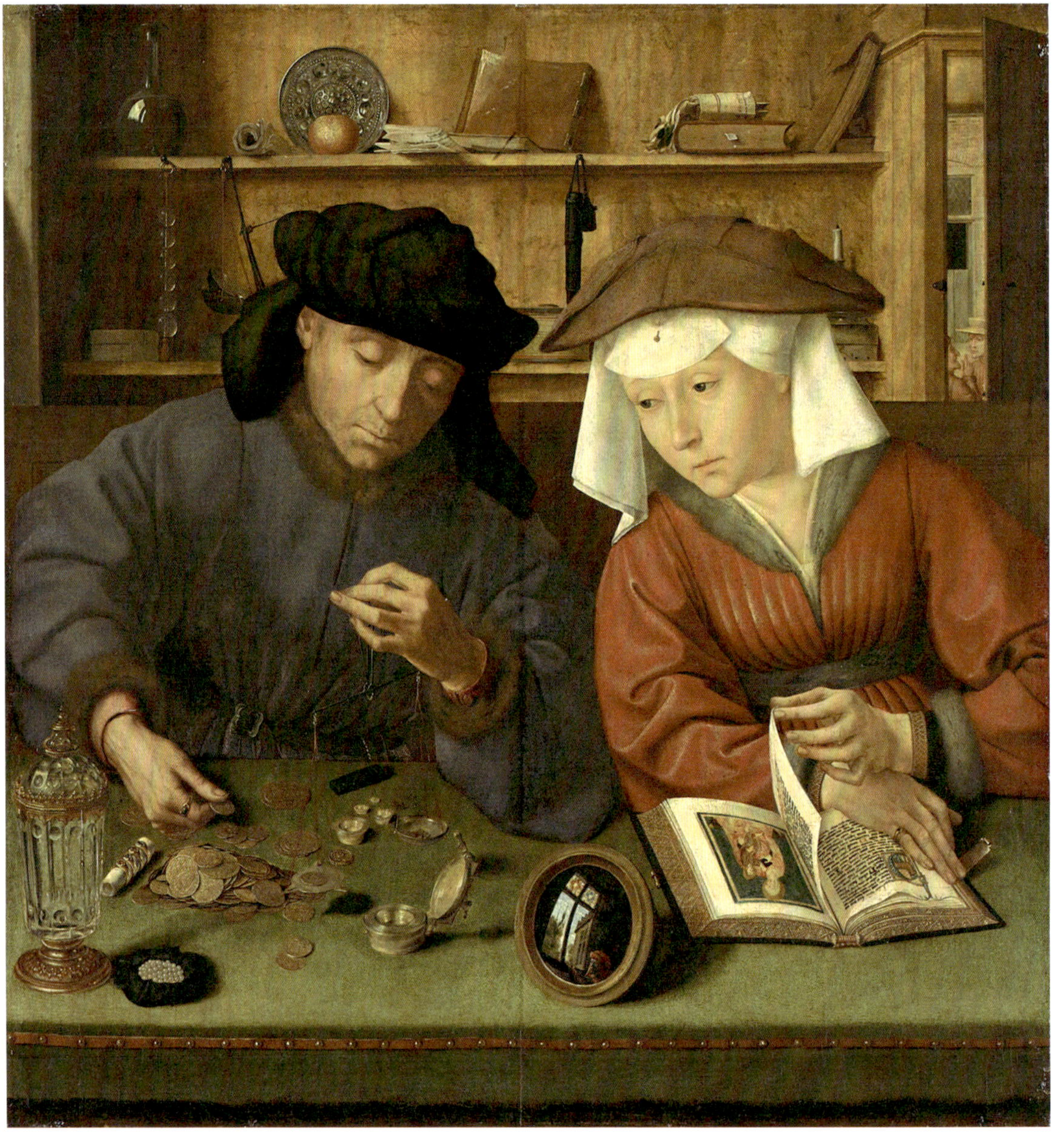

fig. 41 Quinten Metsys, *The Money Changer and His Wife*, 1514, oil on panel. Paris, Louvre, inv. 1444.

A Writing Revolution

Four centuries earlier, such a setting would have been unthinkable. Throughout most of the Middle Ages, and certainly until the early thirteenth century, literacy and education were largely dominated by an ecclesiastical elite. Manuscripts primarily contained theological, historiographical, liturgical and hagiographical texts, which were preserved and copied, mainly in monasteries – when the aristocracy required written charters they relied on clerics to produce them. In most of Western Europe, particularly on the continent, Latin remained the dominant written language well into the twelfth century, making it inaccessible to the majority of laypeople. Education, too, was largely monopolised by monastic and cathedral schools, which focused mainly on educating boys who aspired to careers in the clergy. Noble families who wished to provide their sons or daughters with some degree of literacy could, however, hire private tutors.

From the twelfth century onwards, interest in vernacular literature grew within aristocratic circles. This shift was closely tied to the rise of courtly culture, in which *chansons de geste*, troubadour poetry and chivalric romances became particularly popular. In some cases, nobles even took up the pen themselves.[2] Within the Church – especially from the thirteenth century onwards – there was also a growing recognition that simple texts in the vernacular, such as saints' lives, could reach a broad audience, particularly among laypeople and female religious communities. At the same time, semi-religious women, including Beguines such as the renowned poet Hadewijch and the controversial Marguerite Porete (later burnt at the stake for heresy), became active contributors to vernacular devotional literature.

When historians refer to a writing revolution from the thirteenth century onwards, however, they generally focus on the rapid and widespread emergence of a more practical and everyday form of literacy. In this transformation, writing was no longer essentially in the service of theology, memory or literary aesthetics; instead, it became an essential tool for managing information in daily life. This shift was particularly evident in book production, where older texts were compiled, rewritten, reorganised and abridged in entirely new ways to serve as practical tools for new audiences. The rise of Books of Hours and prayer books fits naturally within this context. This revolution in the written word also existed in royal and urban administrations, in the world of commerce, craft guilds and other corporations.[3]

The Secularisation of Literacy and Education

In the late Middle Ages, literacy among laypeople increased significantly, particularly in the highly urbanised Low Countries. From the late twelfth century onwards, this region was marked by the growing influence of local urban governments and their expanding administrations. Towns and cities also became key centres of economic growth, which also increased the importance of enhanced literacy and numeracy (fig. 42). To participate in public life and pursue a successful professional career, children needed to learn to read and write, perform arithmetic and bookkeeping, and communicate effectively in multiple languages, both orally and in writing. Consequently – initially in Flanders, Hainaut and Brabant – merchant elites and urban authorities began developing initiatives to provide educational opportunities that addressed these new needs.

From the thirteenth century onwards, the importance of education was increasingly emphasised. This is evident in literary texts, such as Jacob van Maerlant's *Heimelijkheid der heimelijkheden* (The Secret of Secrets), written around 1266, in which Maerlant advises the young Floris V, Count of Holland (r.1266–1296): '*In steden dire mogenthede / mac scolen, ende doe leren mede / die kinder van dinen lande*' (In cities where you hold authority, establish schools and ensure that the children of your land receive an education). In the fourteenth century, Jan van Boendaele, a city clerk from Antwerp, similarly argued that as many children as possible should attend school from an early age '*om lesen leren ende scriven*' (to learn to read and write), stressing that this would benefit everyone – servants and masters alike.[4] Education and training not only contributed to the transmission of knowledge and the development of professional skills, but also played a crucial role in the socialisation of children.[5]

The older monastic and cathedral schools, along with the more recently established parish schools, faced increasing pressure from the gradual secularisation of education. This process was not without friction between the ecclesiastical authorities and the urban elites. It typically resulted in agreements in which schoolmasters or magisters who wished to establish their own schools had to sign a contract with the municipal magistracy, submit to visitation by the *scholaster* or priest of the local chapter or parish school, and allocate a portion of their income to the chapter or presbytery.[6] Over time, and particularly in the Northern Netherlands, municipal governments increasingly took control of parish schools, appointing schoolmasters and schoolmistresses. This led to the development of a diversified school system in the Low Countries, characterised by numerous local variations and regulations.[7]

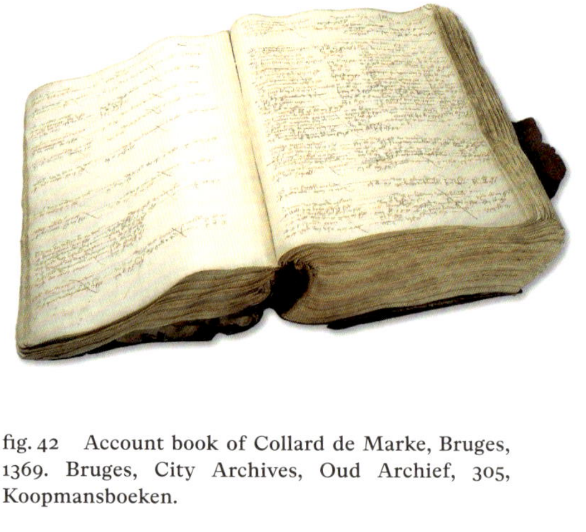

fig. 42 Account book of Collard de Marke, Bruges, 1369. Bruges, City Archives, Oud Archief, 305, Koopmansboeken.

Schooling in the Late Middle Ages

Young children typically began their schooling around the age of five or six. They could be homeschooled or, more commonly, attend a so-called *cleyne* (small) or *Dietsche* (Dutch-language) school, or a writing school in their area until about the age of eight. These small, often co-educational schools frequently arose from private initiatives (fig. 43). Male and female teachers instructed children in the basics of reading, writing, praying and singing in the vernacular (*Dietsch* was used as a collective designation for regional variants of Middle Dutch, including Flemish, Brabantian, Hollandic and Limburgish) (fig. 44).

Boys, particularly those from middle-class and wealthy families, could then continue their education at a Latin school from around the age of seven to ten. There, they were taught the liberal arts, which were generally limited to the *trivium*: grammar, logic and rhetoric. Traditional textbooks for this education included *Ars Grammatica* by Aelius Donatus and the *Disticha Catonis*, a collection of moral sayings erroneously attributed to Cato.[8] These Latin schools could be administered by various institutions and often offered boarding opportunities for children from rural areas. Some had evolved from traditional chapter schools, where pupils frequently took part in the liturgical services conducted in the associated chapter church. Others were established by parishes or municipal governments.[9] From the fifteenth century onwards, communities of the Brethren of the Common Life played an important role in many towns and cities. Initially, they focused on establishing boarding houses for both the poorer and the somewhat better-off schoolboys. They were sent to the local Latin schools but received additional guidance from the Brethren. They also took part in aspects of their religious life inspired by the reform movement of

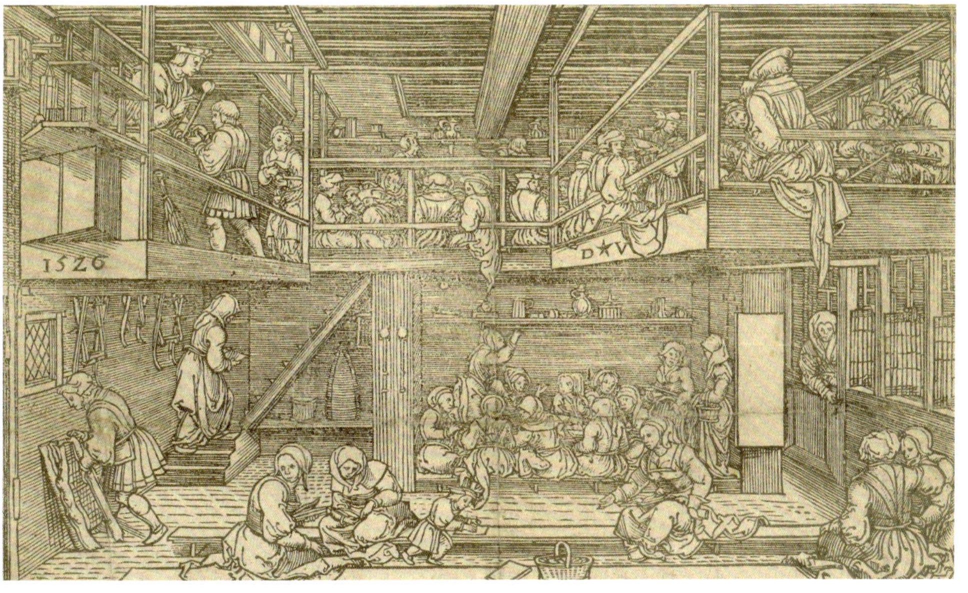

fig. 43 Dirk Jacobsz Vellert, *A 'cleyne' school for boys and girls*, Antwerp, 1526, woodcut. London, British Museum, 1857,0520.7.

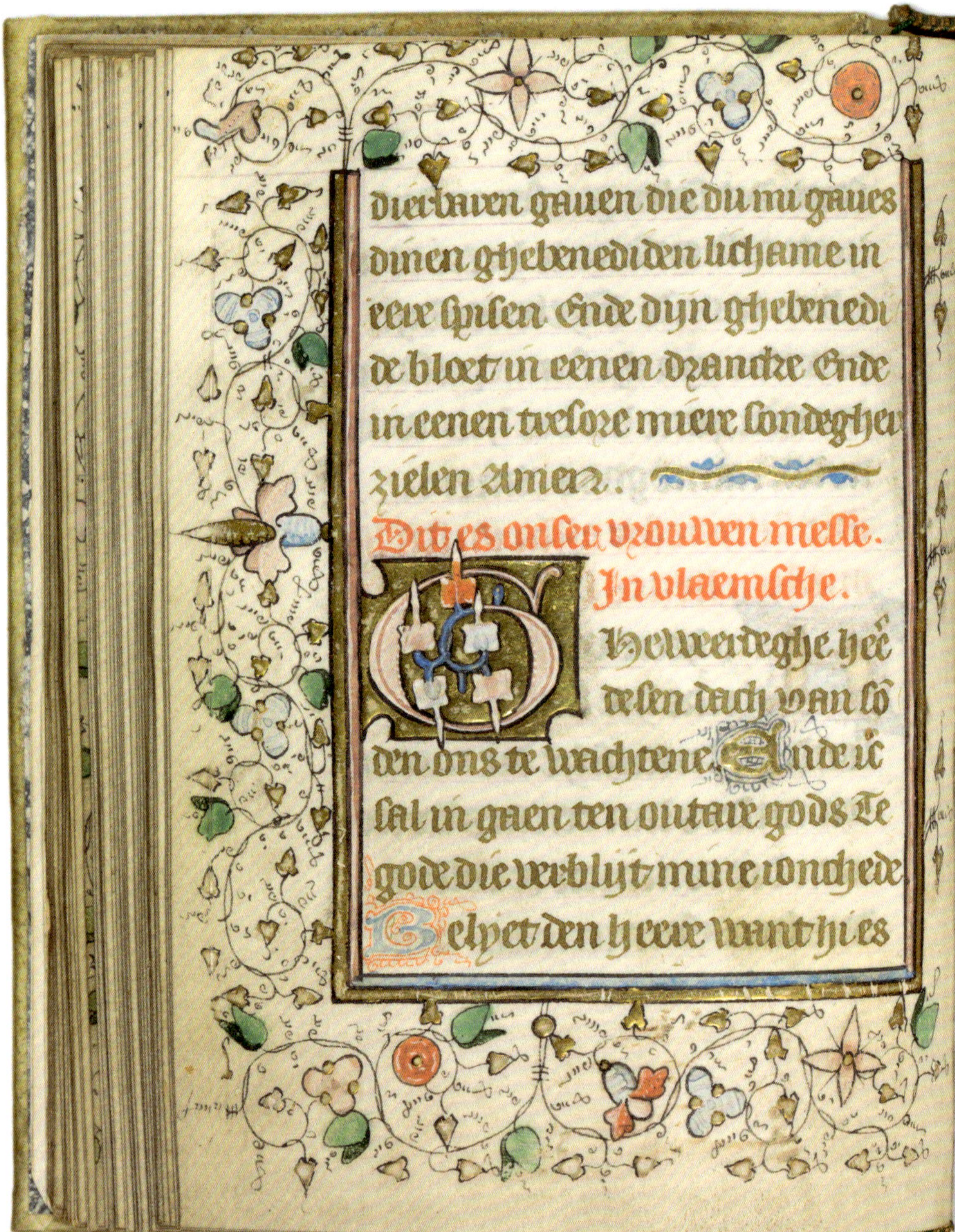

fig. 44 Marian Mass *'in Vlaemsche'* (in Flemish), in Book of Hours, Master of Guillebert de Mets, Ghent (?), c.1428. Bruges, Public Library, Jean van Caloen Foundation Collection, Ms. 1, f. 39v.

the Devotio Moderna. Particularly in the Southern Netherlands, the Brethren eventually organised their own schools.[10]

In addition to Latin schools, other educational pathways also existed. Some schoolmasters specialised in training young people for careers in trades or crafts. At these so-called *Walsche* or French schools, the curriculum included not only French and other modern languages but also subjects such as bookkeeping, arithmetic and letter writing. Bilingual textbooks, such as the more commercially orientated *Livre des mestiers / Bouc vanden ambachten* (Book of Trades) (fig. 45) or the *Leere van hoveschede* (Teachings of Courtliness) intended for future domestic servants, were likely particularly useful in this context.[11] Parents who enrolled their children in such private supplementary schools not only paid tuition fees but also compensation to the magister of the official Latin school.

Poorer children, for whom school fees were a barrier, could, in some towns and cities, attend so-called *bonifanten* schools (derived from *bons enfants*), where municipally funded teachers provided them with basic reading and writing skills and, most importantly, vocational training.[12] In Bruges, the municipal *bogardenschool* ('Beghard' school) offered similar vocational education from 1513 onwards. Young people could also receive training in specific crafts within guilds after signing an apprenticeship contract. Acquiring reading and writing skills within such contracts, however, was rare. If literacy were required, a schoolmaster could be hired, as was common in a *cleyne* school.[13] At the other end of the social spectrum, among the nobility, it was customary for children to receive home schooling from resident chaplains or specially appointed and paid magisters. Some noble children were sent to Latin schools, though this was certainly not standard practice.[14]

For a very small group – no more than 2.5% of the population – the Latin school could serve as a stepping stone to university, typically around the age of fourteen. For students from the Low Countries, the most common destinations were Paris and Cologne, and from 1425 onwards, Leuven. There, a small intellectual elite, sometimes supported by a municipal grant, could further specialise in the liberal arts, particularly the *quadrivium* (astronomy, geometry, arithmetic and music), as well as theology, law or medicine. Many students were members of the clergy.[15] Some nobles and courtiers also attended universities, sometimes receiving additional financial support from the Duke of Burgundy.[16]

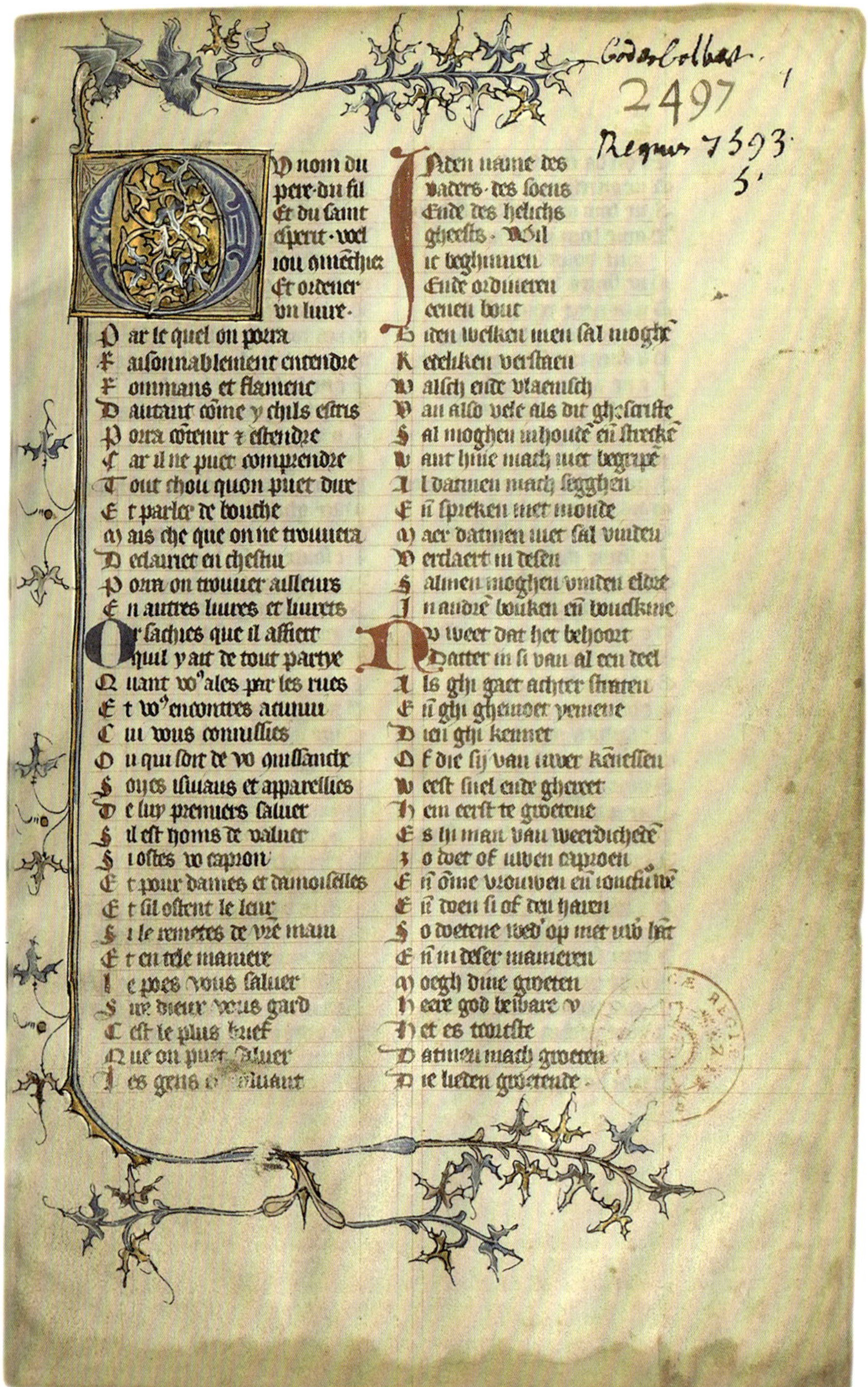

fig. 45 Opening page from the *Livre des mestiers / Bouc vanden ambachten*, a French-Dutch conversation book, Bruges, c.1370. Paris, Bibliothèque nationale de France, Ms. néerlandais 16, f. 1r.

fig. 46 Saint Anne teaching her young daughter Mary to read, in Book of Hours of Loys van Boghem, Lyon (?), 1526. Bruges, Archives of Ten Duinen Major Seminary, Ms. 66/35, f. 53v.

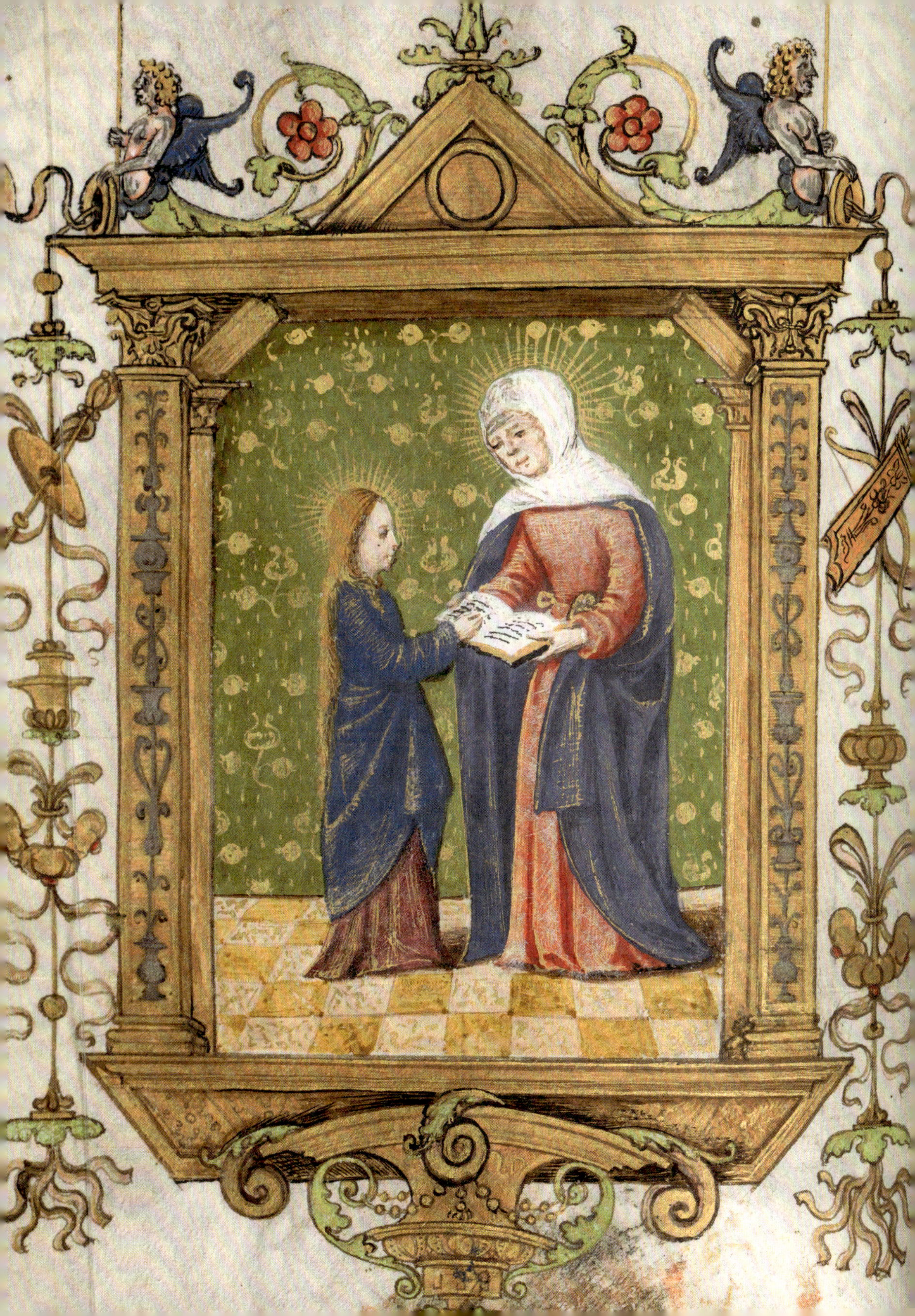

Female Literacy

The extent to which girls had access to education is difficult to determine. While they could certainly attend a *cleyne* school (co-educational or not), Latin schools in many towns and cities remained reserved for boys. This, however, was not the case everywhere: in Brussels, for example, a big (Latin) school for girls had existed since at least 1320. In the early fifteenth century, the renowned female author Christine de Pizan, who herself enjoyed a privileged position at the French royal court, passionately advocated for greater educational opportunities for girls. According to her, they should be regarded as intellectually equal to boys.[17] Nevertheless, most older girls likely relied more on home schooling or schooling in convents, where instruction was heavily religious in nature. Depictions of Saint Anne teaching her daughter Mary to read suggest that literacy was sometimes passed down from mother to daughter within the household (figs 46 and 47).[18]

It is therefore unsurprising that, on average, girls had less knowledge of Latin than boys. This is evident from book ownership and the writing culture within late-medieval religious communities, about which we have relatively detailed information. In male monasteries, where members had usually attended Latin school, books and original texts were generally written in Latin. In female religious communities, however, collections consisted almost exclusively of texts in the vernacular. The few known female authors of late-medieval religious literature also wrote almost entirely in the vernacular.[19]

There is indirect evidence, however, that laywomen actively participated in a reading and writing culture. Wills and colophons in preserved manuscripts indicate that women owned and passed down books. The widespread popularity of images depicting a reading Virgin Mary (fig. 48) and portraits of female patrons with books, reflects the devotional reading culture among women.[20] Rare surviving spiritual guidelines also suggest that laywomen structured their day around prayers from the Book of Hours and meditations on the Passion of Christ, found in *goeden Dietschen boeken* (good Dutch books).[21] The Devotio Moderna movement particularly encouraged the reading of devotional literature in the vernacular, both among religious women and laypeople. The Middle Dutch translation of the Latin Book of Hours by Geert Grote, one of the founding figures of the Devotio Moderna, became especially popular in the Low Countries (fig. 49).

Finally, women were also involved in economic life and administrative tasks, although they typically only appear in historical records after becoming widows, when they could legally continue their late husband's business under their own name. Women also worked as scribes in the book trade.[22] There were even female money changers, as evidenced by the account book of the fourteenth-century Bruges money changer Willem Ruweel. Willem only entered the financial sector after marrying Margriet van Ruuslede, who had inherited and managed her parents' exchange business. While Margriet oversaw daily operations, Willem focused on investments, ultimately leading to his bankruptcy. Afterward, Margriet was able to continue running the exchange business independently, as it had been part of her dowry.[23]

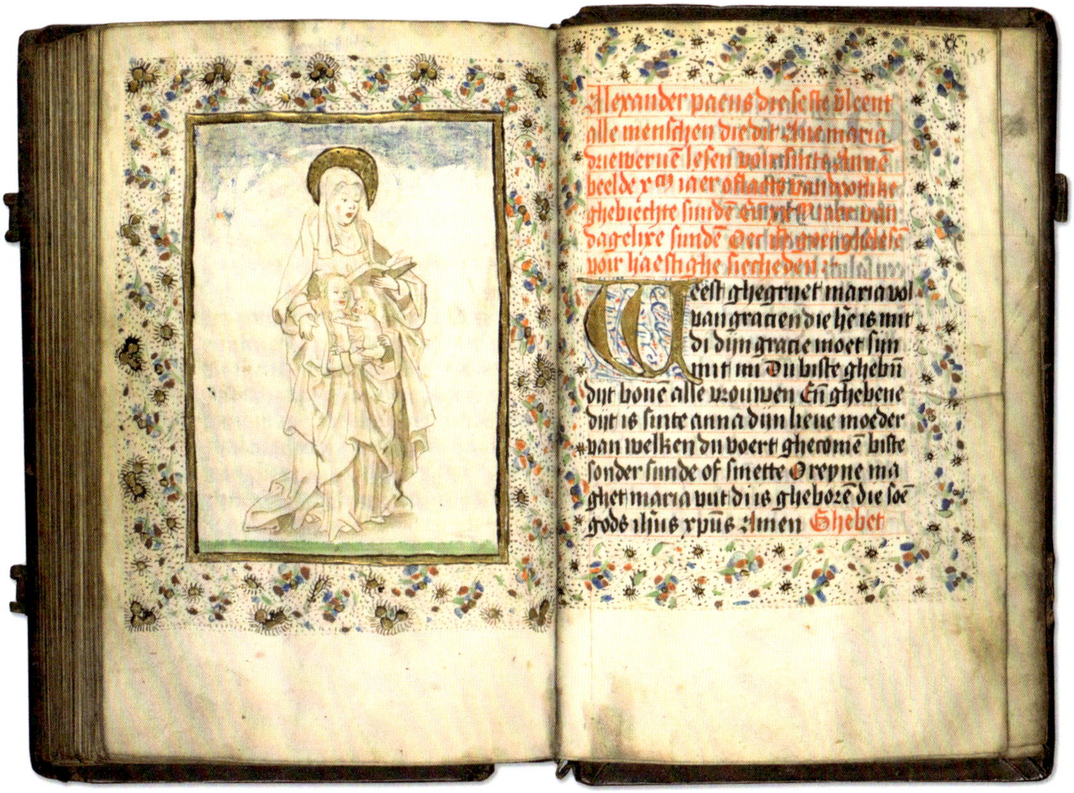

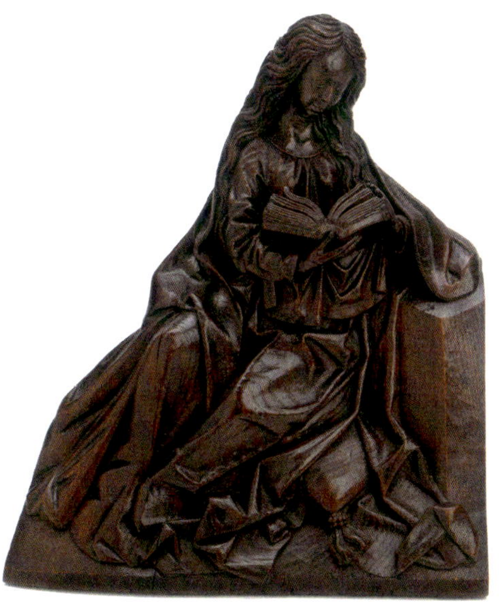

fig. 47 Middle Dutch indulgence prayer for Saint Anne, with an image of Anne, Mary and Christ reading together, South Holland, c.1492– c.1503. Bruges, Public Library, Jean van Caloen Foundation Collection, Ms. 8, ff. 137v–138r.

fig. 48 Adriaen van Wesel, *Mary Reading*, Utrecht, c.1475–c.1477, wooden sculpture. Bruges, Musea Brugge, V.O.0154.

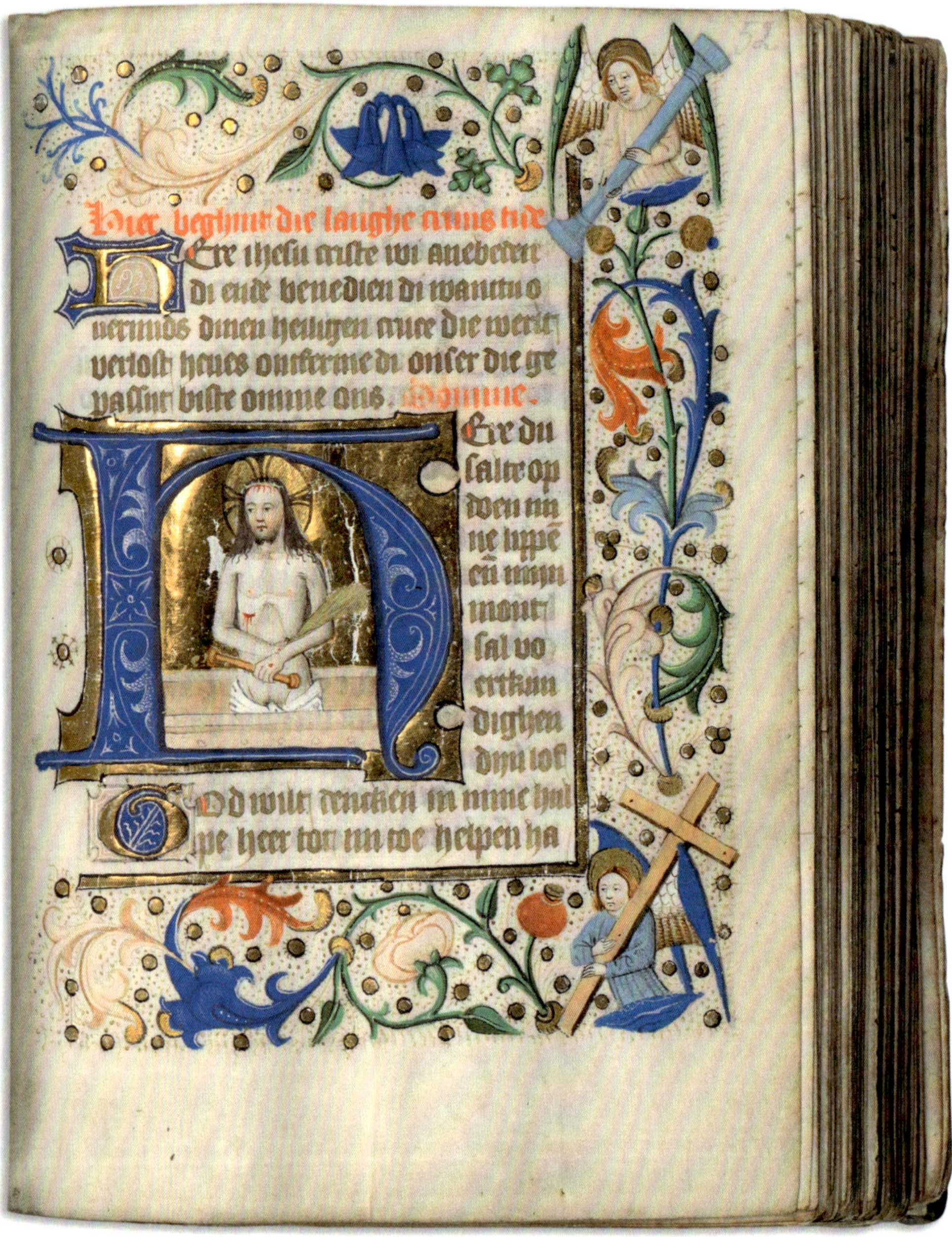

fig. 49 Book of Hours and Passion of Christ in the Middle Dutch translation by Geert Grote, Zwolle, c.1465–c.1485. Bruges, Public Library, Ms. 673, f. 52r.

Conclusion

In 1567, the Italian traveller Lodovico Guicciardini marvelled at the high level of education in the Low Countries. He believed that nearly everyone there could read and write. Estimates for smaller towns and cities in the Northern Netherlands, such as Alkmaar, Gouda and Kampen, suggest that 30 to 60% of boys aged seven to fourteen attended urban schools.[24] The literacy rate in the Low Countries was likely among the highest in Europe, although illiteracy certainly persisted, particularly among unskilled labourers.

Although the expansion of writing was initially driven by administrative and economic needs, late-medieval society saw the emergence of a diverse, multilingual literary culture.[25] Mendicant orders and, later, the Devotia Moderna promoted religious awareness, in which both collective rituals and private devotion – along with individual reading – played a significant role. Middle-class groups, organised into craft guilds and confraternities, also fostered an equally influential form of 'civic religion', in which the written word held an important cultural place. 'Chambers of rhetoric' (*rederijkerskamers*) contributed significantly to this development.[26]

By the end of the Middle Ages, and especially in towns and cities, books had become objects that had fully integrated into daily life, as seen in the office of Metsys's money changer and his wife. Moreover, the rise of the printing press made them increasingly affordable.[27]

1. Woodall, '*De wisselaer*'.
2. Aurell, *The Lettered Knight.*
3. Bertrand, *Documenting the Everyday.*
4. Willemsen, *Back to the Schoolyard*, 33–40, 293–94.
5. Lynch, 'Marking Time'.
6. De Munck, De Ridder-Symoens, 'Education and Knowledge', 224–27.
7. De Ridder-Symoens, 'Education and Literacy'.
8. Willemsen, *Back to the Schoolyard*, 21–26.
9. Van Buuren, 'Want ander konsten'.
10. Van Engen, *Sisters and Brothers*, 144–54.
11. Hugen, 'Van lesboek naar leesboek'.
12. De Munck, De Ridder-Symoens, 'Education and Knowledge', 227–29.
13. De Munck, De Ridder-Symoens, 'Education and Knowledge', 229–31.
14. Naber, 'Bourgonische edelen', 245–47.
15. De Munck, De Ridder-Symoens, 'Education and Knowledge', 244–48.
16. Naber, 'Bourgonische edelen', 248–49.
17. Willemsen, *Back to the Schoolyard*, 22–23, 28–31.
18. See also Chapter 5.
19. Scheepsma, *Medieval Religious Women.*
20. See Chapter 5 and Miles, 'The Origins and Development of the Virgin Mary's Book at the Annunciation', 659.
21. De Jong, 'Read Some Good Dutch Books', 38.
22. See Chapter 2 and de Hemptinne, 'Des femmes copistes'.
23. Murray, 'Family, Marriage and Money-changing'.
24. Willemsen, *Back to the Schoolyard*, 15–16.
25. Demets, 'Bruges as a Multilingual Contact Zone'.
26. Marnef, Van Bruaene, 'Civic Religion', 145–51.
27. Hauwaerts, *Colard Mansion.*

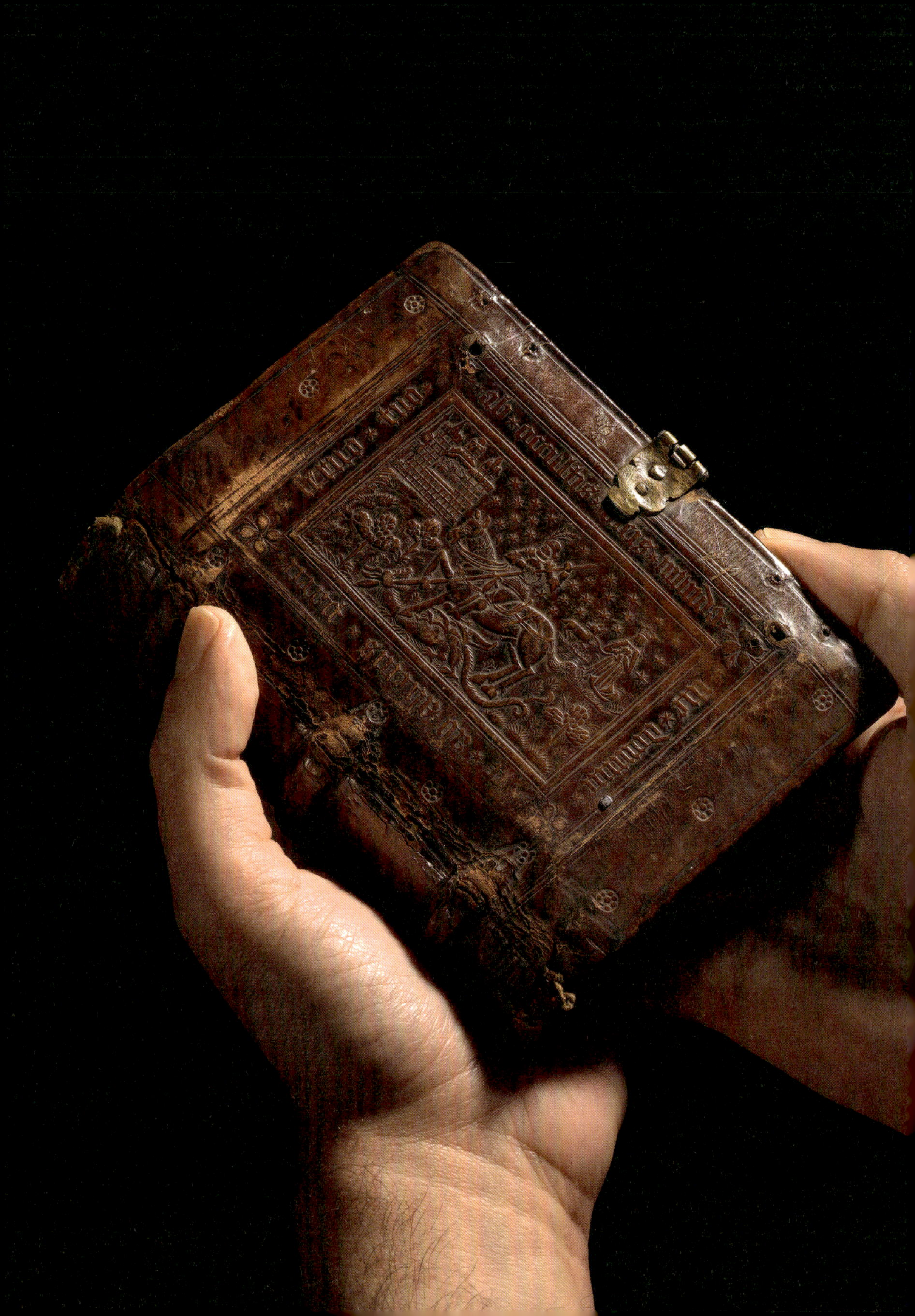

5. # DEPICTIONS OF DEVOTIONAL BOOKS IN WORKS OF ART

From Icon to Object

Like depictions of clothing, jewellery and architecture, representations of books by artists of the fifteenth century always combine observations of real-life objects with the fantasy afforded by artistic licence. In a situation unique to the Low Countries, the Eyckian optical revolution – made possible through the full adoption of the oil painting medium – combined with the growing commercial production of books, to the extent that artists increasingly had both the capacity and the inspiration to represent these objects in astonishing detail. This chapter will examine such depictions, primarily through the lens of artworks present in Bruges. Rather than comparing the represented objects with actual surviving books to gain insights into codicology and material facture, this essay will primarily discuss how such painted (and carved) books are shown in use by devotees, biblical figures and saints. Who is seen manipulating these items, these costly indicators of literacy and rank? How might their interactions resemble or differ from real-world practices? Do depictions of books in use represent an unreachable ideal, or are they a true reflection of actual habits? Since we cannot transport ourselves back to the fifteenth century, answering such questions is difficult, yet ultimately, by close examination of historical evidence, we can arrive at some preliminary answers.

Nicholas Herman

fig. 50 Panel-stamped decoration showing *Saint George Slaying the Dragon* and Ps. 18, Book of Hours, Ghent, c.1500. Bruges, Public Library, Ms. 823.

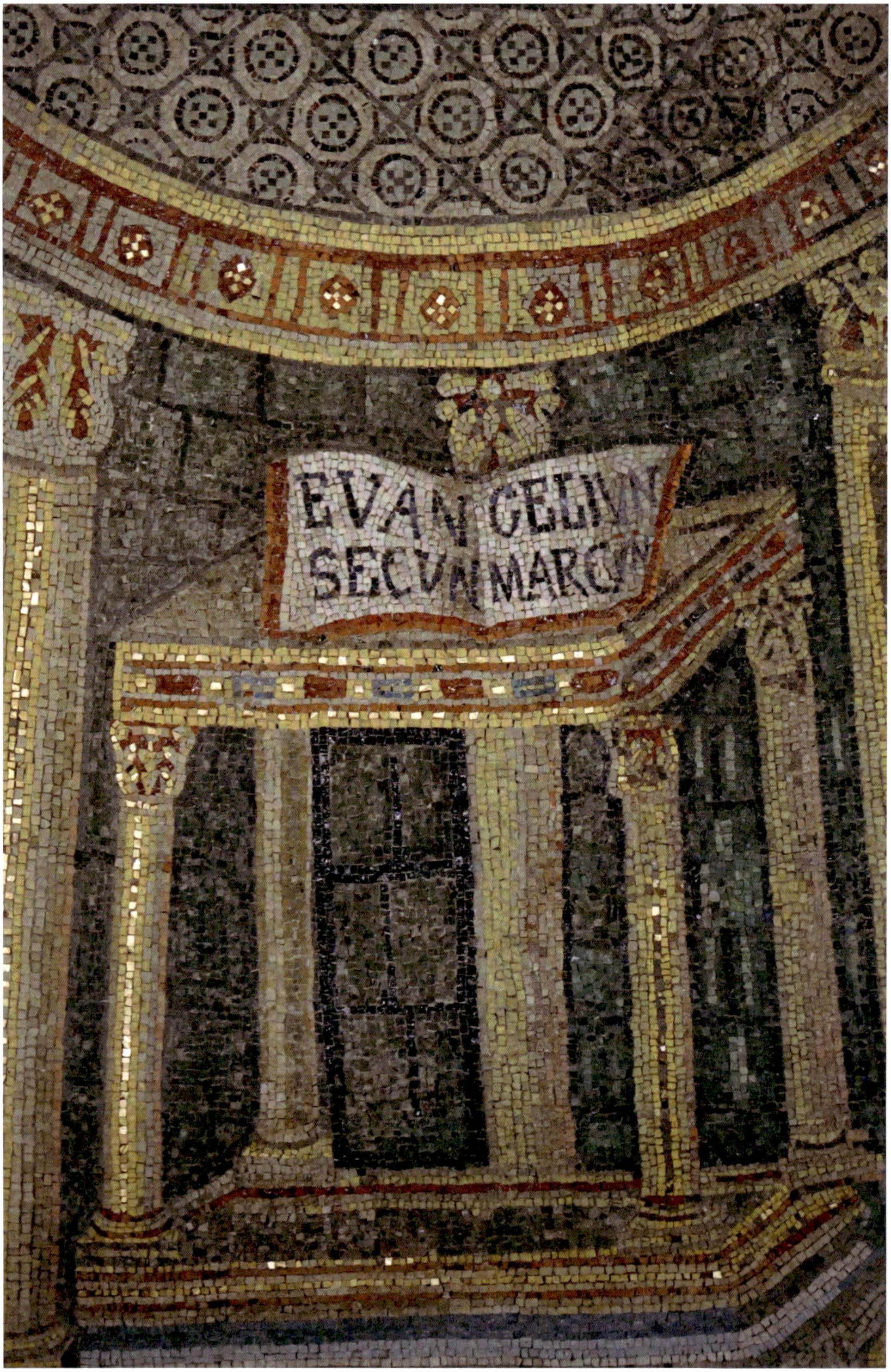

fig. 51 Gospel according to Mark open upon an altar, detail of mosaic, c.470. Baptistery of Neon, Ravenna.

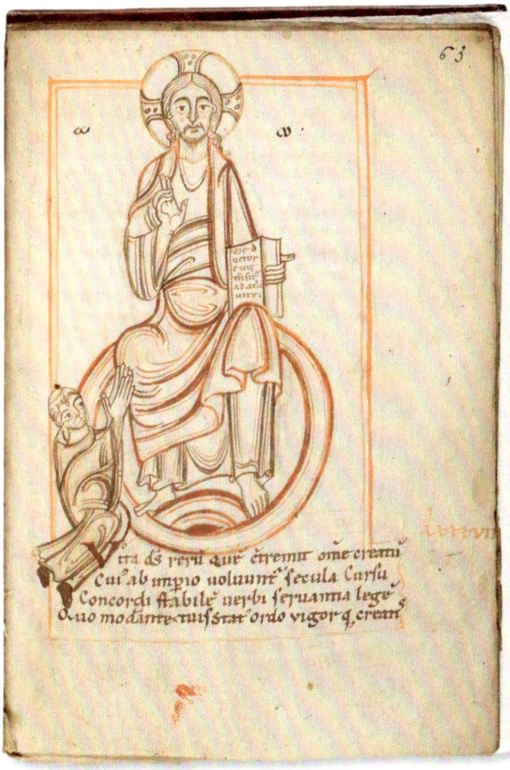

By the year 1500, the codex had existed for more than a thousand years and had been depicted in early Christian, Byzantine and Western medieval art with increasing frequency (fig. 51). A general trend can be observed over the course of this millennium. The book, which in earlier centuries had an almost exclusively iconic presence as an attribute or marker of sanctity, religious authority and internalised wisdom began, by the late Middle Ages, to acquire additional meaning in certain contexts: a real object, tangible, knowable and (increasingly) readable by a broader section of society. Accordingly, whereas in previous centuries the book, so often the purview of God and the saints alone, would be held shut, displayed outwardly like an avatar, or written in by an authorial figure (fig. 52), individuals are shown manipulating, leafing through and reading the book with increasing frequency. This change is, of course, a reflection of interconnected macroscopic historical trends: increasing literacy by lay people, a greater desire for personal participation in religious rituals, and the production of enormous numbers of Books of Hours to satisfy these demands. A close analysis of surviving representations, however, also demonstrates that artists continued to use the book as a vessel for symbolic meaning, even in pictures that appear seductively true to life.

fig. 52 Christ enthroned with a book, in *Vita Gregorii metrica*, Germany (?), c.1150. Bruges, Public Library, Ms. 406, f. 63r.

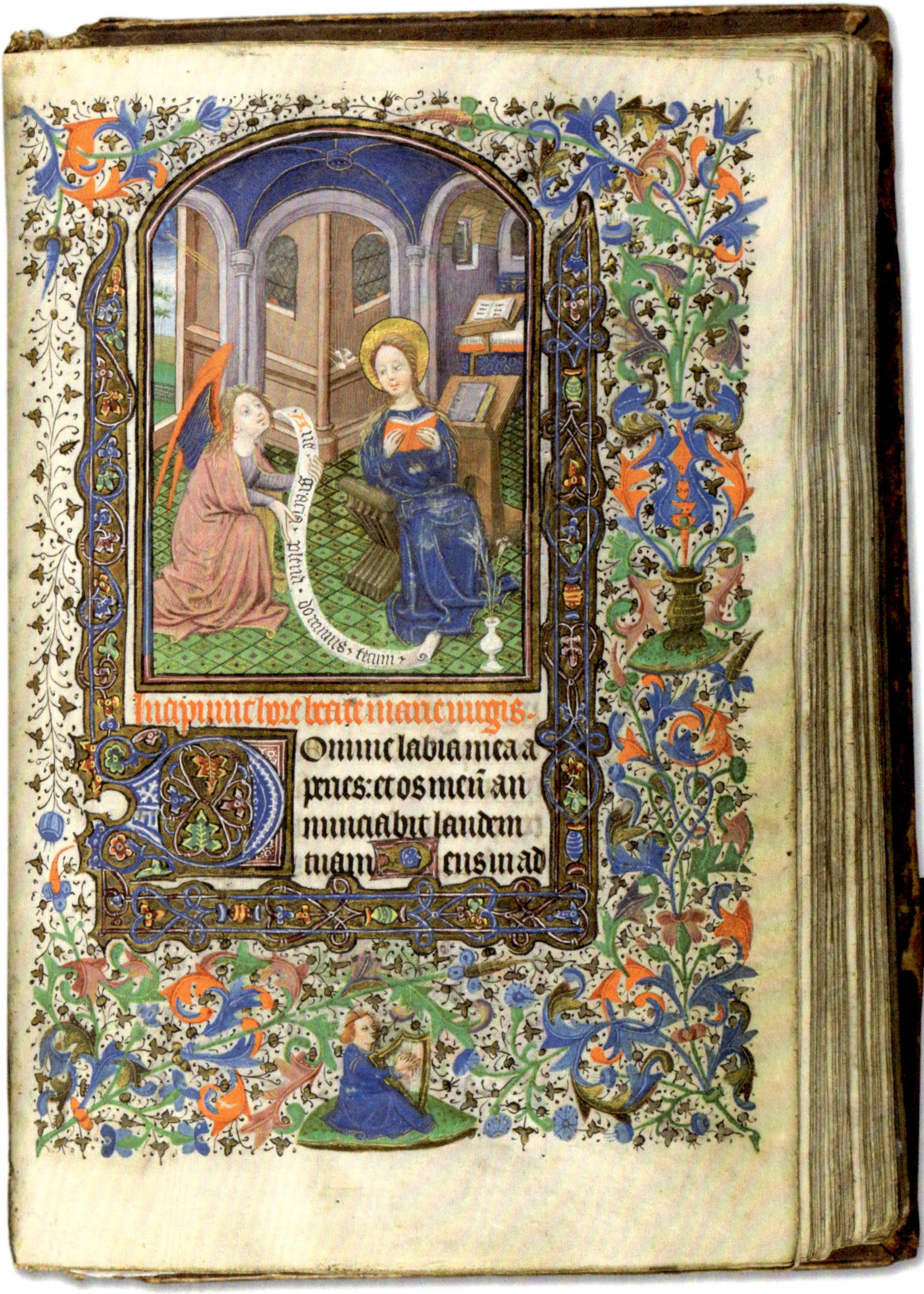

fig. 53 *Annunciation*, in Book of Hours, Master(s) of the Gold Scrolls, Bruges, c.1440–c.1450. Bruges, Public Library, OCMW O.L.V. ter Potterie Collection, Ms. 5, f. 30r.

Dos and Don'ts

The fundamental archetype for devotional behaviour was the Virgin Mary, whose wisdom and piety are exemplified by the presence of a book in thousands of late-medieval Annunciation scenes (fig. 53) Through such details, the Biblical narrative is transposed into a contemporary upper-class domestic setting: codices, an invention of late antiquity, did not exist in first-century Palestine. While the fact of Mary's studiousness is totally absent from the Gospel narrative of the angel appearing to Mary (Luke 1:26–38), in the visual imagination of late-medieval Europe the story of salvation began with an act of reading, or more precisely of divinely interrupted reading. This was not always the case: earlier depictions of the event often had the Virgin spinning yarn, a prototypically female activity typologically associated with the work that Eve – Mary's antetype – had to perform upon her expulsion from Eden. Only between the ninth and twelfth centuries did the trope of the Annunciate Mary with a book become normalised.[1] Whereas in more modern times reading has on occasion been considered transgressive and potentially dangerous for women, in the Middle Ages and early-modern period the opposite was true.[2] Engagement with texts which were almost invariably religious in nature was perceived as a sign of humility. Before the era of the Protestant reformers – and long before the age of the libertine novel – the opportunities for illicit literature were few and far between.

In Petrus Christus's *Annunciation*, Mary's physical association with the book is underlined pictorially by her impossibly voluminous mantle (fig. 54). It billows over the small bench before her and serves as a cushioned pillow supporting an open book, whose text is illegible except for an initial E that suggests either Isaiah's prophetic verse, *Ecce virgo concipiet* (Behold, a Virgin

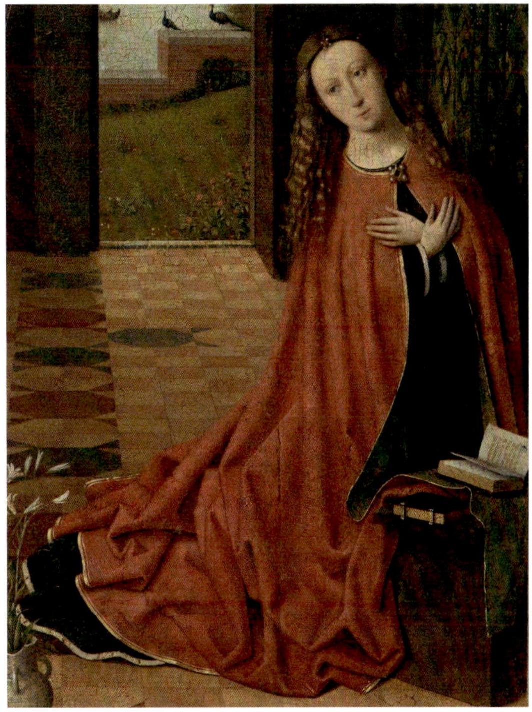

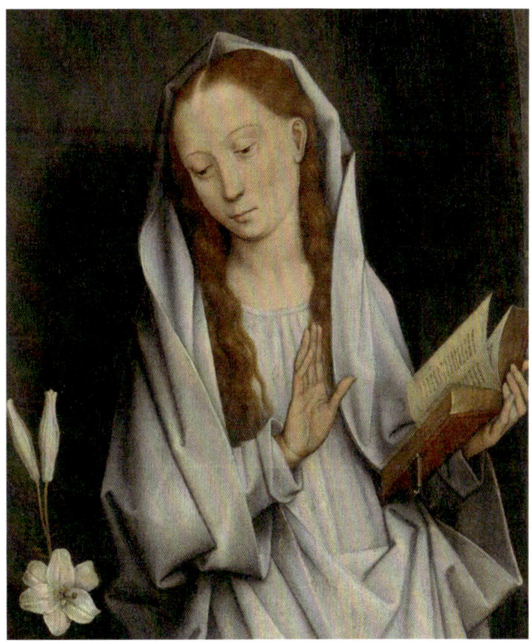

fig. 54 Petrus Christus, *Annunciation* (detail), 1452, oil on panel. Bruges, Musea Brugge, 1983.GRO0019.I.

fig. 55 Hans Memling, *Annunciation* (detail), c.1467, oil on panel. Bruges, Musea Brugge, 0000.GRO1254.I-1255.I.

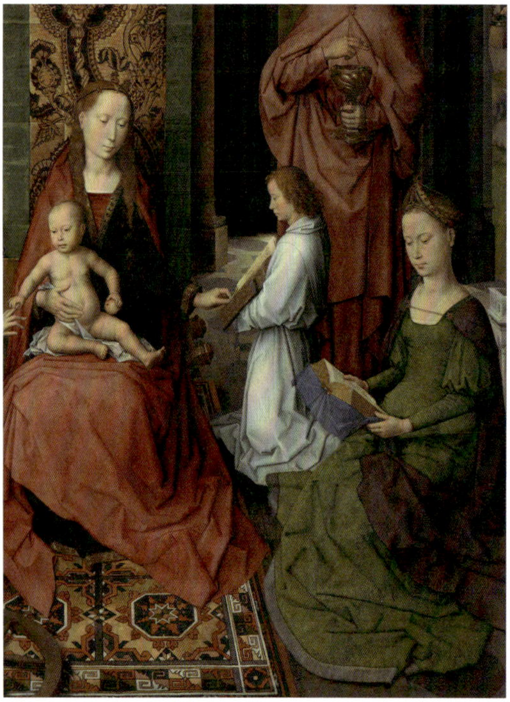

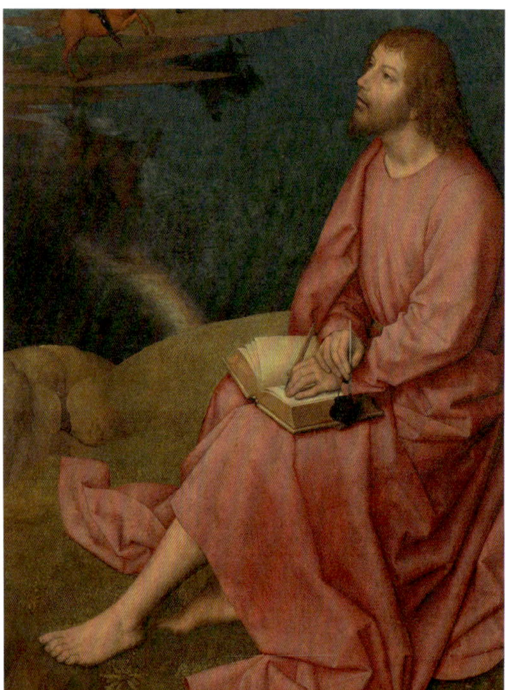

fig. 56 Hans Memling, *Triptych of John the Baptist and John the Evangelist* (central panel, detail: the Virgin and Saint Barbara; right panel, detail: John the Evangelist), 1479, oil on panel. Bruges, Musea Brugge, O.SJ0175.I.

shall conceive – Isaiah 7:14), or Mary's response to the Angelic salutation *Ecce ancilla domini* (Behold the handmaiden of the Lord – Luke 1:38). She literally cannot step away. This is not a plausible or convenient way of configuring a book, as in Hans Memling's standing Virgin Annunciate from the exterior of the Crabbe Triptych, where Mary is balancing a book rather precariously on her left palm as she turns to greet the angel (fig. 55). The composition appears graceful at first, but upon careful consideration we see that ergonomics have been sacrificed for visual balance and symbolism.

Increasingly believable objects should not trick us into believing that they are being employed in historically accurate ways. Memling's *Triptych of John the Baptist* is a case in point (fig. 56). The Virgin is multitasking: as she supports her child, an attendant angel holds open a book for her momentary perusal, much as a deacon might proffer a liturgical tome during a procession. This is not a gesture that can be sustained for longer than a few moments. Saint Barbara elevates a smaller but still substantial book in mid-air – not an easy task for anyone who attempts it for an extended period of time. On the right-hand wing, Saint John the Evangelist performs an action often repeated in iconography of the period: he is writing, implausibly, within a fully bound book of several hundred folios propped upon his knees, dipping a quill into a wobbly inkpot while holding a pen knife at the ready to correct errors. While compact and ready-to-inscribe notebooks did exist, this method of production for such a substantial tome is far-fetched. Sometimes, artists had John writing in a scroll, which at least had the sheen of antiquity: prophets from the Old Testament often hold banderoles to distinguish them from codex-bearing saints of the Christian epoch. What we can infer from these historically impossible configurations, however, reinforces subtle messaging within Memling's picture. Mary's book has two columns, like the book in Jan van Eyck's *Annunciation* (Washington, DC), suggesting a Bible or perhaps a breviary – in any event, a more complex theological or liturgical tome in comparison to Barbara's single-columned Book of Hours, which has a chemise binding redolent of refined portability. The angel, mimicking a deacon, reinforces Mary's role as a symbolic priestess. The Virgin is familiar enough with the text to flip to the relevant passage. Barbara, on the other hand, uses a multiple strand bar-type bookmarker that can be seen anchored into the top of her book, the sign of repetitive but rote use. To the side, John's impromptu workspace reinforces the immediacy of the revelation he witnesses in the distance.

A final and unequivocal *don't* of book handling is evident in a Virgin and Child by the Master of the Embroidered Foliage (fig. 57), in which the infant rather nonchalantly ruffles the pages of a rubricated prayer book. Such depictions of the baby as biblioclast, inspired by Rogier van der Weyden's *Durán Madonna* (now in the Prado), survive in considerable numbers, and have been intelligently interpreted not as true-to-life renderings of toddler tantrums, but rather as mystical, symbolic gestures. The infant Christ skips ahead or flips back within the text, pointing either to the prophecies or to their fulfilment.[3] This detail is equivalent to the Christ Child twisting his limbs into a cross-shape, playing with a blood-red coral necklace, or other such disguised prefigurations of his fate that abound in fifteenth-century painting.

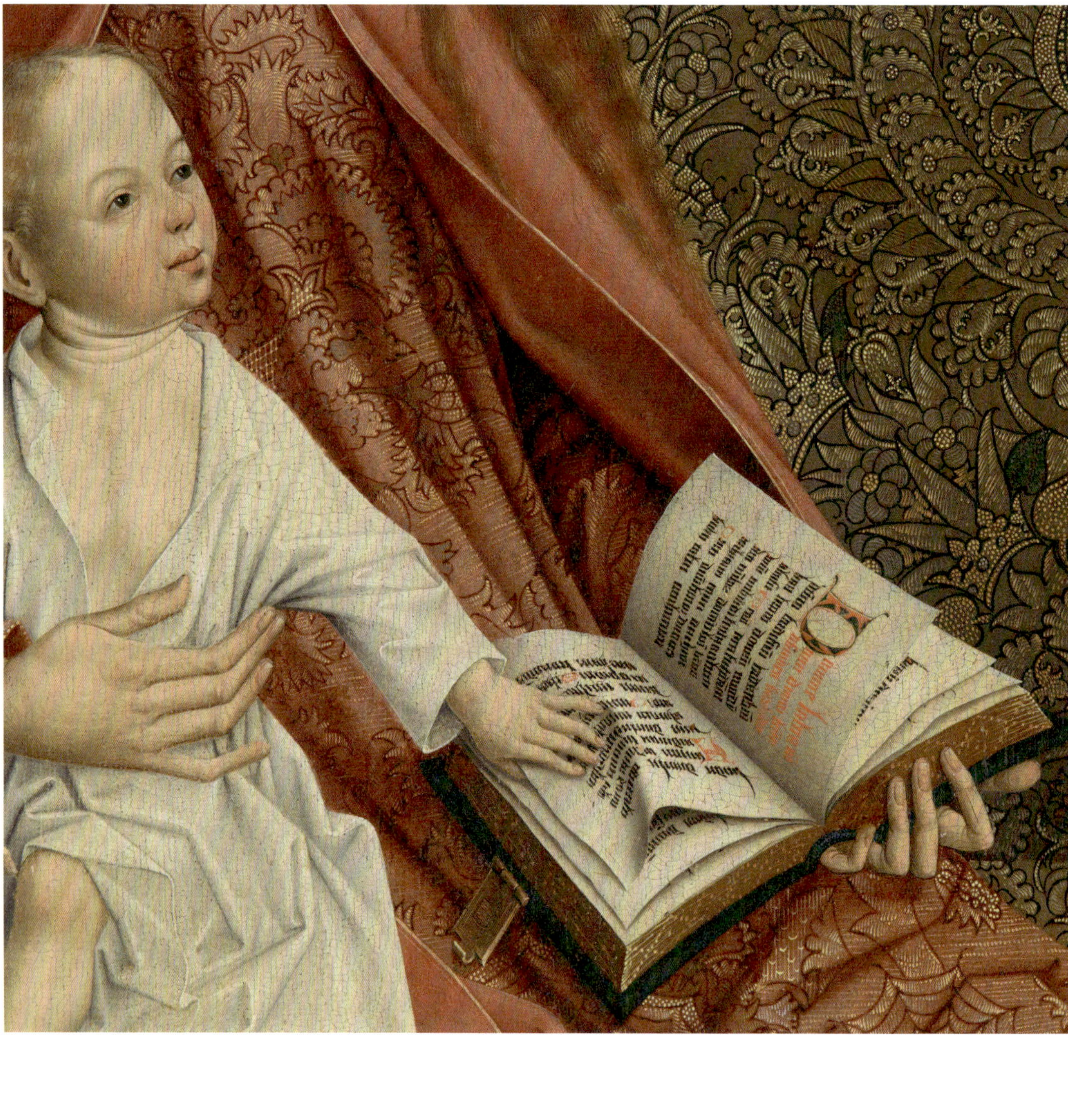

fig. 57 Master of the Embroidered Foliage, *Virgin and Child* (detail), c.1476–c.1482, oil on panel. Bruges, Musea Brugge, 0000.GRO1660.I.

Models of Behaviour

If the books held by holy figures were included more for reasons of symbolic association than as reflections of everyday practice, the opposite can be said of books included alongside representations of supplicants, those modern-day patrons of works of art: these depictions represent a high watermark of good devotional behaviour, something to aspire towards. The Low Countries, being an epicentre of book production and of the Devotio moderna spiritual movement, were the setting for increasingly frequent demonstrations of this type over the course of the fifteenth century. Many examples show devotees engaging in behaviour that mimics that of the central, saintly characters in some way. In the *Moreel Triptych*, for example, the donors Willem Moreel and Barbara van Vlaenderbergh kneel at a prie-dieu with an open devotional book, matching the actions performed by Saint Giles and especially Saint Maurus, who himself is absorbed in the act of reading (fig. 58). Again, the saintly figures are momentarily standing still, but the supplicants benefit from the convenience of perfectly positioned bookstands.

Whilst the saints demonstrate behaviour for the nearby supplicants, those supplicants in turn model comportment for us, the external viewers. Another couple on the wings of a triptych, whose identities are not known to us, displays the accoutrements of devotion (figs 59 and 82): the husband's prim Book of Hours bears a miniature of King David introducing the Penitential Psalms (though the initial 'A' is out of place), and nearby are a rosary, another multiple-strand bookmarker, and a set of eyeglasses removed from their case. Yet why are he, his wife opposite, and so many others not absorbed in reading, and not even touching the book? The answer may lie in the vernacular devotional manuals and sermons of the period which, intended for the laity, stress the use of text and images merely as an initial aid in devotional training to be superseded by a state of imageless and wordless contemplation. This influential notion had its roots in the writings of the theologian and preacher Geert Grote (1340–1384)

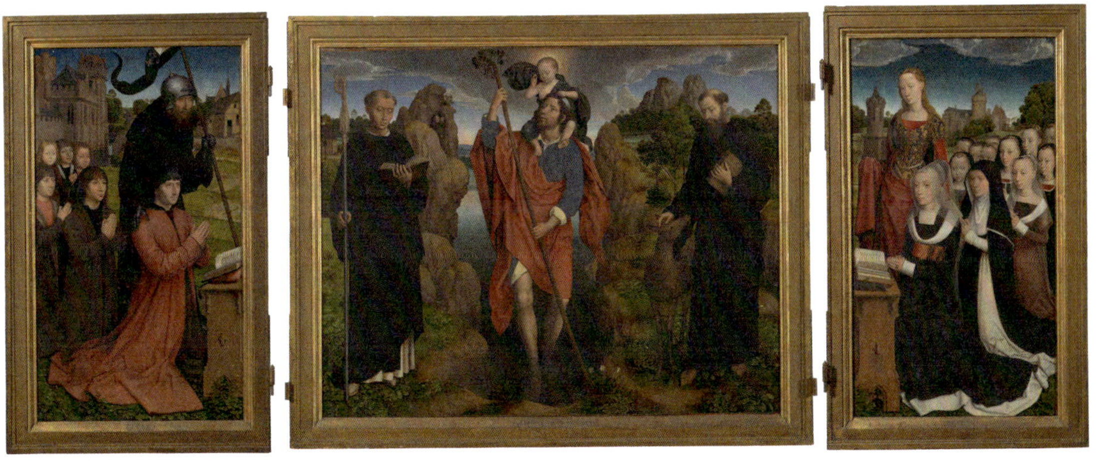

fig. 58 Hans Memling, *Moreel Triptych*, 1484, oil on panel. Bruges, Musea Brugge, 0000.GRO0091.I-0095.I.

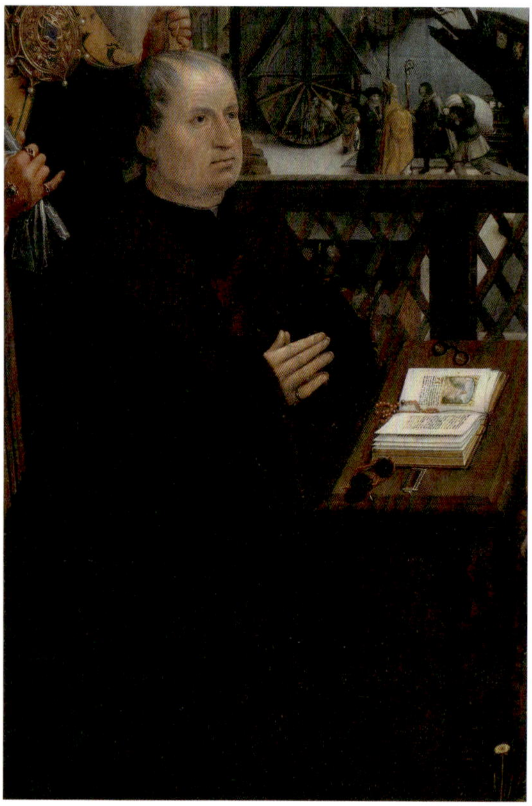

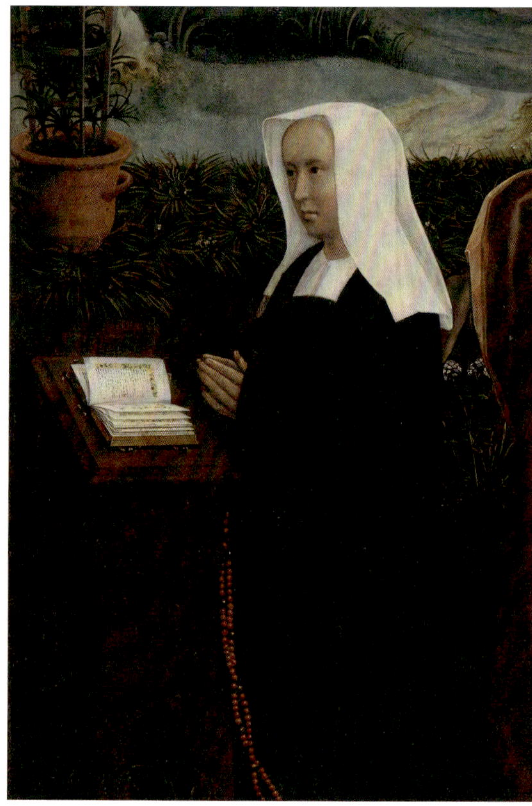

fig. 59 Jan Provoost, *Portrait of a Donor and Saint Nicholas* and *Portrait of a Donor and Saint Gudula* (details), c.1515–c.1521. Bruges, Musea Brugge, 0000.GRO0216.I-0217.I.

who, in addition to translating the Hours of the Virgin into Dutch and founding the Brethren of the Common Life, also wrote a Latin treatise, derived from a sermon, which provided a template for meditative self-perfection: *De quattuor generibus meditabilium* (On Four Kinds of Matter for Meditation).[4] Famously, Grote contended that images, both mental and real, are necessary as a first step to aid the feeble human mind as it gradually ascends from particulars towards a more abstracted realm of universals.[5] This directive is why many supplicants are shown neither reading nor looking fixedly towards the depicted object of their devotions, but instead staring blankly into space. That Maarten van Nieuwenhove and Joris van der Paele seem to miss their visual target in famous works by Hans Memling and Jan van Eyck is not an accident (figs 60 and 61). Their minds are not empty but rather transposed to a higher state of being after progressing through those steps prescribed by Grote, each using a prayer book as a stepping stone. Van der Paele, like the anonymous husband mentioned above (fig. 59), has just removed his spectacles, another sign of the frailty and unreliability of the senses, a filter and a crutch that must ultimately be abandoned. The most sophisticated painters of the age, Memling and Van Eyck among them, harnessed this ideal to prompt us, the viewers, to imagine the differences between the flat painted surface before us, the objects of our devotion and the formless principles of the spirit.

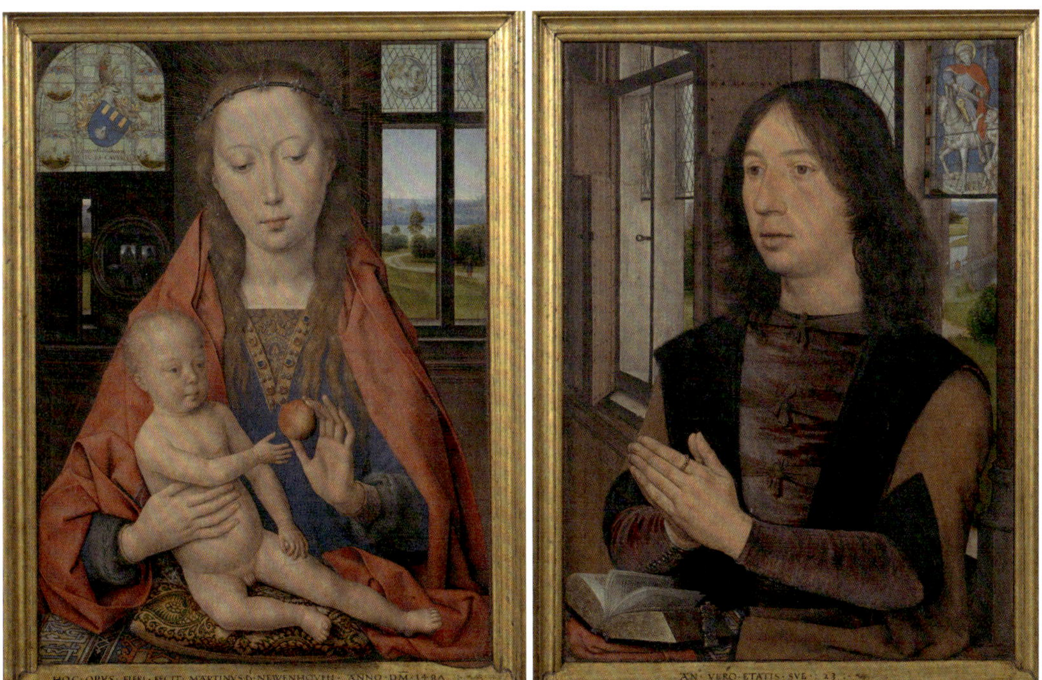

fig. 60 Hans Memling, *Diptych of Maarten van Nieuwenhove*, 1487, oil on panel. Bruges, Musea Brugge, O.SJ0178.I.

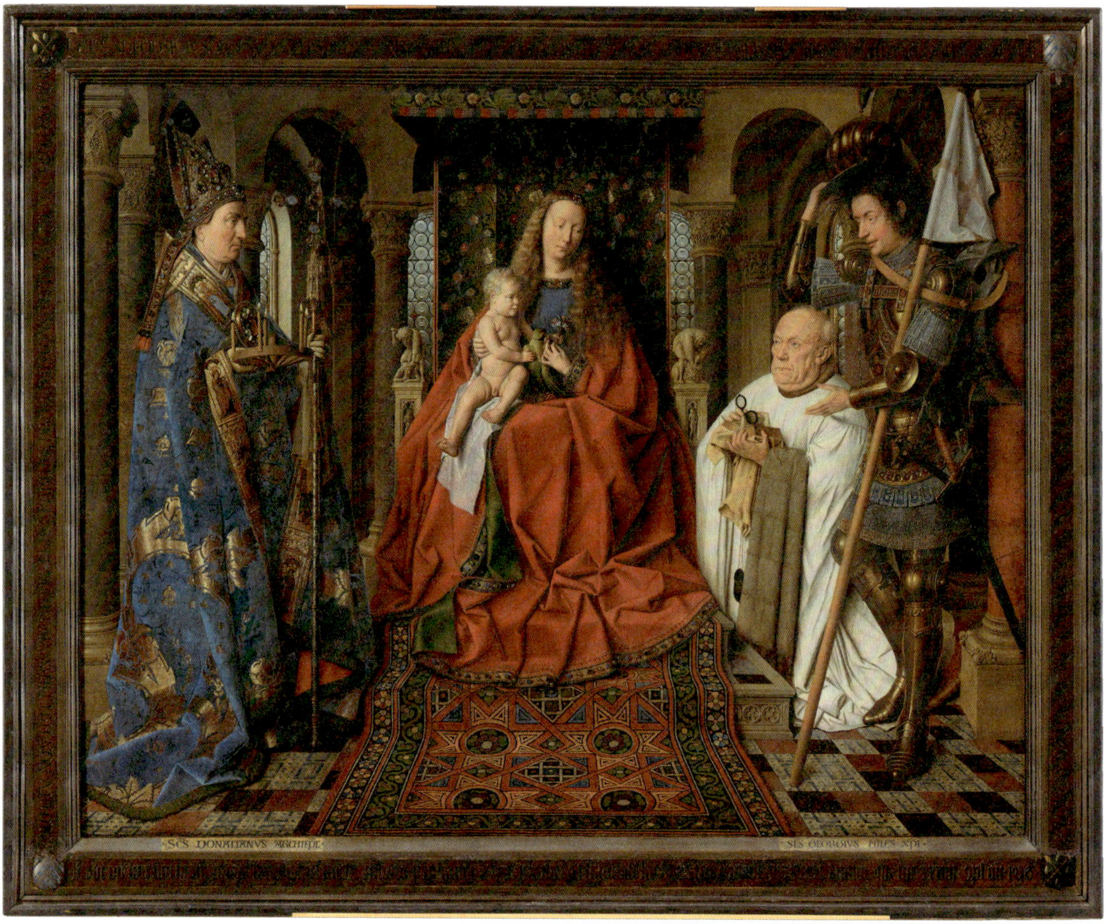

fig. 61 Jan van Eyck, *Madonna with Canon Joris van der Paele*, 1436, oil on panel. Bruges, Musea Brugge, 0000. GRO0161.I.

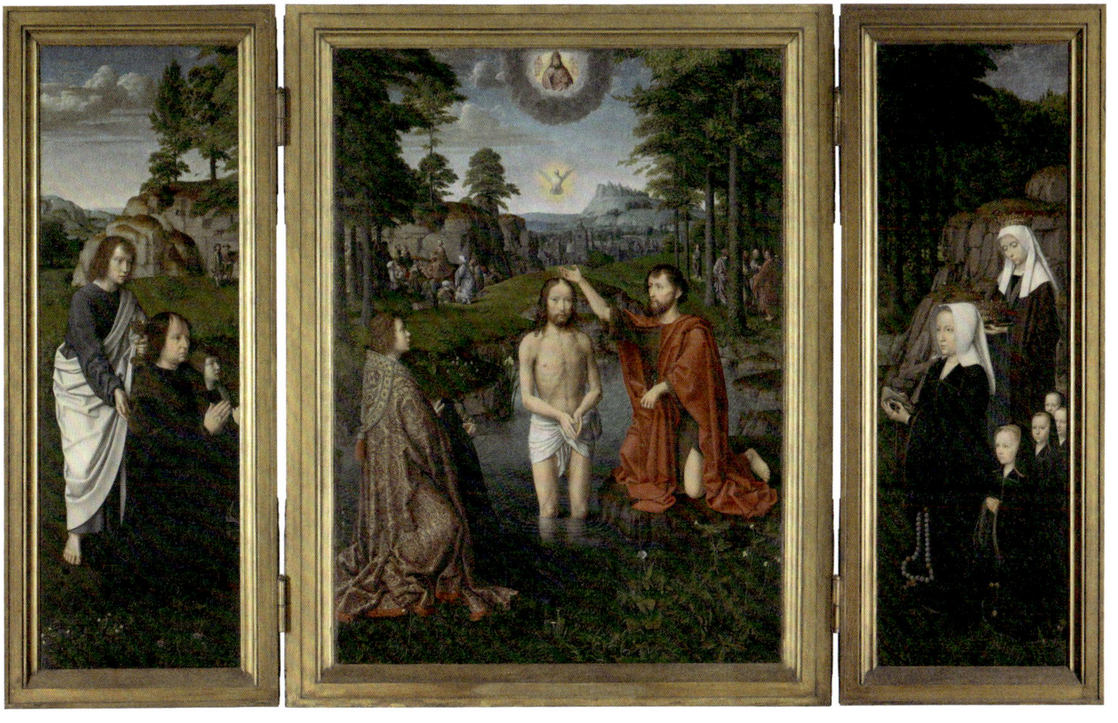

fig. 62 Gerard David, *Baptism of Christ*, c.1502–c.1508, oil on panel. Bruges, Musea Brugge, 0000.GRO0035.I-0039.I.

Gendered Difference?

An interesting dichotomy sometimes arises in works of art that show both a male and female supplicant, usually husband and wife, at either side of the central iconographical group. Predominantly, the man will be to our left (the heraldic dexter), the privileged position 'at the right hand of God', while the woman will be on the right. While we have seen examples of spousal parity in depictions, the hierarchical placement is often emphasised by the divergence in how books are portrayed before each respective supplicant. In some cases, the male has a closed book or even no book before him, indicating his achievement of a higher form of imageless devotion. Correspondingly, the female is more frequently shown with a book, usually open, and sometimes being read even while a sacred scene is unfolding before her. Witness the triptych representing Jan de Trompes and his wife Elisabeth van der Meersch beholding the baptism of Christ (fig. 62). His hands are devoutly joined in prayer while hers cradle a prayer book (fig. 99) – a symbol of piety, yes, but also of spiritual frailty, according to the logic of Grote.

The message here is not necessarily misogynistic. Sometimes the composition implies a special feminine kinship with the Virgin.[6] We can certainly detect such privileged access in the triptych of Joachim Christiaans and Jossine Lamsins by the Master of the Holy Blood (fig. 64). The central panel depicts what seems to be a version of the *Virgo inter Virgines* iconography, but is actually the Rest on the Flight into Egypt, with a diminutive Joseph in the distance. Saint Catherine holds a twin-columned Book of Hours on her lap, open at a miniature of King David. On the right wing, Jossine is presented directly by Saint Judoc, who gently touches her. She has a similar prayer book (fig. 98), open at a verso-side image of the Virgin and Child, a cropped version of what unfolds a few feet in front of her. Even though Jossine is deeply engaged in imageless devotion, her prayer book here provides a paratactic link to the sacred figures. Her husband, however, has no book, and even though his prayerful gesture mimics that of Saint Catherine, he is somehow at a greater remove. Saint Joachim, behind him, reads from a book, decidedly on the periphery (as he often is). That Jossine appears more fully present in the work of art is no coincidence: both Joachims had been painted over Jossine's first husband, Jan van Cattenbrouck, following his death.

Images of household education from the period, as opposed to scenes of male-dominated classroom learning, overwhelmingly consist of family portraits of Saint Anne teaching the Virgin to read, with the occasional addition of the Christ Child (figs 63, 46 and 47).[7] The clear message is that education is matrilineal. Here, the book is intended both symbolically as an intergenerational link, and behaviourally as a reflection of contemporary practice. The theological emphasis on Christ's Davidian ancestry melds with the fifteenth-century realities of familial knowledge transfer, which we know from the survival of a limited number of primers or alphabet books for aristocratic children, usually commissioned by their mothers.[8]

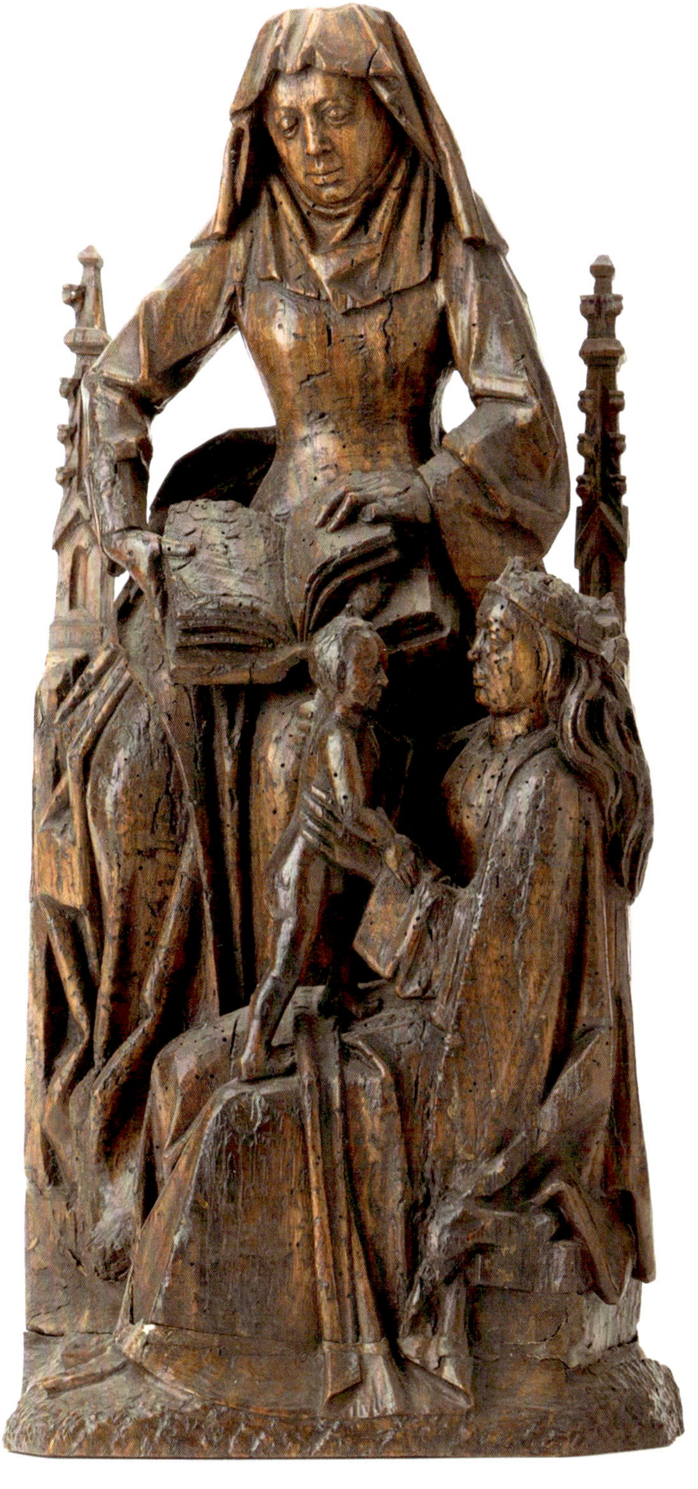

fig. 63 Netherlandish sculptor, *Saint Anne, the Virgin and the Christ Child*, c.1475–c.1500, oak. Bruges, Musea Brugge, V.O.0092.

Signalling Virtue

As modern-day viewers, it is difficult if not impossible for us to assess the intentions of these many supplicants shown engaging with books. In our own era of hyperactive self-promotion and ubiquitous social media, it is tempting to dismiss such depictions as the performative signalling of identity-affirming pieties, rather than the reflection of sincerely held beliefs. After all, portraits can be deceptive. Our own professional headshots, posted and circulated online, tend to show us proudly posing in front of well-ordered shelves of impressive-looking books, even if the majority of our workday is actually spent glaring at screens and typing on keyboards.

In an economy of salvation, however, genuine practices and outward showiness could co-exist. We have confirmation of this from a recent, pathbreaking scientific analysis of patterns of fingerprint dirt found in the margins of late-medieval Books of Hours from the Low Countries.[9] Far from being untouched status symbols, Books of Hours, particularly those of more modest quality, often bear physical traces of frequent, heavy use. The patterns of wear are not consistent between books and appear to be based on the individual owner's predilection for specific offices, suffrages and – especially – miniatures. The highest status, most artistically significant Books of Hours, however, are often in remarkably pristine condition. It is tempting to imagine sociological explanations for this discrepancy: perhaps wealthier owners kept their fingers cleaner, or used delicate chemise bindings to cradle their delicate books, or indeed kept such items merely as status symbols without ever consulting them. Yet, given the iconographic evidence of so many well-off supplicants envisioning the divine without even needing to touch their books, perhaps we could imagine that lords, ladies and the emergent mercantile elite, benefiting from religious edification inaccessible to most, and confident in their own piety, used their Books of Hours by learning not to use them at all.

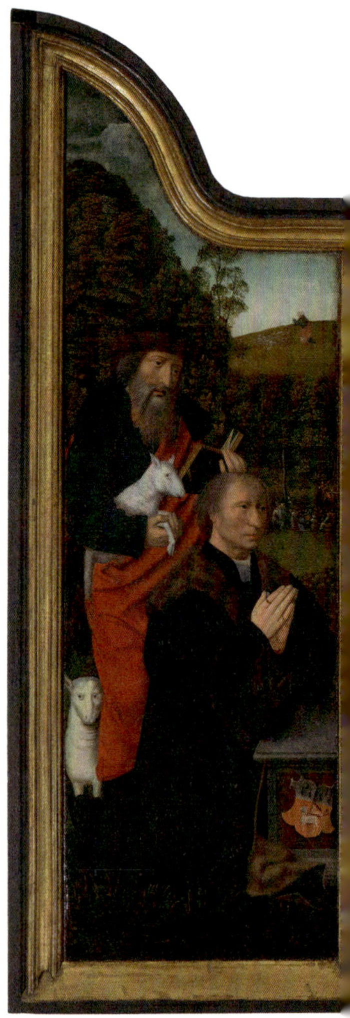

1. Miles, 'The Origins and Development of the Virgin Mary's Book at the Annunciation'.
2. Bollmann, *Women Who Read Are Dangerous*.
3. Acres, 'Rogier van Der Weyden's Painted Texts'.
4. Van Herwaarden, 'Between Saint James and Erasmus'.
5. For a nuanced, recent discussion, see Falque, *Devotional Portraiture and Spiritual Experience*, esp. Chap. 5.
6. Clanchy, 'Images of Ladies with Prayer Books'.
7. On this topic, see Linton, 'Reading the Virgin Reader'; Sheingorn, 'The Wise Mother'; Alexandre-Bidon, 'La lettre volée'.
8. Wieck, 'The Primer of Claude de France'; see also Chapter 4.
9. Rudy, 'Dirty Books'.

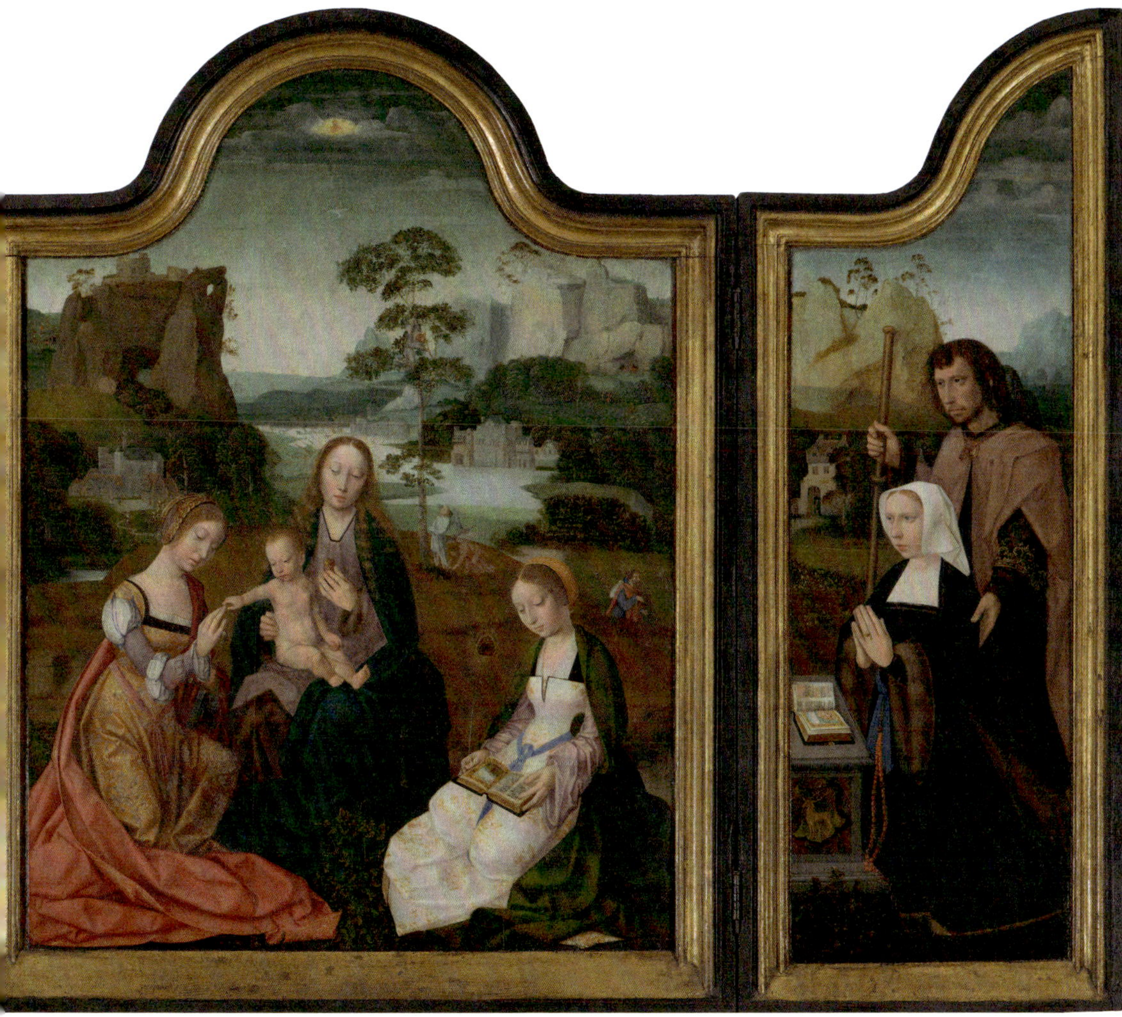

fig. 64 Master of the Holy Blood, *Madonna with the Saints Catherine and Barbara*, c.1509–c.1529, oil on panel. Bruges, Musea Brugge, 1991.GRO0008.I.

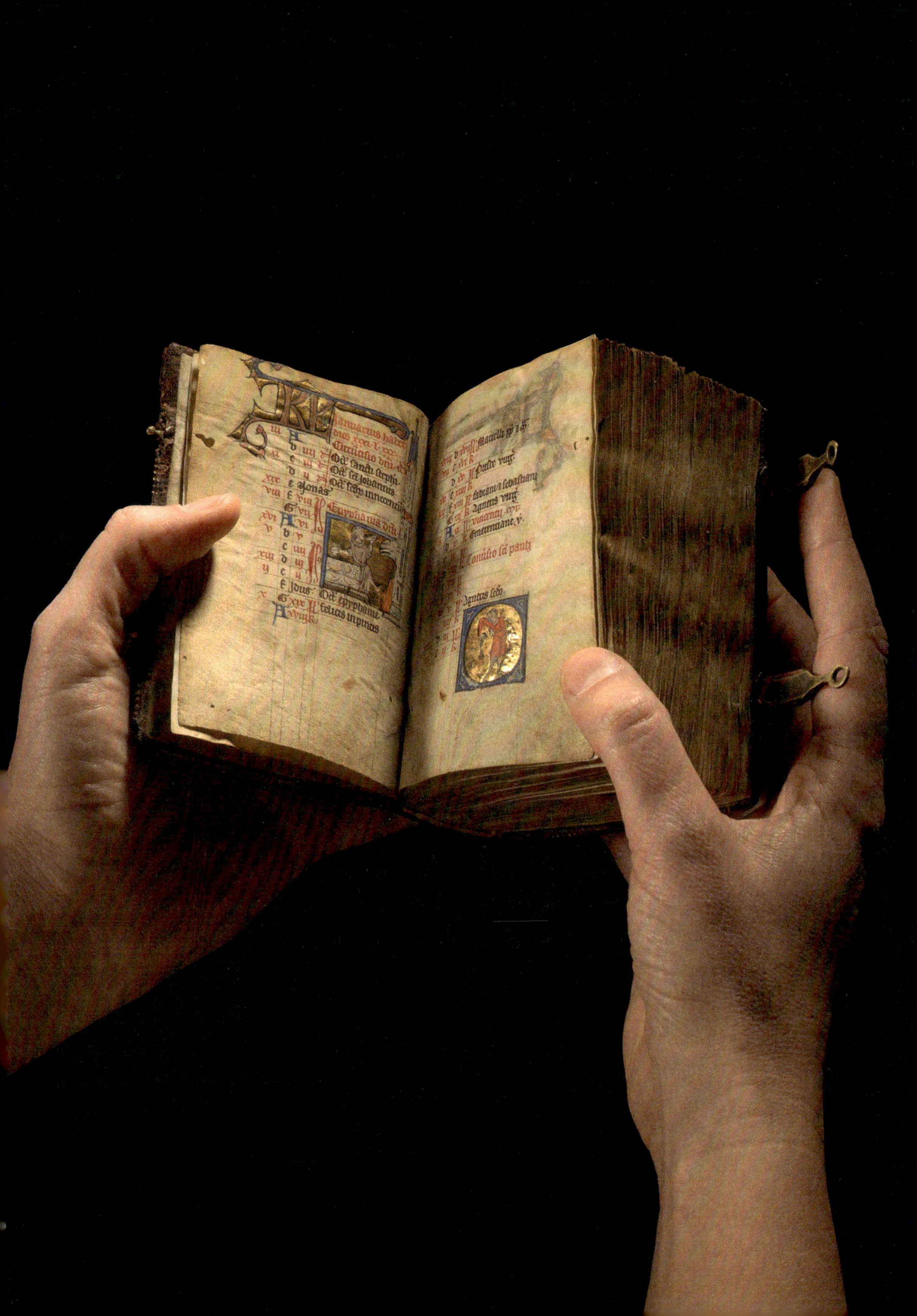

6. DROLLERIES IN THE MARGINS OF HOLY TEXTS

Elena Lichmanova

David vs the Monkey

Folio 19v of the Psalter that once belonged to Margaret II, Countess of Flanders and Hainaut (c.1202–1280),[1] displays a combination of apparently incongruous scenes (fig. 66). While King David in the initial 'D' of *Dominus* points at his eyes and kneels before God in response to the words of Psalm 26, 'The Lord is my light',[2] a monkey dressed as a cleric reads a parchment that hangs from the beak of a blue crane in the lower margin. This latter scene, a whimsical product of medieval imagination that, to a modern eye, looks completely extraneous to the religious text it decorates, is probably a parodic counterpoint to King David in the initial 'D'. True knowledge that comes from God, that of salvation, is contrasted with inverted knowledge presented by an ape who mimics the ability to read – perhaps a reference to the superficial learning of certain clerics.[3] Such humorous depictions started to appear in the margins of luxurious, primarily devotional books in the mid-thirteenth century. Why, the question arises, did medieval nobility find it appropriate and desirable to have their Psalters and Books of Hours, symbols of piety and status, adorned with parodic and seemingly profane marginalia?

fig. 65 Psalter of Margaret II of Flanders, Ghent (?), c.1250–c.1280, Dampierre Master(s). Bruges, Public Library, Ms. 820 (Flemish Community Collection), ff. 1v–2r.

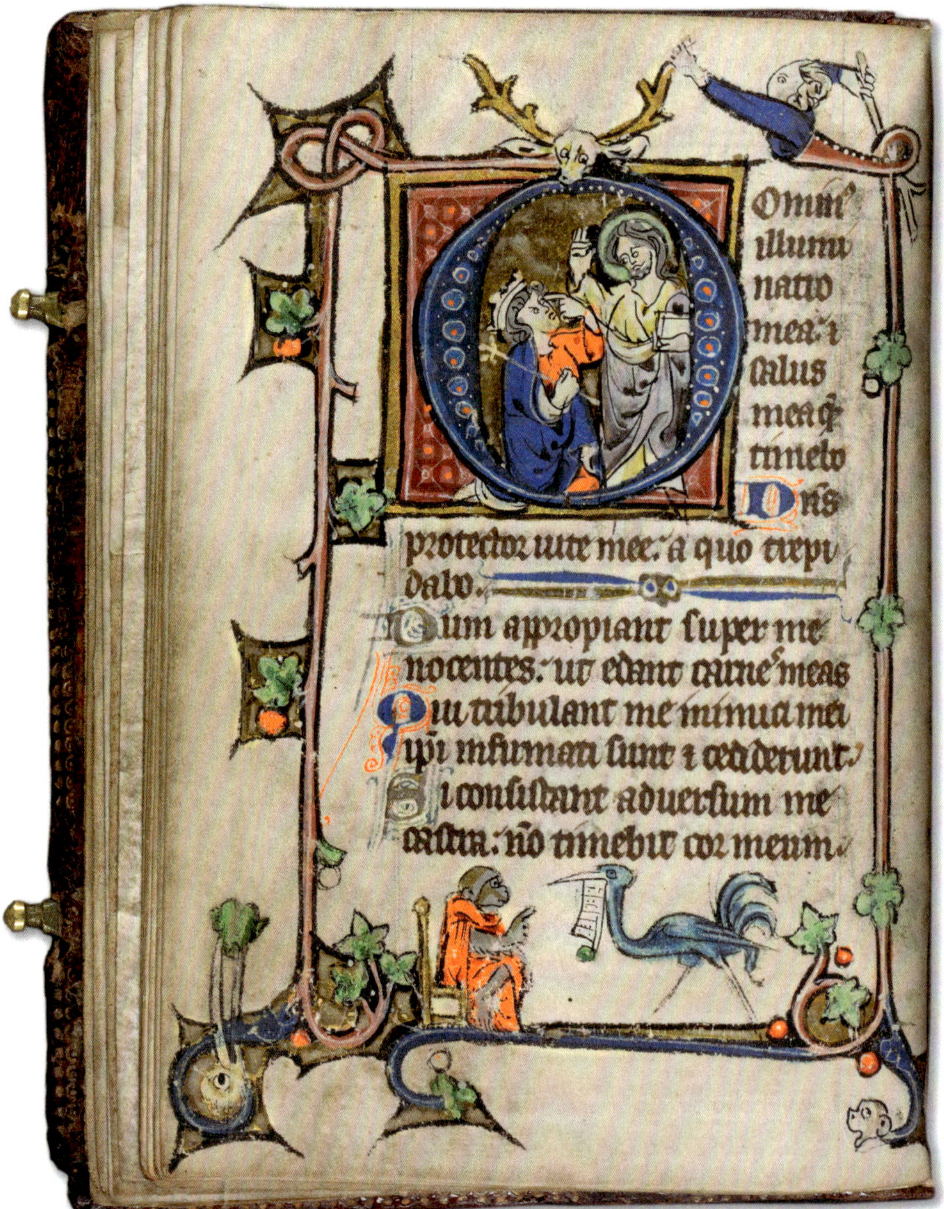

fig. 66 Beginning of Ps. 26, *Dominus illuminatio mea*, in Psalter of Margaret II of Flanders, Ghent (?), c.1250–c.1280, Dampierre Master(s). Bruges, Public Library, Ms. 820 (Flemish Community Collection), f. 19v.

One Question, Many Theories

Following Lilian Randall's seminal publication of 1966,[4] various answers to this question have been offered over recent decades. Michael Camille saw the page as a reflection of social hierarchies and its margins as a field for the carnivalesque.[5] Lucy Freeman Sandler has suggested that many marginal images were inspired by specific phrases of the texts they illuminate.[6] Mary Carruthers proposes that marginalia constituted memory cues,[7] while Ruth Mellinkoff considers some marginal images as apotropaic signs.[8] Paul Binski argues that marginalia were the inventions of witty and highly educated clerical or university communities.[9] Madeline Caviness is among those who regard the margin as a personalised space that expresses the individual concerns of book owners, and the focus on the audience response has dominated the field for the last thirty years.[10] Publications by Kathryn Smith, Elizabeth Moore Hunt and others have examined the question from various angles, with a primary emphasis on manuscript patrons and readers.

Reflection of the Patron's World

The study of the audience builds on the hypothesis that books for private devotion were reflections of their owners' identities, and that the manuscript margin developed into a space where patrons' individualities shone brightest. Indeed, it is in the margins of Margaret of Flanders's Psalter that we find images strongly connecting this book to Margaret's world. Saint Margaret, her patron saint and the only female saint in the manuscript, conquers the devil in the form of a dragon in the margin of folio 196r (fig. 67). On folios 40v and 190v, two of the three Flanders blazons appear in the margins, making a statement about Margaret's identity as a ruler of the powerful county. A man placing a laurel on the head of a lady in the margin of folio 116r in Margaret's Psalter complements the scene in the initial opening Psalm 80 where King David, playing chimes, embodies the Psalm's second verse, 'Rejoice to God our helper: sing aloud to the God of Jacob':[11] the praise to the Lord is visually likened to the adoration given to a lady (fig. 68). The marginal image relates the sacred content of the Psalter to Margaret's secular interests: the crowning of the lady evokes motifs from Margaret's favourite romances and alludes to her courtly surroundings in which romances and their love codes played a significant role.[12]

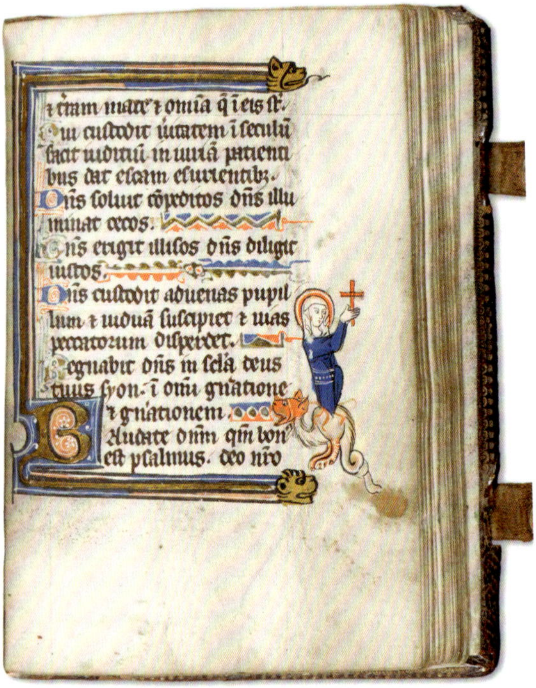

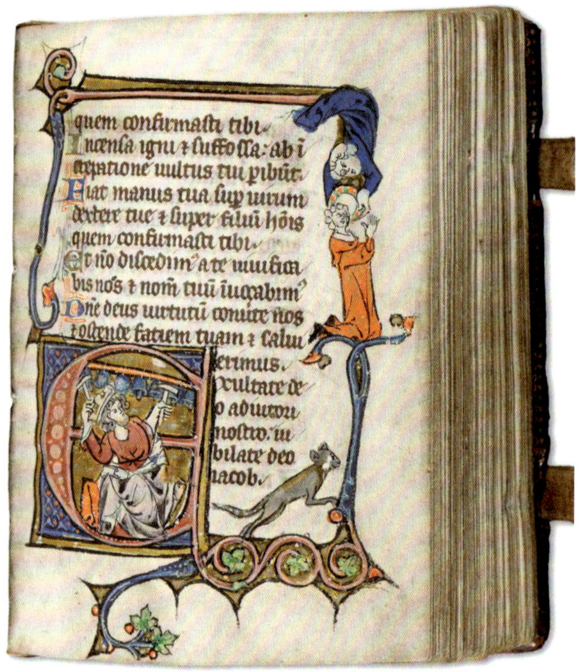

fig. 67 *Margaret of Antioch emerges from the body of a dragon* in the margin at the beginning of Ps. 146, in Psalter of Margaret of Flanders, Ghent, c.1250–c.1280, Dampierre Master(s). Bruges, Public Library, Ms. 820 (Flemish Community Collection), f. 196r.

fig. 68 Beginning of Ps. 80, with King David playing chimes in the initial and two lovers in the margin, in Psalter of Margaret of Flanders, Ghent, c.1250–c.1280, Dampierre Master(s). Bruges, Public Library, Ms. 820 (Flemish Community Collection), f. 116r.

From Preachers' Tales to the Manuscript Page

Yet the focus on the audience – and on monographic studies of single manuscripts – has tended to distract attention from bigger questions. While certain images indicate the preferences of book owners, many marginalia rehearse variants on recurring subjects from manuscript to manuscript.[13] This fact evidently reflects the practice of manuscript workshops, but it also raises a wider issue: how did the Christian culture of the thirteenth century reconcile parodic monkeys and courtly scenes with religious texts – marginalia's secular flair with piety and devotion? Lilian Randall proposed that many marginal scenes emerged from exempla – anecdotes that preachers used to make their sermons more relatable and entertaining to lay audiences.[14] Randall's hypothesis of 1957 has subsequently attracted limited attention but deserves, as I will demonstrate below, further consideration. Religious storytelling, spread in the thirteenth century especially by the new mendicant orders, was characterised by three features also encountered in Gothic marginalia: a variety of sources, the use of stories that originated in the secular realm for religious edification, and humour.

Popular Religious Themes in the Margins

Not only do the margins of Margaret of Flanders's Psalter reflect Margaret's world, they also refer to popular stories, metaphors and themes in contemporary preaching and broader religious discourse. When Margaret opened the page with Saint Margaret emerging from the dragon (fig. 67), she might have remembered a dramatic retelling of this story by preachers who used it to illustrate the miraculous power of a strong faith.[15] Looking at the image of two lovers (fig. 68), Margaret of Flanders might have recalled not only her favourite romances but also preachers' exempla about the perils of earthly love.[16] Seeing King David glorifying God through his music in the initial on the same page would have helped her direct her intentions to the love of God rather than the world. Female vanity, a topic that medieval preachers treated with unwavering gusto,[17] is embodied in a lady holding a mirror on folio 124r, a visual cue reminding Margaret of the importance of coping with her own vain tendencies (fig. 69). Preachers compared vain women to peacocks who have beautiful feathers but ugly voices,[18] and a message of a similar kind might have been exemplified by a peacock on folio 21r of Margaret's Psalter.

Sirens, some wearing contemporary female headgear and performing music, fill multiple pages of Margaret's manuscript (fols 69v, 103v, 163v–164r, 174r, 186r, fig. 70). Medieval preachers would have told Margaret that sirens and their music are like women who tempt men to sin.[19] Preachers may have also encouraged Margaret to flee temptation using the metaphor of a dog pursuing a hare.[20] To strengthen herself in her spiritual journey she may have asked for this metaphor in visual form in her manuscript (fol. 9r). Psalm 97 on folio 138v urges the reader to glorify God who 'hath done wonderful things'[21] by singing a new song to Him. A marginal image of a deer hunt on the same page, a common metaphor of spiritual combat,[22] illuminated for Margaret an idea that she should praise the Lord, first and foremost, by her piety (fig. 71). Images of falconry (fols 15r, 93r, 181r) might have evoked in Margaret's memory both her own recreations and courtly literature (where falconry scenes often symbolised an amorous quest). She might also have recalled religious stories in which a bird of prey flying away from its master is compared to stubborn men 'flying away' from God.[23] Similarly, a bird in a cage on folio 114v may be visualising a flexible Christian metaphor used by preachers to mean both a trap set by Christ for the devil[24] and a trap set by the devil for the human soul.[25]

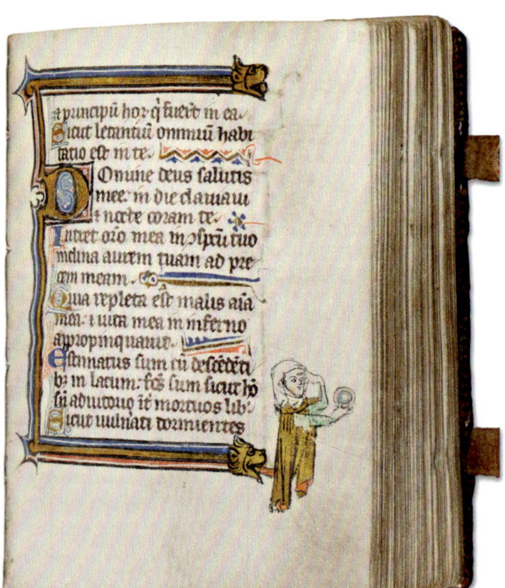

fig. 69 *Lady holding a mirror*, in Psalter of Margaret of Flanders, Ghent, c.1250–c.1280, Dampierre Master(s). Bruges, Public Library, Ms. 820 (Flemish Community Collection), f. 124r.

Secular Motifs for Spiritual Instruction

Considered in the context of religious storytelling, marginal images represent an ingenious devotional tool. They pleased audiences' eyes with delightful and familiar subjects that related the content of Psalters and Books of Hours to the audiences' knowledge of the world, and simultaneously pierced readers' hearts with instructive and pious messages. In many cases, it is impossible for modern scholars to know the exact meaning of these messages – not least because they were probably not supposed to be read in any one way.[26] What is certain, however, is that religious storytelling which used entertaining secular motifs for spiritual instruction became a primary tool for thirteenth-century preachers. Fables, episodes from romances, stories involving games, music, dance, hunts and tournaments alongside saints' lives and stories from the Bible were retold to explain religious truths and doctrines. In that context, the presence of playful, 'profane' and yet edifying marginal imagery in Margaret of Flanders's Psalter may have been encouraged and approved by preachers Margaret knew personally. Indeed, she was much exposed to preachers' tales, being a prominent patron of both Cistercians and Dominicans, members of whose orders authored extensive collections of exempla.[27] Margaret's support of contemporary preaching culture may be the reason why we see Saint Francis preaching to the birds and a preaching monk in the margins of her devotional book (fols 72v, 139r, figs 71 and 72).

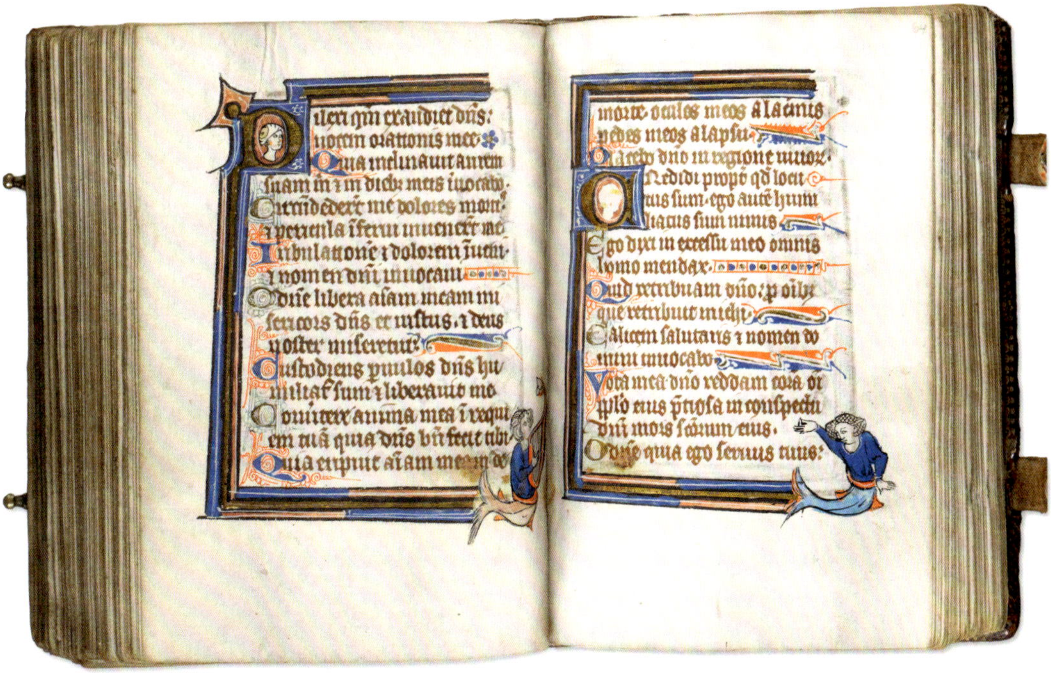

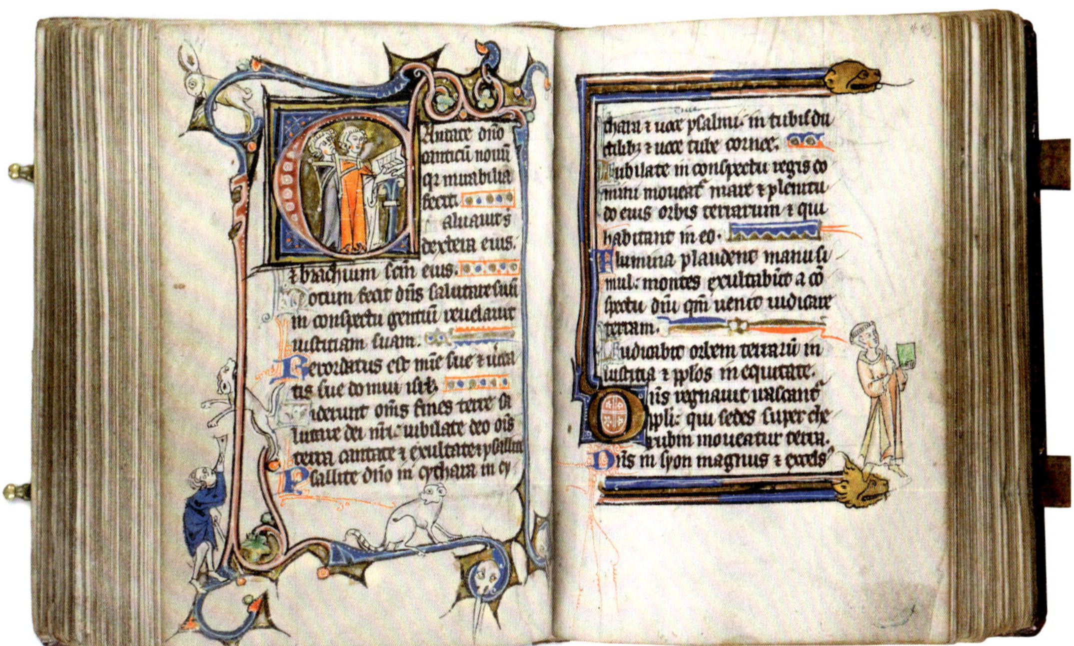

fig. 70 Sirens playing music and dancing; one is wearing contemporary female headgear, in Psalter of Margaret of Flanders, Ghent, c.1250–c.1280, Dampierre Master(s). Bruges, Public Library, Ms. 820 (Flemish Community Collection), ff. 163v–164r.

fig. 71 Deer hunt (to the left) and a preaching monk (to the right), Ps. 97 and Ps. 98, in Psalter of Margaret of Flanders, Ghent, c.1250–c.1280, Dampierre Master(s), Bruges, Public Library, Ms. 820 (Flemish Community Collection), ff. 138v–139r.

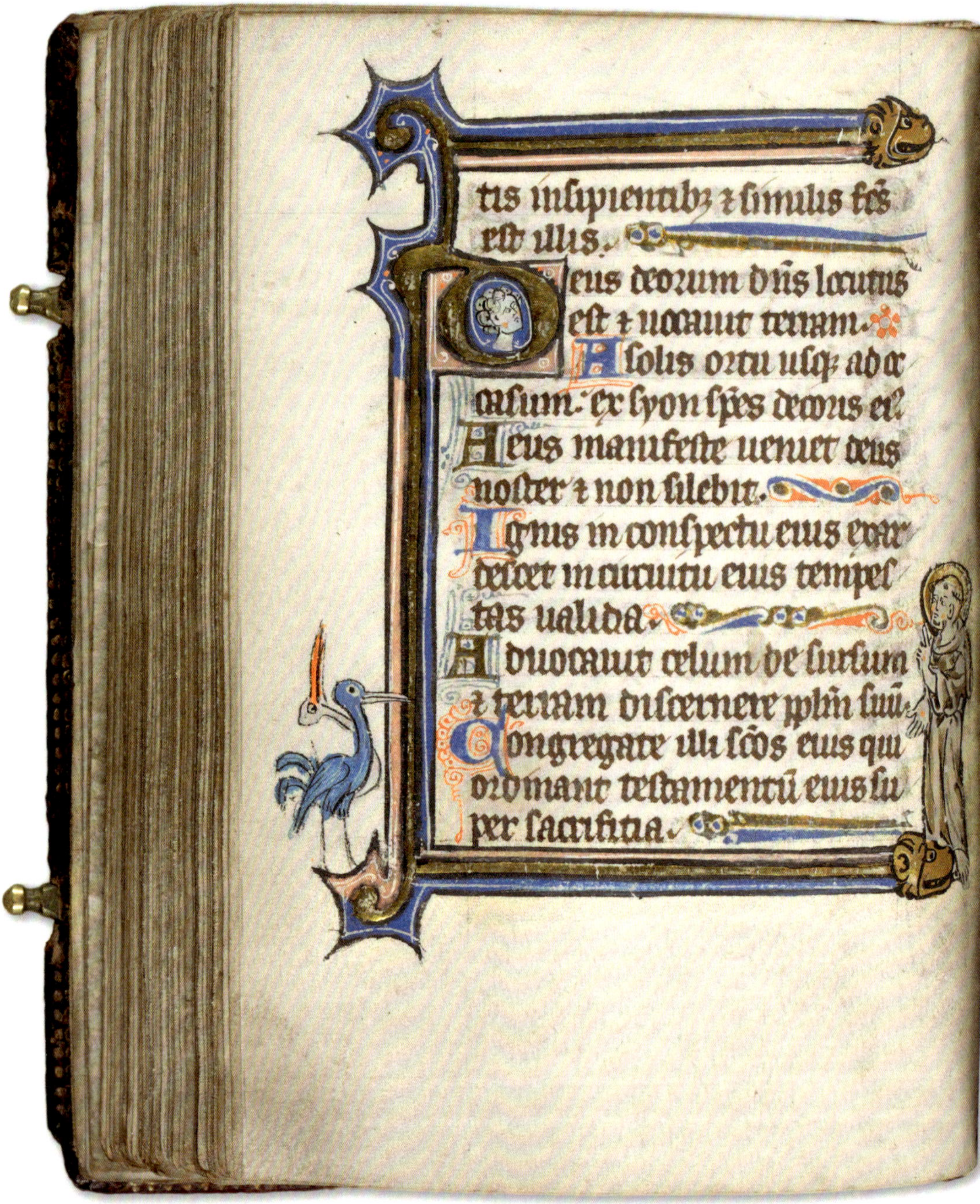

fig. 72 *Saint Francis preaching to the birds*, Ps. 49, in Psalter of Margaret of Flanders, Ghent, c.1250–c.1280, Dampierre Master(s). Bruges, Public Library, Ms. 820 (Flemish Community Collection), f. 72v.

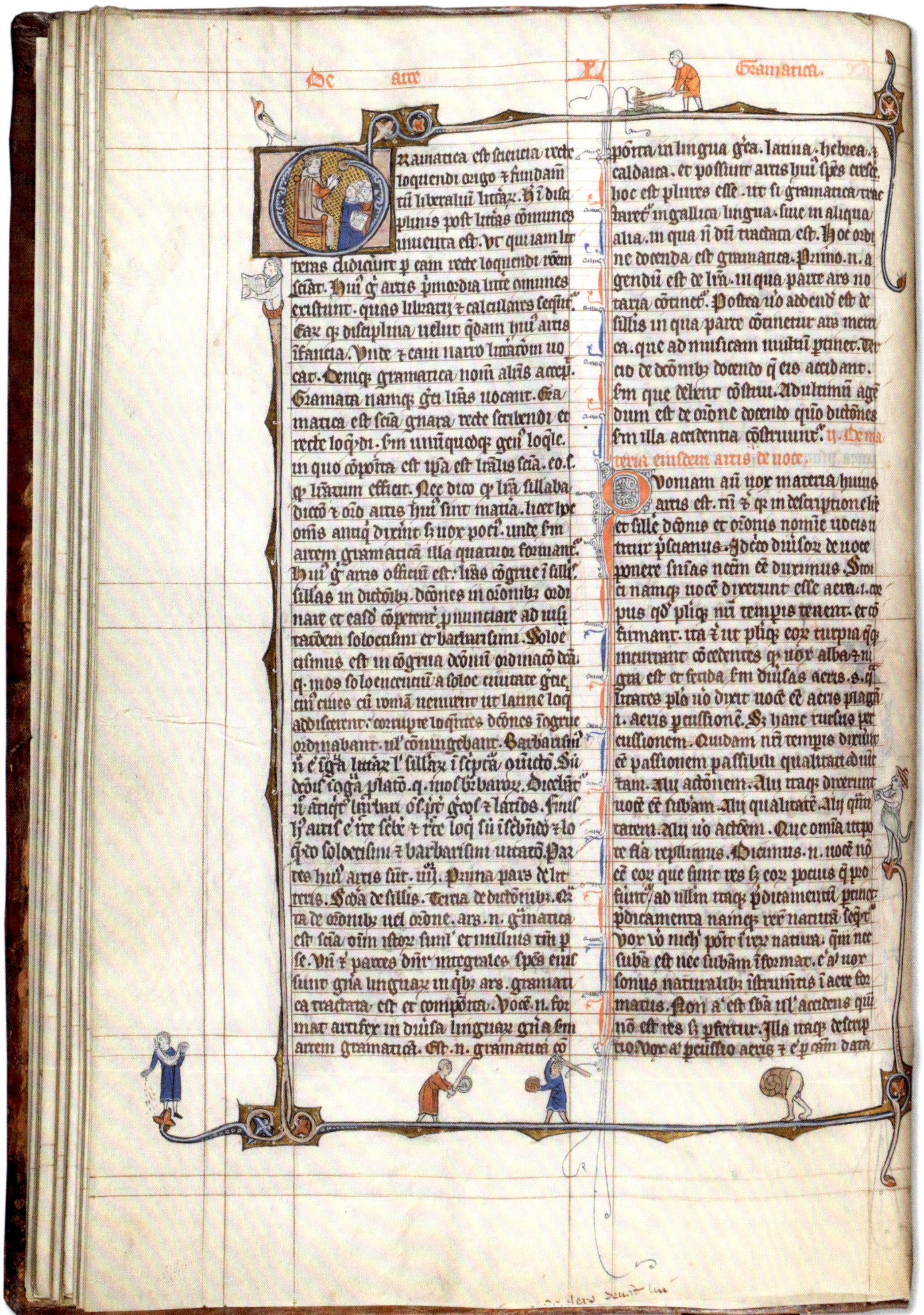

fig. 73 Beginning of the book on Grammar, in *Speculum doctrinale* by Vincent of Beauvais, France, Douai (?), late 13th century. Bruges, Public Library, Ms. 251, f. 54v.

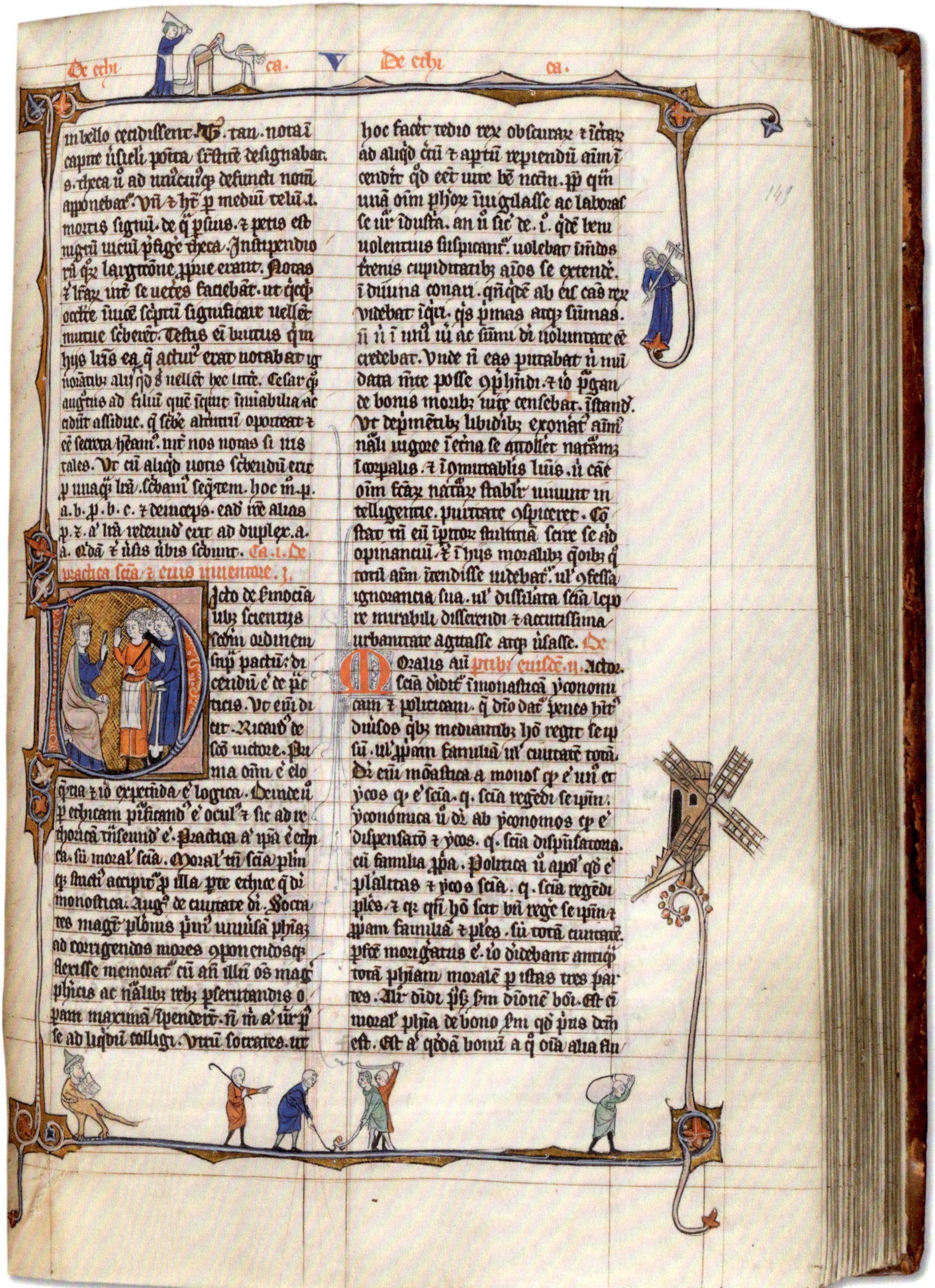

fig. 74 Beginning of the book on Ethics, in *Speculum doctrinale* by Vincent of Beauvais, France, Douai (?), late 13th century. Bruges, Public Library, Ms. 251, f. 149r.

Different Margins for Different Books

The metaphors and stories which inspired margins varied between different types of book. Playful marginalia frame the beginning of each section in a Cistercian (?) manuscript of the *Speculum doctrinale*.[28] Written by the Dominican Vincent of Beauvais (c.1190–1264), this manual for students deals with subjects ranging from grammar to ethics and politics. Unlike the devotional imagery in Margaret's Psalter, the decoration in the *Speculum* manuscript is built around the theme of learning. Historiated initials portray teachers and students in classrooms, masters instructing their apprentices, and scholars passing on their knowledge to everyone from princes to children (e.g. figs 73 and 74).

Rather than visualising social contexts of pedagogy, marginalia here seem to provide creative metaphors that comment on the joys and struggles of learning. Folio 54r which begins the book on the art of grammar is illuminated by images of sowing seeds and harrowing crops, while folio 149r shows a man carrying grain into the mill (fig. 74). These may be metaphors of knowledge that must be planted and diligently cared for, as the seed life cycle was widely used as an allegory of the power of the word, spiritual progression and learning.[29] Physical combat, as a pervasive analogy for inner struggle,[30] may be depicted in the lower margin to represent another aspect of learning, namely study as a battlefield (fig. 73). A naked man who tries to escape this battle by hiding in a snail shell might be a visualisation of the lazy student: snails were humorous and popular symbols of cowardice and avoidance.[31] Lack of diligence was probably an enduring issue, as the same theme continues on folio 149r where a teacher reproaches idle boys playing with a ball instead of studying (fig. 74).

None of these metaphors is mentioned in the *Speculum*. Artists designed marginalia that, although rarely responding to specific passages in the text, visualised tropes that were thematically appropriate for the function of each book: study and knowledge in the case of the *Speculum*, and virtues, vices and piety in the case of the Psalter. As with allegorical stories in preaching, images in the margins were only associatively connected to texts, enriching reading with vivid metaphors, memorable characters and humour.

Edifying Humour

Laughter must have been a natural response to the slothful student hiding in a snail shell or the monkey-cleric simulating reading (figs 73 and 66). Humour in marginalia was often based on deceived expectations and the subversion of the natural order.[32] What creature is a better contrast to pretentious scholars than a monkey who can imitate human behaviour but can never truly be human (fig. 66)? The artificiality of intellectual – as opposed to spiritual – knowledge was a concern of preachers. The futile knowledge of letters is laughed at in a story about a shepherd who, observing a toad, stated to a cleric that he himself thanked God every day for creating him a human in His likeness and not making him as ugly as this toad.[33] Hearing this, the cleric was amazed at the shepherd's wisdom, and felt that he himself had spent his father's money on studying in Paris for nothing. This anecdote tells us that preachers did not shun humour as a tool of persuasion, and that humour in the margins and humour in preaching, though manifested in different forms, could have touched upon similar subjects. In the thirteenth-century Dominican and Cistercian milieu, to which both Margaret of Flanders's Psalter and the *Speculum* manuscript are deeply connected, laughter was seen as a positive force and even an expression of spiritual triumph over evil.[34]

Manuscript margins participated in a religious culture in which almost any subject could be used for edification. Further research, however, is required to explore the manifold connections between marginalia and contemporary religious storytelling, including the implications for the reading practices to which the marginal stories attest. A fuller story of images in the margins of Gothic books remains to be written.

1. The combination of the arms of Flanders on ff. 40v and 190v and the arms of Hainaut on f. 103v and the date before 1300 point to Margaret as the only plausible commissioner of Ms. 820. For a general description, see: Hauwaerts, 'The Psalter of Countess Margaret'; Hunt, *Illuminating the Borders*, 46–48; Christie's catalogue https://www.christies.com/en/lot/lot-5334918 (accessed 8 January, 2025).
2. Ps. 26:1, Douay-Rheims translation.
3. For instance, Alexander Neckam (c.1157–1217) drew a connection between apes and hypocrites, see: Pietrini, 'Apes as Jesters in Medieval Imagery', 81. See also: Janson, *Apes and Ape Lore*, 163–86; Wirth, 'Les singes dans les marges à drôleries', 429–44.
4. Randall, *Images in the Margins*.
5. Camille, *Image on the Edge*, interprets marginalia based on the idea of the carnivalesque proposed by Mikhail Bakhtin in *Rabelais and His World*.
6. Sandler, *Studies in Manuscript Illumination*, 45–75, 127–94.
7. Carruthers, *The Book of Memory*, 309–24.
8. Mellinkoff, *Outcasts*.
9. Binski, *Gothic Wonder*, 283–306.
10. Caviness, *Patron or Matron*, 333–62; Camille, *Mirror in Parchment*; Stanton, *The Queen Mary Psalter*; Smith, *Art, Identity, and Devotion*; Hunt, *Illuminating the Borders*; most recently, Carns, *Making and Unmaking Love*.
11. Ps. 80:2.
12. Demets, 'French Literature', 30–60.
13. A point raised in Wirth, 'Problèmes de méthode', 11–43.
14. Randall, 'Exempla', 97–107.
15. Stephanus de Borbone, *Tractatus*, 164, 446, no. 157.
16. Jacobus de Voragine, *Sermones aurei*, I, 128a–b, 134b.
17. Étienne de Bourbon, for instance, tells a story about a priest whose mother appeared to him from Hell and related her hellish tortures to her vain love of adornments: Stephanus de Borbone, *Tractatus*, 124, 426–27, no. 113.
18. *The Exempla of Jacques de Vitry*, 114–15, 253, no. 273.
19. Stephanus de Borbone, *Tractatus*, 349, 537, no. 404; Peter of Limoges, *The Moral Treatise on the Eye*, 104.
20. Nicolas Bozon, *Contes moralisés*, unedited, London, British Library, Harley Ms. 1288, f. 103v; *Ci nous dit*, II, 244, no. 769.
21. Ps. 97:1.
22. Helsinger, 'Images on the Beatus Page', 161–76.
23. Jacobus de Voragine, *Sermones aurei*, I, 46a.
24. Jacobus de Voragine, *Sermones aurei*, I, 165b.
25. Stephanus de Borbone, *Tractatus*, 363, 541, no. 418; *The Exempla of Jacques de Vitry*, 46, 176, no. 101.
26. See 'The Study of Marginal Imagery: Past, Present, and Future', first published in 1997, reprinted in Sandler, *Studies in Manuscript Illumination*, 76–126.
27. Jordan, *Women, Power, and Religious Patronage*, 61–111.
28. The manuscript is discussed in: De Poorter, *Catalogue*, 292; Busine, *Le vaste monde*, 151, no. 33; Hunt, *Illuminating the Borders*, 148, 161–70.
29. Mk 4:26-32; Jean Gobi, *La Scala coeli*, 573, no. 957; Hunt, *Illuminating the Borders*, 113, 163.
30. 1 Tim 1:18, 6:12; Eph 6:10–12; Acts 14:21; Mt 10:34; Ps. 17:35, 23:8, 26:3, 143:1.
31. Randall, 'The Snail', 358–67.
32. On theories explaining the mechanics of humour: Martin and Ford, *The Psychology of Humor*, 55–67, 82–95.
33. *Ci nous dit*, I, 286, no. 349.
34. Horowitz and Menache, *L'humour en chaire*, 66-78; Jones, 'Preaching Laughter', 171.

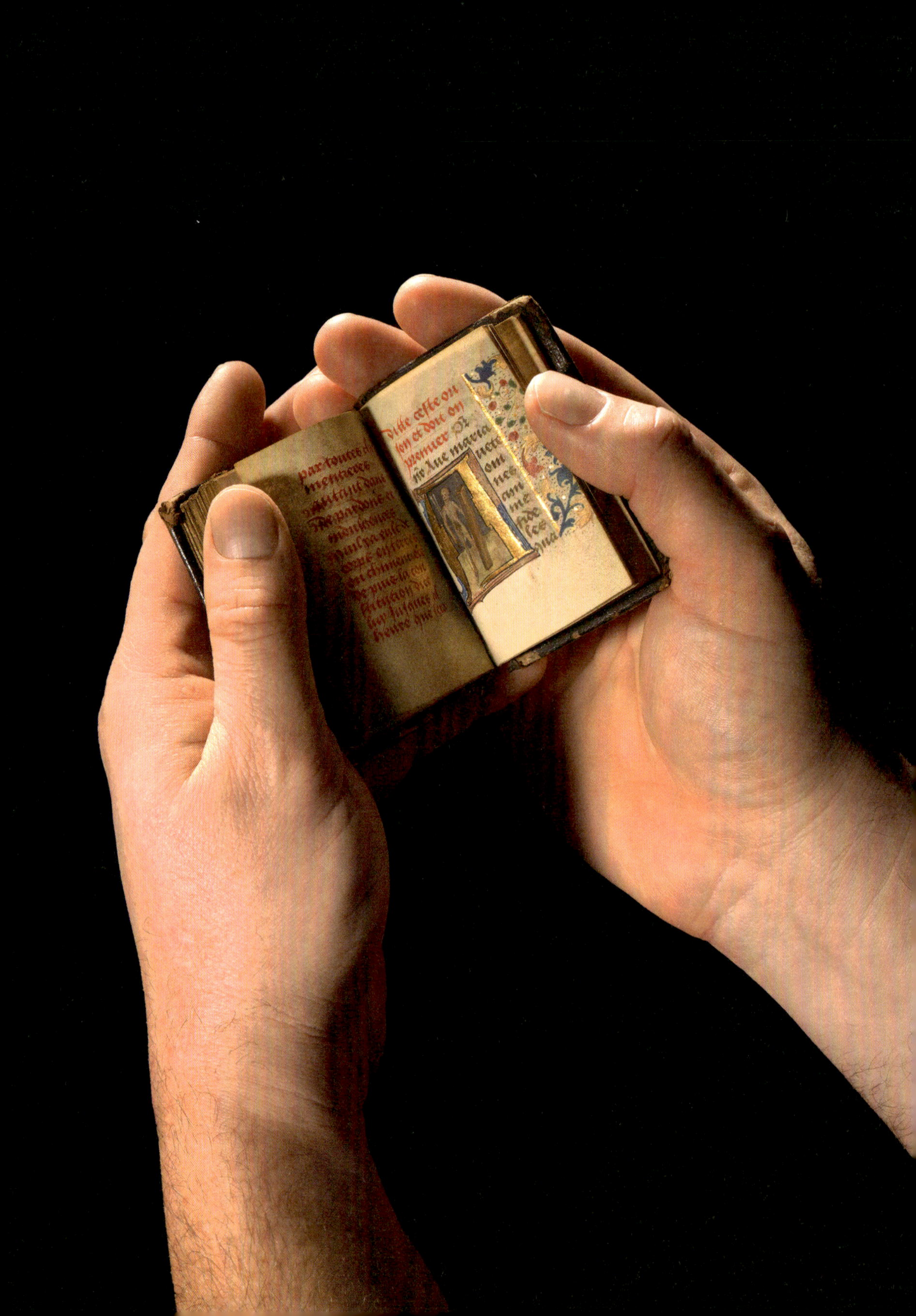

7. READING GLASSES IN THE MIDDLE AGES

Larissa van Vianen

Due to their compact size, Books of Hours were often written in small script, making them difficult to read – especially for the elderly. Scribes and miniaturists also likely found it challenging to work at such a small scale. Fortunately, they had tools to aid their vision. By the thirteenth century, an ingenious solution had been developed: two magnifying lenses mounted on the nose with a hinge, giving rise to the invention of spectacles.[1]

In the Low Countries, archaeological finds of medieval spectacles are, unfortunately, scarce, with discoveries limited to Raversijde (fig. 80), Middelburg, Haarlem and Windesheim.[2] These visual aids, however, are well represented in paintings.[3] One of the most famous examples is the pair worn by Canon Joris van der Paele in his portrait by Jan van Eyck (fig. 78). Van Eyck (1390–1441) meticulously captures the way convex lenses distort text when held at the wrong angle. The depiction of the distortion is so precise that opticians have been able to determine the strength of the lenses: +2.50, equivalent to modern reading glasses.[4] Yet, the canon's spectacles raise intriguing questions: how did he come to possess such a visual aid, and were spectacles only accessible to the upper classes?

fig. 75 Pocket-size Book of Hours (bifolium 8 x 11 cm), Cambrai (?), c.1470–c.1480. Bruges, Public Library, Jean van Caloen Foundation Collection, Ms. 15, ff. 121v–122r.

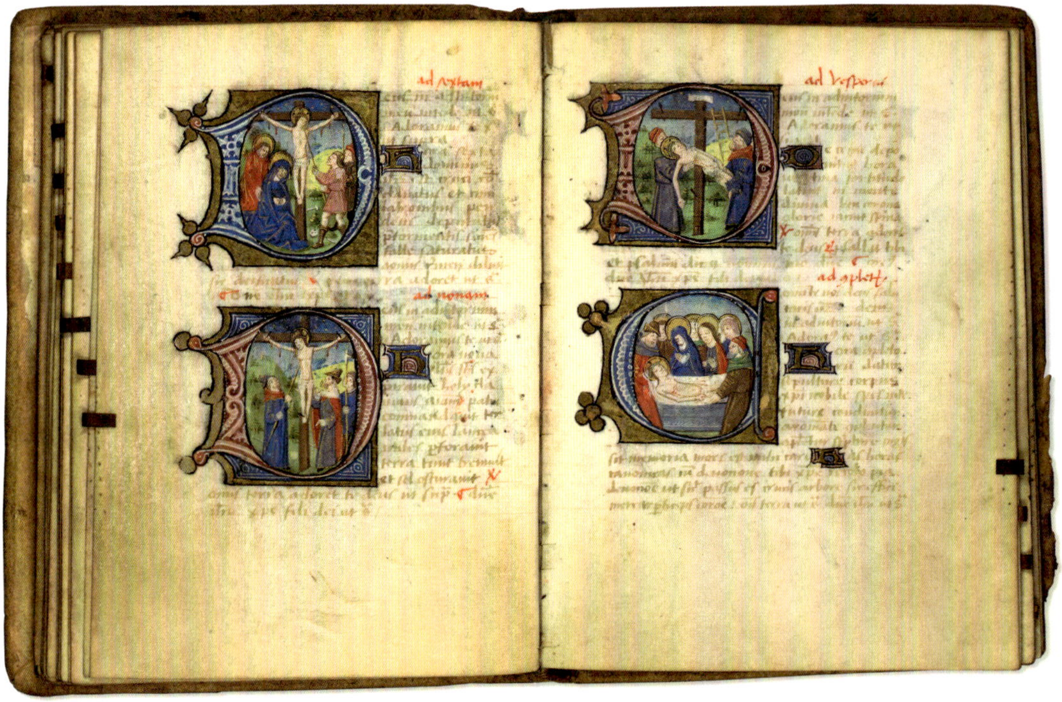

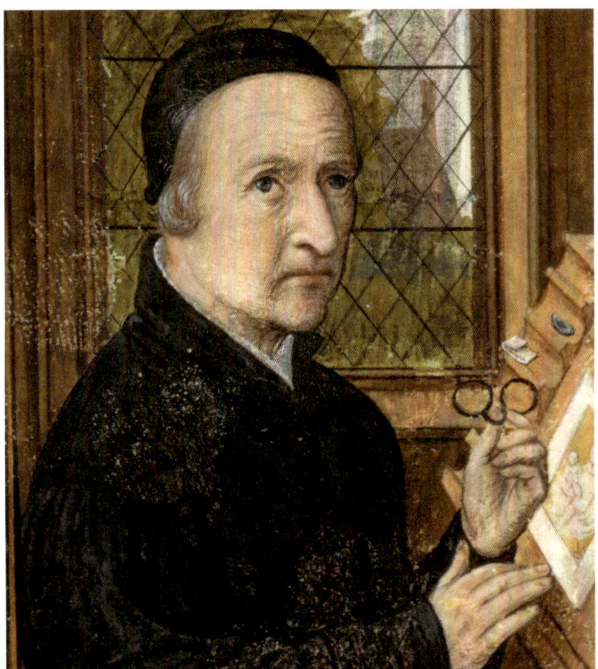

fig. 76 Barely legible text and four detailed miniatures on a small surface (14 x 22 cm), in Book of Hours, Besançon (?), c.1470. Bruges, Public Library, Jean van Caloen Foundation Collection, Ms. 7, ff. 28v–29r.

fig. 77 Bruges miniaturist Simon Bening holding spectacles. Simon Bening, *Self-Portrait* (detail), 1558, tempera on parchment. New York, The Metropolitan Museum of Art, 1975.1.2487.

A Necessary Invention

The earliest recorded mention of spectacles comes from the Dominican friar Giordano da Pisa (c.1255–1311) who, in 1306, preaching at Santa Maria Novella in Florence, hailed the invention as one of the greatest and most essential in the world – a true testament to human ingenuity.[5] The brilliance of spectacles lay not so much in the lenses themselves but in the frame that secured them to the head. The magnifying properties of lenses were already known. In 1021, Ḥasan Ibn al-Haytham (c.965–1040), also known as Alhazen, wrote about lenses made from quartz or beryl. Around 1265, Roger Bacon (c.1214–c.1294) described convex lenses in his work *Perspectiva*, explaining how they could help older individuals or those with poor eyesight read fine script.[6] Their theoretical understanding was flawed, however, as it was based on the mistaken belief that vision was centred within the eye itself.

Glassmakers, already familiar with convex lenses but unencumbered by medieval optical theories, may have been the first to experiment with frames for magnifying glasses.[7] Alternatively, historian Vincent Ilardi suggests that anyone possessing two magnifying lenses might have conceived the idea of mounting them together.[8] The depiction of spectacles in a thirteenth-century Ghent psalter (fig. 79) raises questions about how quickly the invention spread and whether spectacles were invented independently in different parts of Europe.[9] From the thirteenth to the sixteenth century, traders, missionaries and colonists played a key role in disseminating the concept of spectacles across the world.[10]

During the thirteenth century, the demand for visual aids grew rapidly, driven by the increasing specialisation of trades and professions. As European cities expanded during the High Middle Ages, so did the need for literate individuals.[11] Not only clerks, but craftsmen such as goldsmiths also relied on sharp eyesight to carry out their work. Spectacles with convex lenses offered a solution, allowing people to extend their careers by an average ten to fifteen years.[12] It was not until the mid-fifteenth century that spectacles with concave lenses appeared, designed for the short-sighted. To distinguish between the two types, they were referred to as either 'glasses for young people' (for short-sightedness) or 'glasses for older people' (for long-sightedness).[13]

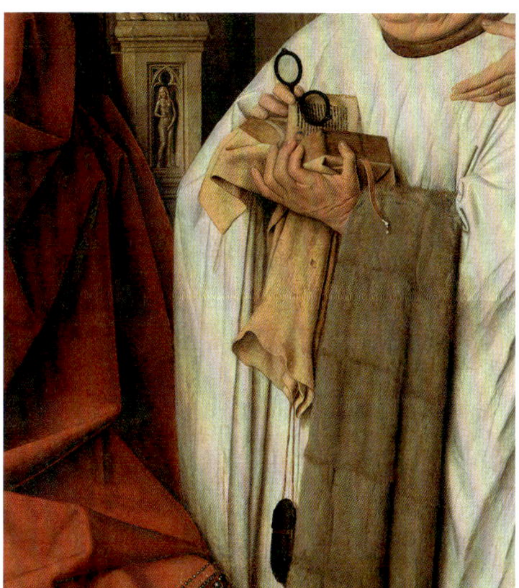

fig. 78 Spectacles and spectacle case attached to a string. Jan van Eyck, *Madonna with Canon Van der Paele* (detail), 1436, oil on panel. Bruges, Musea Brugge, 0000.GRO0161.I.

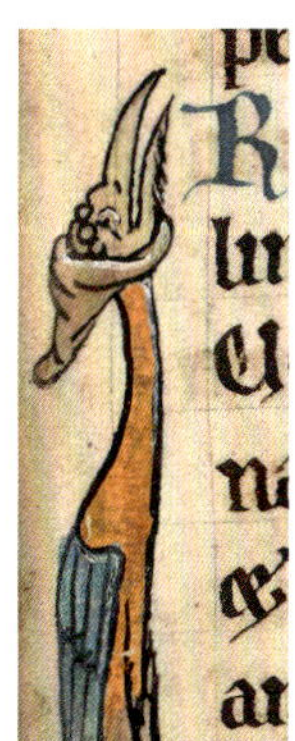

fig. 79 Bird with spectacles, in Psalter, Ghent, c.1240–c.1290. Brussels, KBR, Ms. 5163-4, f. 32r.

The Frame

The main advantage of spectacles over magnifying glasses was that they freed the hands. For the design to be effective, the frame had to hold the lenses securely in place on the nose. The earliest designs featured a scissor-like mechanism, with a pin or rivet holding the lenses together. This structure, however, proved too weak for frequent use. This likely explains why many depictions show spectacle wearers holding their glasses in place by hand.[14] To secure the scissor-style spectacles, one could also attach them to the brim of a hat or fasten them with a cord around the head.[15]

From the second half of the fourteenth century, a new type of spectacle frame appears in painting: the round nose bridge. This design, still in use today, not only fits more comfortably on the nose but also ensures that the lenses stay properly aligned. The frame was usually made from a single piece of material, which could be bone, wood, leather or even gilded metal. The edges of wooden or bone frames were often notched to secure the lenses in place.[16] The strongest and most comfortable frames, however, were made from horn, a tough, keratin-rich material found in hooves, nails and horns. Bovine horn was used to make figurines, combs, spectacles and other items.[17] To create a secure setting for the lenses, craftsmen would heat the horn to shape a groove – as the material cooled, it would contract, firmly holding the lenses in place without visible seams.[18] The spectacles worn by Canon Van der Paele appear to have been made using this technique.

Spectacle Cases

Spectacle cases were often made from the same materials as the frames. While most were made of wood or leather, some were crafted from gilded metal, horn or ivory.[19] Hinged cases, similar to those used today, only became common in the sixteenth century. Prior to that, the most common type of case was the one depicted by Jan Provoost (fig. 82). The string holding the two parts together allowed the case to be easily attached to a belt or bookbinding. Other storage methods were also used. Spectacles with rivets, for example, were sometimes kept in a drop-shaped case, in which they could be folded for safekeeping.[20] The Book of Hours of Loys van Boghem even has a cut-out in the back cover specifically designed to hold a pair of reading glasses (fig. 81).

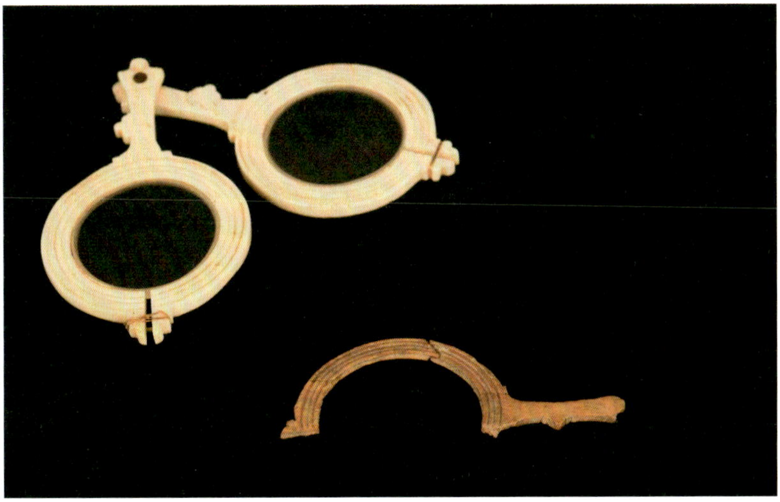

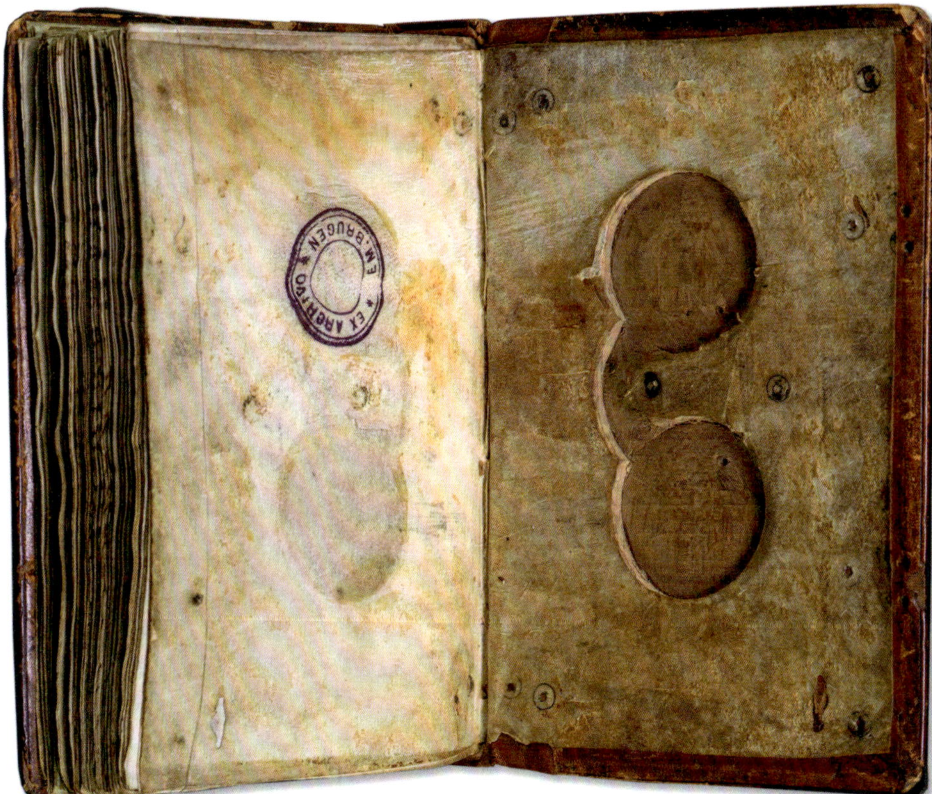

fig. 80 Fragment of bone spectacles from the medieval fishing village of Walraversijde (and contemporary facsimile), animal bone (ox), 15th century. Ostend, Atlantikwall Raversyde (West Flanders Province), WR00074 (94RAV714).

fig. 81 Cut-out for reading glasses, in Book of Hours of Loys van Boghem, Lyon (?), 1526. Bruges, Archives of Ten Duinen Major Seminary, Ms. 66/35.

Beryl, *Vitrum blanchum*, *Waldglas* and Crystal

Advancements in medieval glassmaking, particularly in what is now Italy and Germany, led to the production of glass refined enough to replace the precious stone, beryl. Beryl, aside from being rare and expensive, also contained natural imperfections that reduced the transparency of the lenses.[21] *Vitrum blanchum*, produced in northern Italy from the fourteenth century onwards, could be processed to a more consistent transparency and was easier to grind into lenses.[22] Yet despite its good quality making it difficult for the untrained eye to distinguish from crystal, *vitrum blanchum* retained a greyish tinge, even when the finest raw materials were used.[23]

In contrast, German *Waldglas*, or forest glass, primarily used for windows and drinking vessels but also for cheaper lenses, had a distinct greenish tint.[24]

Nonetheless, these colour variations likely did not outweigh the main advantage of glass: its significantly lower production costs.

Crystal lenses, often set in gilded metal or black horn frames, were considerably more expensive: the 1365 inventory of Bishop Giovanni di Magnavia, for example, records that a typical pair of spectacles in Pisa cost between 6 and 15 *soldi*, whereas crystal spectacles were valued at ten times that amount. Records from the Venetian crystal guild, however, reveal that counterfeit glasses were a widespread issue. Glass quality improved significantly from 1375 onwards with the import of pure alkaline ash from Syria and Egypt.[25]

Even six hundred years ago, spectacles were not considered a luxury item. A basic pair with glass lenses and a wooden or leather frame cost roughly the same as a carpenter's daily wages or a good pair of shoes.[26] Moreover, spectacle production was not limited to glassmakers and crystal workers – local craftsmen, such as goldsmiths and leatherworkers, had the skills to make frames from horn, bone, wood or leather. Even monasteries made a profit from manufacturing spectacles.[27]

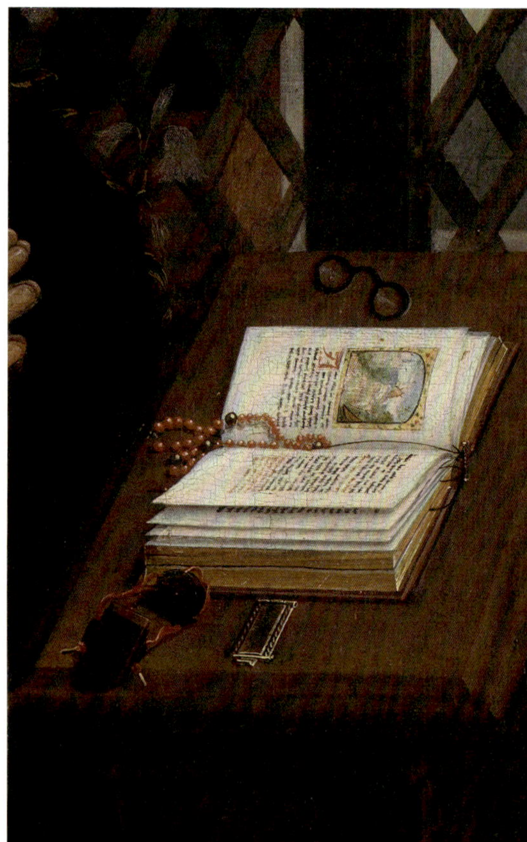

fig. 82 Spectacle case and glasses beside a Book of Hours. Jan Provoost, *Portrait of a Donor with Saint Nicholas* (detail), 1515, oil on panel. Bruges, Musea Brugge, 0000.GRO0216.I-0217.I.

Spectacles in Bruges

Little is known about the spectacle industry in Flanders, but data on the English spectacle market help fill this gap in the archives. Records show that in 1384, 1390 and 1391, thousands of spectacles of varying quality were imported into the port of London aboard Flemish and Dutch ships.[28] The fact that the earliest English spectacle makers bore Flemish names further suggests that the Low Countries had a thriving spectacle industry in the fourteenth and fifteenth centuries, rivalling that of northern Italy.[29] In Antwerp, for instance, glassblowers had already joined forces with artists and goldsmiths in the Guild of St Luke as early as 1382.[30]

English records also highlight the importance of Bruges as a trading hub. It was not until 1669 that spectacles were shipped directly from Italy to England, indicating that in the fifteenth century, most goods – including spectacles – first passed through Bruges before being transported to Southampton and King's Lynn.[31] Like London, Bruges was likely flooded with spectacles and the raw materials needed for their production in the late fourteenth and early fifteenth centuries. From 1425 onwards, Florentine and Venetian ships made annual voyages from Porto Pisano to Sluis, bringing goods such as alum, spices, Murano glass – and spectacles in both glass and crystal.[32]

These Italian spectacles likely provided a higher-quality alternative to the locally produced options in Bruges. For glassblowers, the sale of transparent glass and *vitrum blanchum* was far more lucrative than the labour-intensive production of spectacle lenses, which were then distributed cheaply throughout Europe via monasteries and markets, and by travelling merchants.[33]

Thanks to the wide range of materials and quality, spectacles became an affordable option for nearly all social classes. As a result, they quickly became indispensable, and are essential to our understanding of medieval readers and their books.

1. Rosen, 'The Invention of Eyeglasses', 13–46.
2. Ilardi, *Renaissance Vision*, 140.
3. See Poulet, *Atlas on the History of Spectacles.*
4. Hanley, 'Optical Symbolism', 2.
5. Rosen, 'The Invention', 13–46.
6. Ilardi, *Renaissance Vision*, 41–44.
7. Rosen, 'The Invention', 183–218.
8. Ilardi, *Renaissance Vision*, 25.
9. Neaman, 'The Mystery of the Ghent Bird', 212–13.
10. Ilardi, *Renaissance Vision*, 149–50.
11. Stock, *The Implications of Literacy*, 105.
12. Ilardi, *Renaissance Vision*, 3.
13. Ilardi, 'Eyeglasses and Concave Lenses', 341.
14. See for example Poulet, *Atlas on the History of Spectacles*, 26; Ilardi, *Renaissance Vision*, 271–72.
15. Rosenthal, *Spectacles*, 38.
16. Ilardi, *Renaissance Vision*, 126.
17. Ibidem. Fifteenth-century Bolognese import records even mention spectacles made from water buffalo horn (Ilardi, *Renaissance Vision*, 158).
18. Hardwick, *Discovering Horn*, 37, 145.
19. Ilardi, *Renaissance Vision*, 130, 137.
20. Rosenthal, 'Wooden Eyeglass Cases', 19–20.
21. Rosenthal, *Spectacles*, 11.
22. Ilardi, *Renaissance Vision*, 126.
23. Mentasti, *et al.*, 'Venetian Conical Goblets', 157–59.
24. Pfaender, *Schott Guide to Glass*, 1.6.
25. Ilardi, *Renaissance Vision*, 52, 8, 11.
26. Ibidem, 51–53, 144.
27. Ibidem, 22.
28. Ravenhill, 'The Earliest Recorded Spectacle Makers', 12–13.
29. Rhodes, 'A Pair of Late Medieval Spectacles', 25.
30. Veeckman, Dumortier, 'La production de verres à Anvers', 69; Prims, *Geschiedenis van Antwerpen*, 190–91.
31. Ilardi, *Renaissance Vision*, 143.
32. Ibidem, 135.
33. Ilardi, *Renaissance Vision*, 71, 129.

Penitential Psalms with *Last Judgement* (detail, see p. 32)

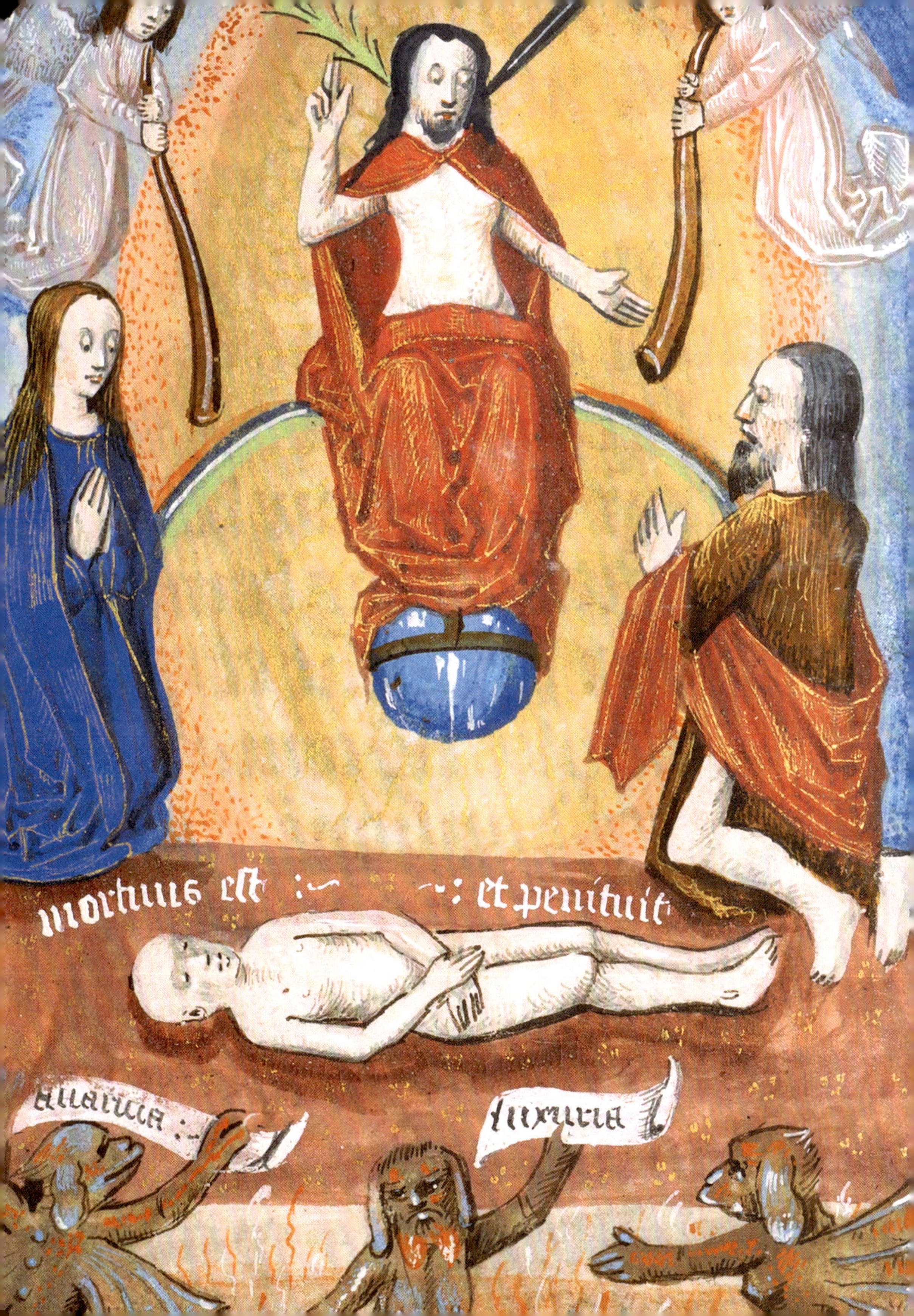
mortuus est
et penituit
auaricia
luxuria

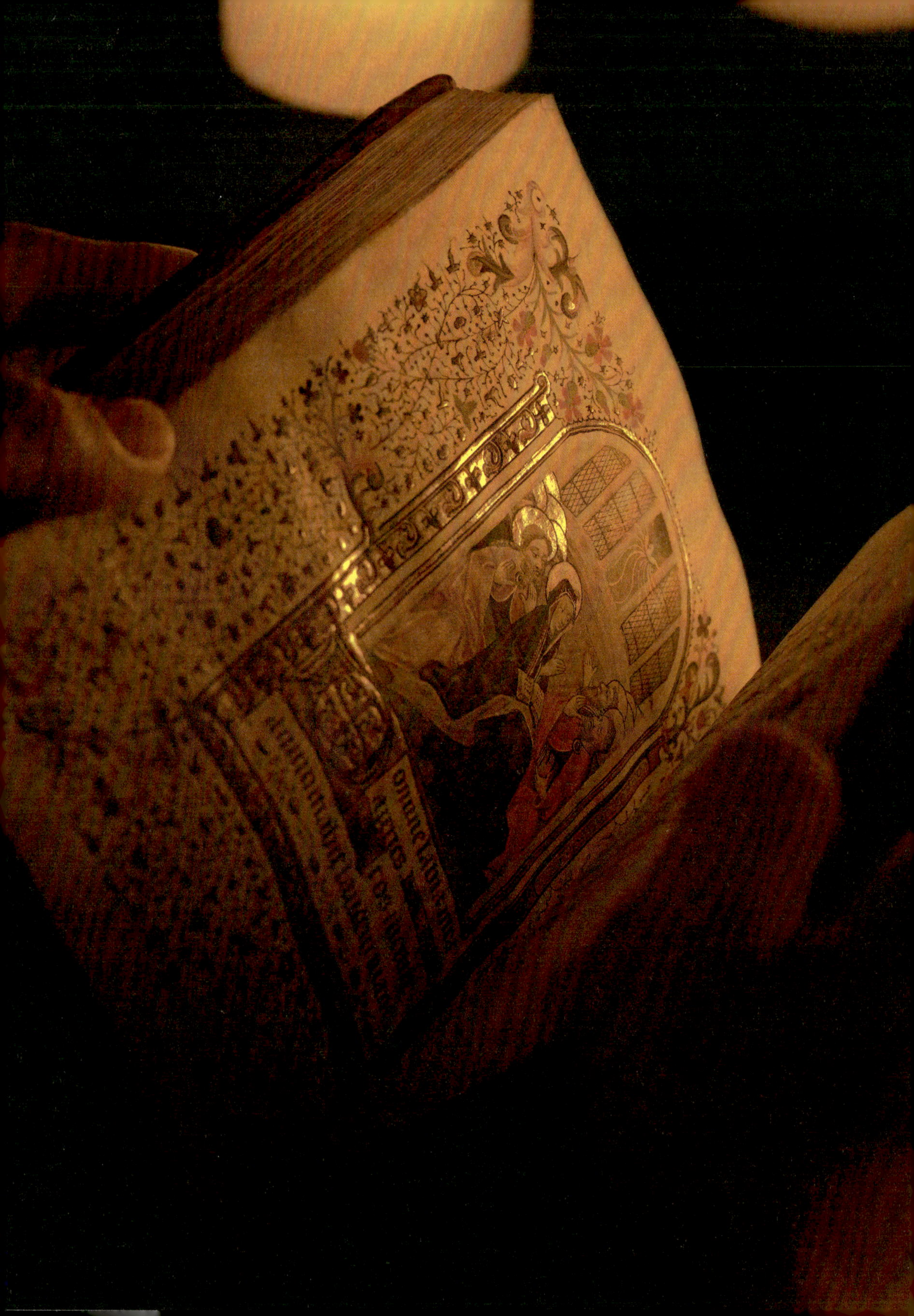

8. READING AFTER DARK: THE MANY LIGHTS OF THE MIDDLE AGES

Whilst the term 'Dark Ages' – which some people still use today to refer to the Middle Ages – evokes a dark landscape in both a metaphorical and a real sense, the cities of the last centuries of the Middle Ages were illuminated after twilight and 'curfew' by thousands of lights. Many people roamed the streets at night: priests, midwives, doctors, officials, soldiers, thieves, bakers and revellers. Indoors, however, lighting illuminated dinners, spinning and weaving, artisan workshops, banquets, bureaucratic tasks, reading, writing and learning. From homes and workshops to palaces, churches and stables, life continued after dark, driven by work, necessity or leisure.

Beatrice Del Bo

fig. 83 Book of Hours, Master of the Bedford Hours, Paris, c.1435. Bruges, Public Library, Jean van Caloen Foundation Collection, Ms. 12, ff. 103v–104r.

A Large Variety of Objects for Three Fuels

Depending on whether one were indoors or outdoors, different shaped artefacts were used to make light, fuelled by three different types of raw material: wax, tallow (e.g. animal fat) and oils of different origins.[1] Outdoor objects were designed to be wind and weather resistant, such as lanterns (small or medium sized, portable, circular, square or polygonal) made of wood or metal, with parchment or glass sides to protect the flame of the candle placed in the centre (figs 84 and 89). Torches were long wooden sticks covered with resin at the top and/or topped with a basket full of flammable substances. Doublets consisted of two/four long tapers joined together. They were mainly used in processions such as that of the Holy Blood which, from the beginning of the fourteenth century, has been held during the day in the streets of Bruges with the participation of all members of society, from the clergy to the guilds.[2] In front of gates to buildings or in open spaces and gardens inside buildings, braziers of various sizes burned, simultaneously heating and illuminating.

Indoors, candles, lamps, chandeliers, candelabra of different sizes and crowns (also circular chandeliers with several turns or 'layers', so much so that today they are called 'wedding cakes') were mainly used, in various shapes, forms and materials – wood, glass, ceramics, precious and semi-precious metals – with candles, torches and tapers made of very expensive and valuable beeswax,[3] often imported from the Baltic coast and the East, where the best quality wax was produced.[4]

Some lamps and chandeliers were fuelled with olive, walnut, fish or whale oil, depending on the local availability of the product. Over the centuries, however, oil was used less and less, because the spread of Christianity promoted the candle as the lighting object *par excellence*. It was still sometimes used in lamps in homes (fig. 86), where animal fat (tallow) could also be used, and especially in churches, where an oil lamp burns perpetually next to the Blessed Sacrament.

fig. 84 Portable polygonal lantern (lower left corner), in Book of Hours, Bruges, c.1400–c.1420, Master of the Tall Figures (Beaufort Group). Bruges, Public Library, Ms. 736 (King Baudouin Foundation Collection), f. 83v.

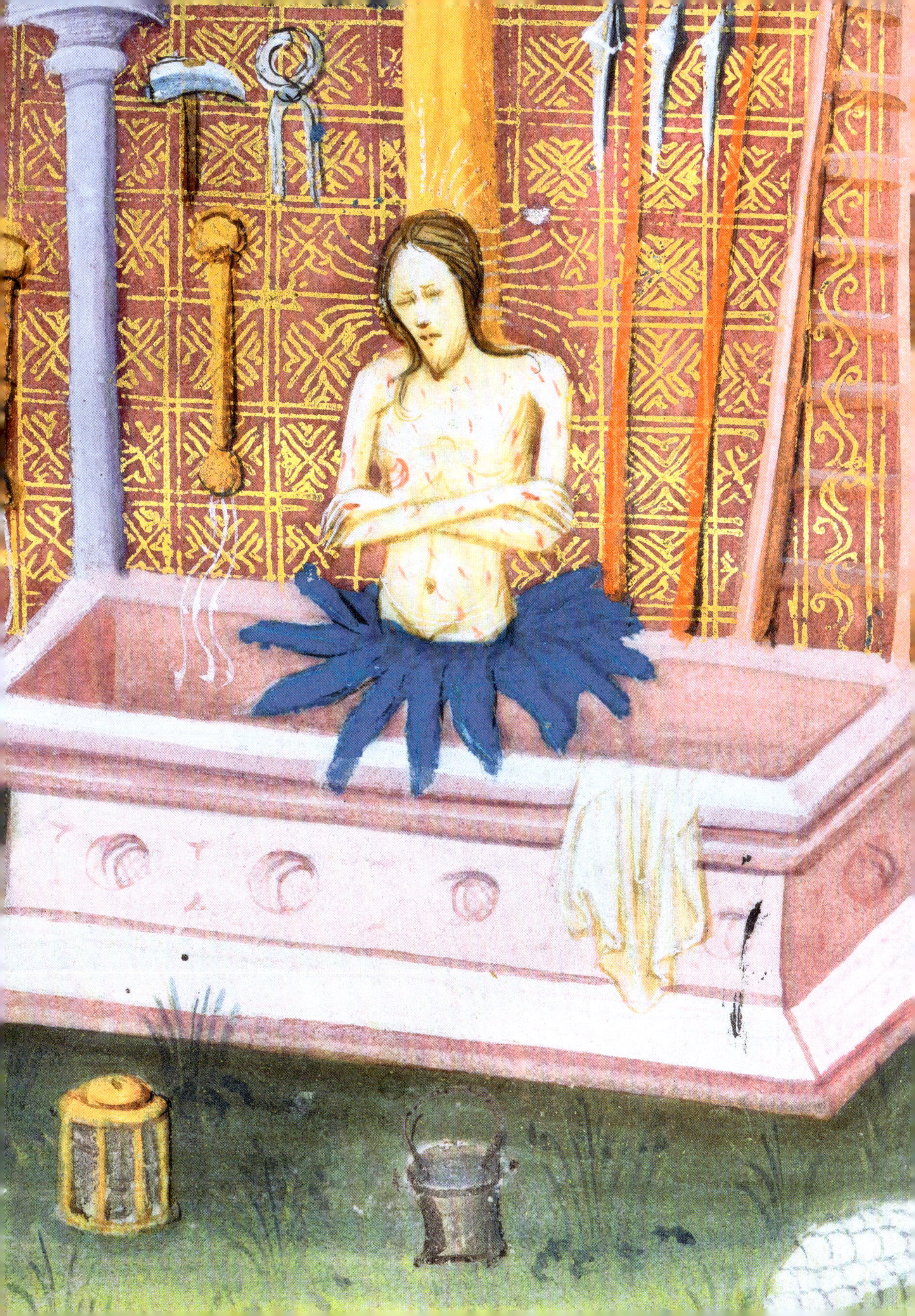

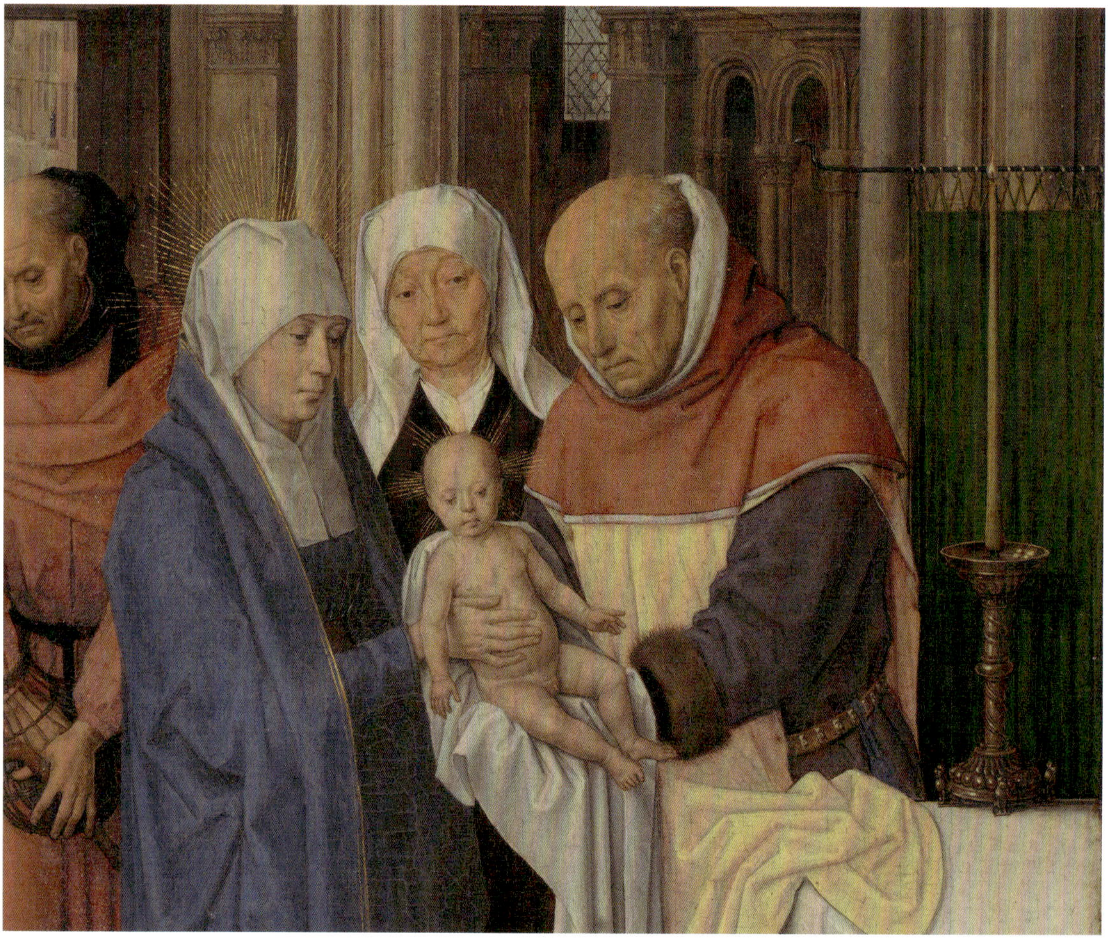

fig. 85 Ornate metal candle holder for indoor use. Hans Memling, *Adoration of the Magi* (detail of right panel), 1479, oil on panel. Bruges, Musea Brugge, O.SJ0173.I.

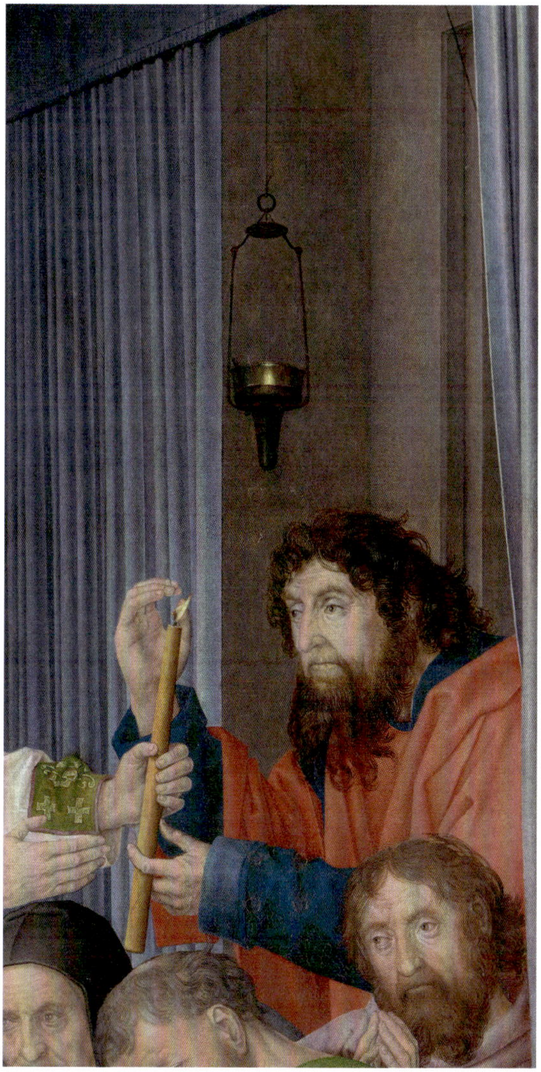

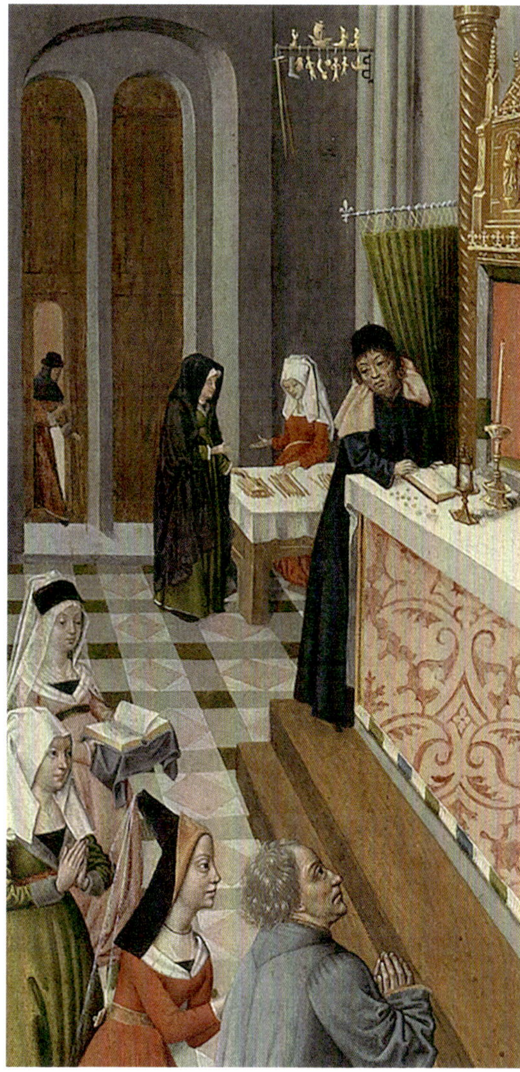

fig. 86 Oil lamp hanging from the ceiling, and taper. Hugo van der Goes, *The Death of the Virgin* (detail), 1475–1482, oil on panel. Bruges, Musea Brugge, 0000.GRO0204.I.

fig. 87 Woman selling candles. Master of the (Bruges) Legend of Saint Ursula, *The Legend of Saint Ursula* (detail lower right panel), c.1482, oil on panel. Bruges, Musea Brugge, 0000.GRO1542.I-1545.I.

Making and Buying Light

The cheapest option was candles made from animal fat or tallow.[5] They could be bought from specialist candle makers. In Italy, even sausage makers are known to have produced such candles using slaughterhouse waste. Tallow candles were about a third cheaper than wax candles, but they emitted a nauseating odour when they burned. As a result, those who could afford better alternatives avoided them or only used them outdoors.

Wax was mostly used for lighting in official and sacred circumstances. The Bruges booksellers' guild, for instance, purchased candles and accessories for lighting their altars, as the fifteenth-century account books show.[6] In the church, one of the few places where the use of candles has survived to the present day, the faithful could buy candles *in situ*; inside the sacred buildings or in the churchyard there were vendors, mainly women, who ran retail stalls.[7] A stunning example can be seen in the lower right-hand panel of the 1482 *Legend of Saint Ursula*, where a female candle-seller is seen near the altar (fig. 87).

Candles were also sold by candlemakers, and street names such as Keersstraat (Candle Street) in Bruges still hint at their importance in medieval cities. This area likely hosted several workshops, easily identified by signs and banners advertising their goods.[8] In cities in the Low Countries, makers of candles were united in guilds. Most often, this was the guild of sellers of *vette waren* (fatty products), but in Bruges they belonged to the guild of 'turners' (chair turners, sieve makers and wax light makers).[9] Wax candle production in Bruges was governed by an ordonnance of 1454, which describes different types according to their use: *stallichten*, i.e. funeral candles, which are placed at the corners of the coffin (fig. 88); *offerkeerssen* and *evenlanghen*, i.e. altar candles; *vrauwen evenlanghen*, perhaps specific candles offered by women in church; *taefelkeerssen* or *dobbelytsen*, long tapers joined together in twos and fours; *ghewronghene keersen*, i.e. torches of twisted shape; and other types.[10] The quality of wax was checked by the authorities.[11]

Alternatively, whether for large supplies or for personal use, one could turn to an apothecary, a spice merchant or a drug manufacturer who, among the various luxury products they dealt with in their shop – silk, parchment, sugar, cakes, exotic fruits – also traded in wax. Apothecaries used this raw material for the composition of therapeutic products, for the manufacture of candles and tapers of various sizes, and for votive objects.

fig. 88 Funeral candles, in Book of Hours, Bruges, c.1430. Bruges, Public Library, Ms. 821 (Flemish Community Collection), f. 119r.

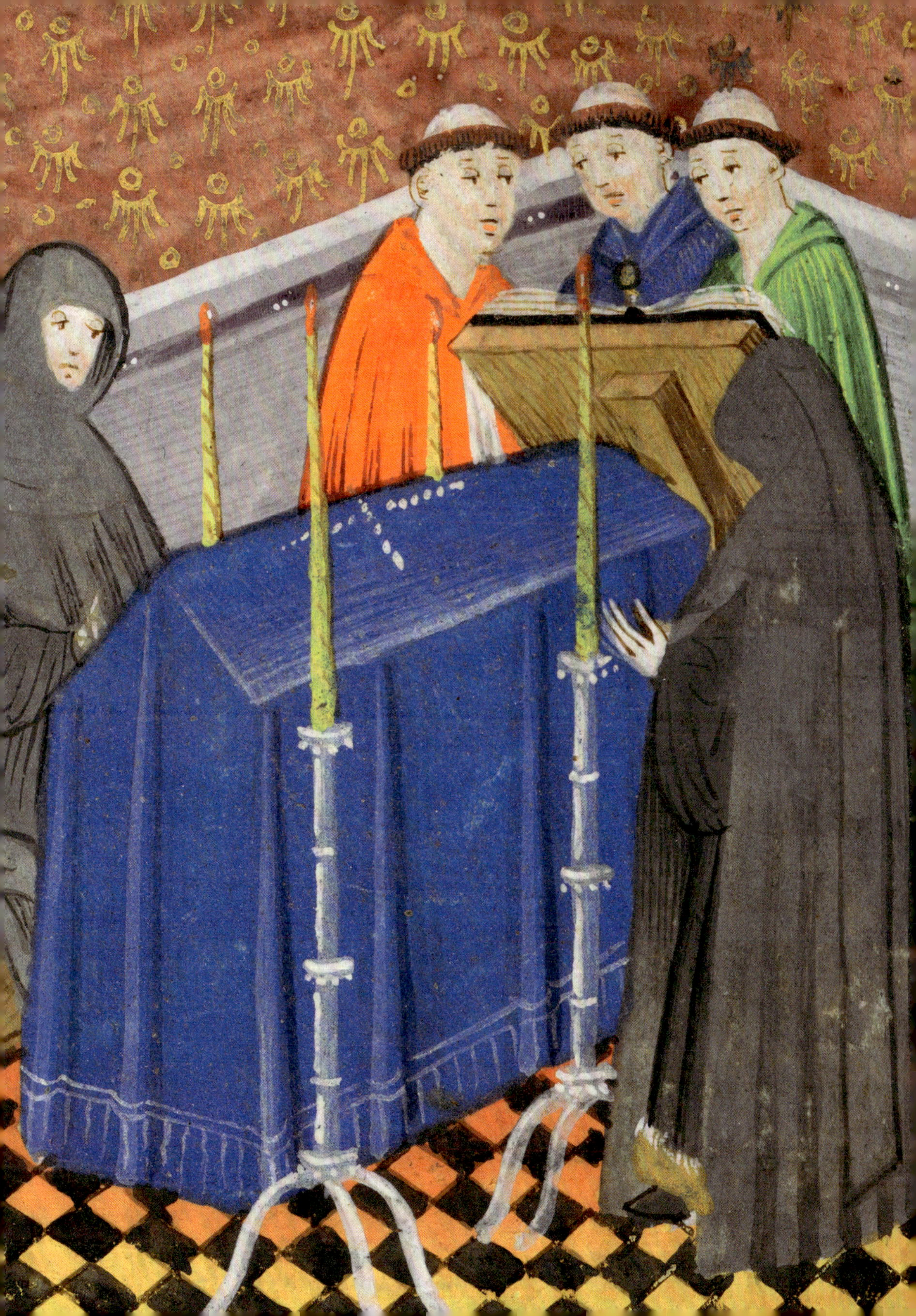

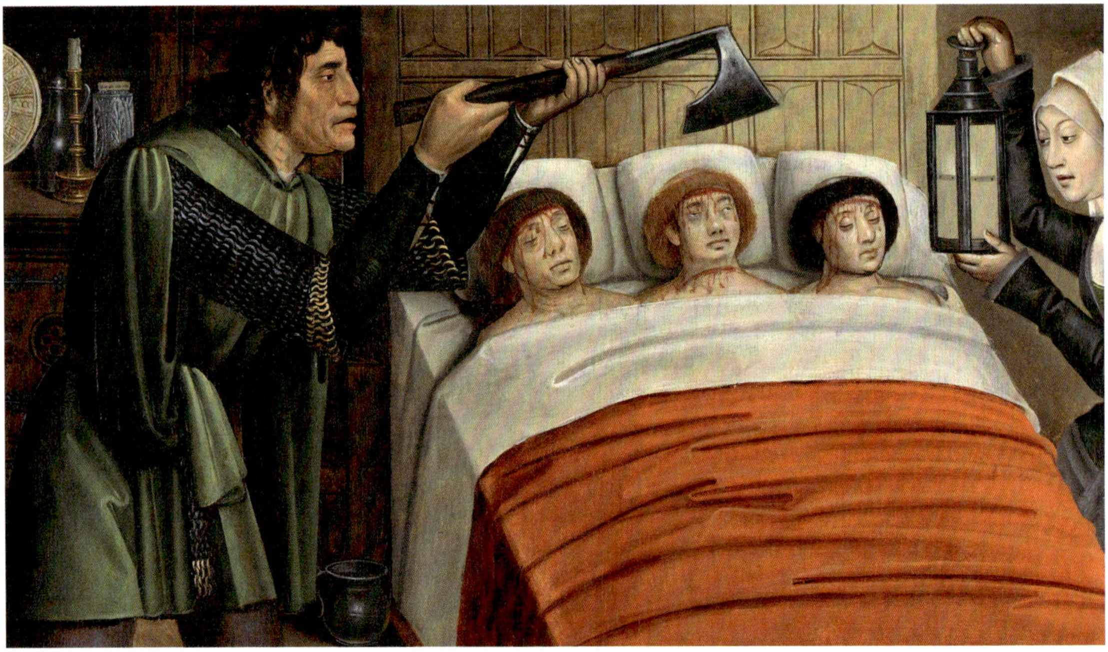

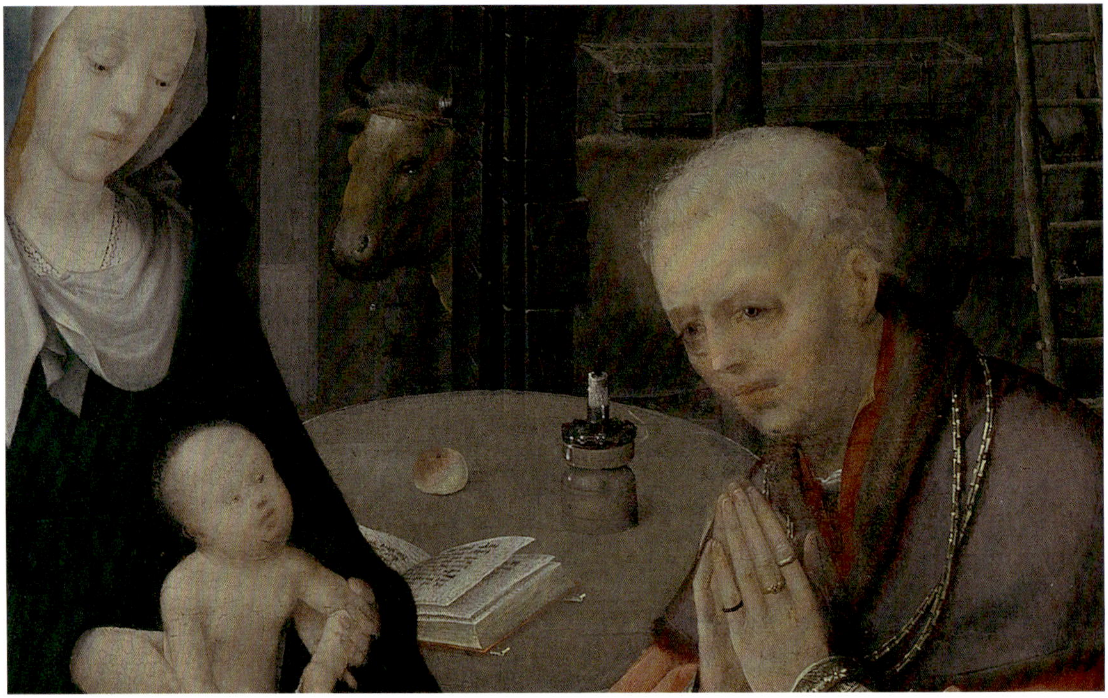

fig. 89 Metal lamp (on nightstand) and pewter lantern (in the woman's hand). Master of the Legend of Saint Lucia, *Retable of Saint Nicholas* (detail), 1479–c.1505, oil on panel. Bruges, Musea Brugge, 0000.GRO0676.I-2008.GRO0002a-2c.I.

fig. 90 Lamp on table. Master of the Bruges Adoration, *The Adoration of the Kings* (detail), c.1501–c.1525, oil on panel. Bruges, Musea Brugge, 0000.GRO0221.I.

Evidence of Widespread Use

Documentary and iconographic sources testify to the great variety of types of artificial light. The simplest and most common were lanterns, i.e. wooden, ceramic, glass or metal holders, into which a candle was inserted. Candelabra were designed to hold several candles. Particularly popular are those made in Dinant – already considered the home of copper, brass, pewter and tin sheet work, hence the generic term '*dinanderie*' [brassware] for objects of this type. Wall sconces, designed to hold one or more candles, were mounted on walls or fireplace lintels. These fixtures often featured mechanisms allowing them to swivel, providing adjustable lighting for various settings. From the ceilings also hung chandeliers made of simple crossed planks fitted with pulleys, with candles at each end, or precious goldsmiths' artefacts of a very refined style (fig. 92).[12]

The small wooden wheel with candles on its rim, an iconographic attribute of Saint Donatian, is unique to Flemish art. It is masterfully depicted by Van Eyck (fig. 93) and later by the Master of the Legend of Saint Lucia (*Pietà Triptych*, c.1475), Gerard David (*Canon Bernardijn Salviati and Three Saints*, 1501) and Jan Gossaert (*Saint Donatian*, 1520).[13] In 390, this type of wheel was placed on the water to help recover the drowned body of Bishop Donatian. From the 9th century, his relics were kept in the Cathedral of Saint Donatian in Bruges where Joris van der Paele (1370–1443), patron of Van Eyck's painting, served as canon.[14]

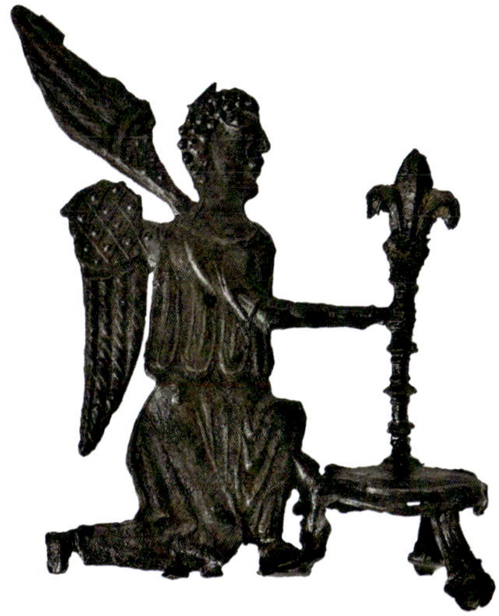

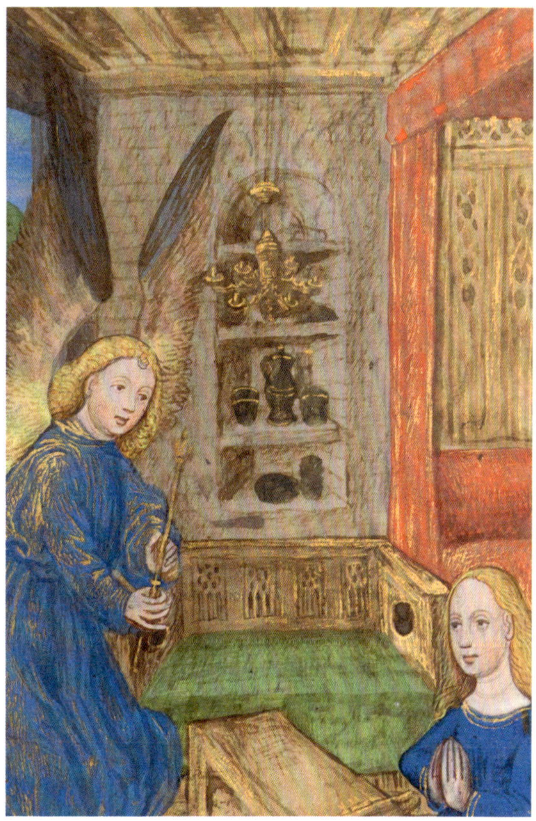

fig. 91 Lamp. Tin-lead alloy, 14th century. Bruges, Raakvlak, inv. col. Beuck/1/1/A/346.

fig. 92 Ornate chandelier, in Book of Hours, Master of the Flemish Boethius, Ghent and/or Bruges, c.1480. Bruges, Public Library, OCMW O.L.V. ter Potterie Collection, Ms. 4, f. 41v.

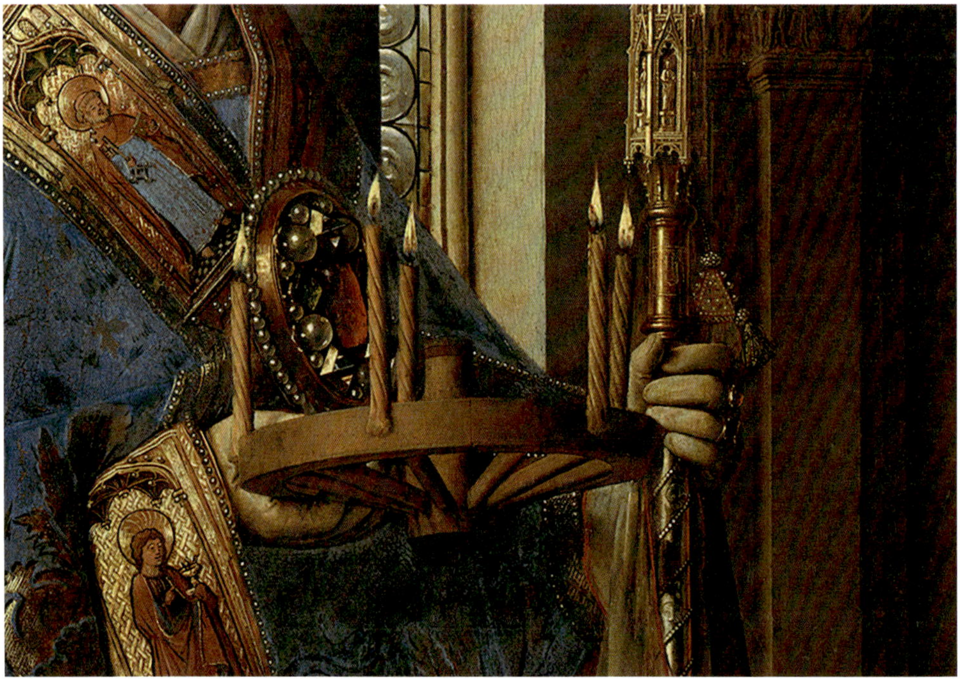

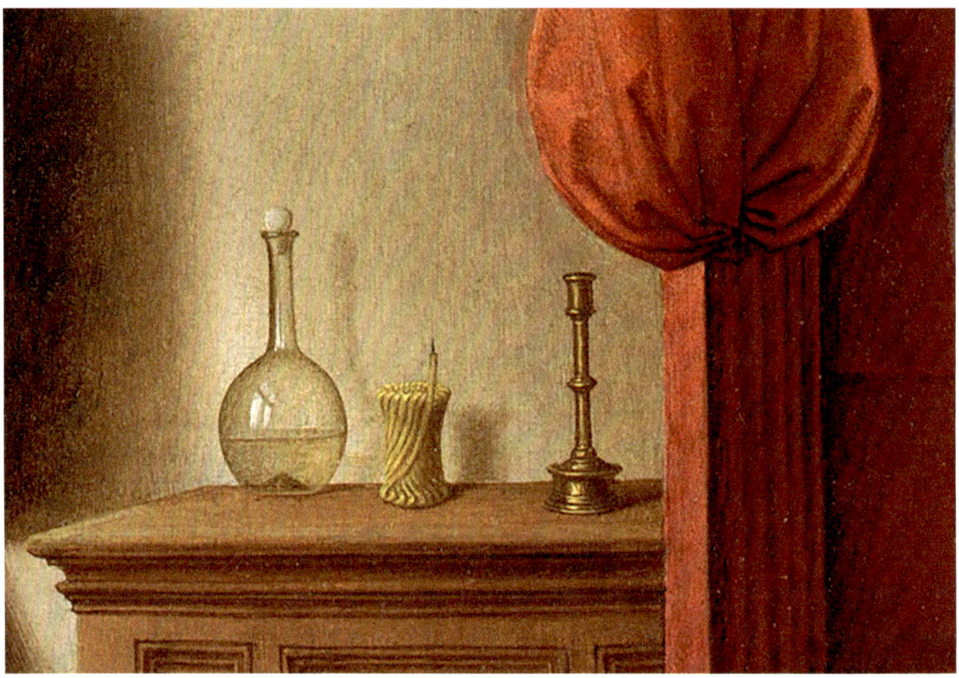

fig. 93 Wooden wheel with candles held by Saint Donatian. Jan van Eyck, *Madonna with Canon Joris van der Paele* (detail), 1436, oil on panel. Bruges, Musea Brugge, 0000.GRO0161.I.

fig. 94 Waxed wick (middle) and candlestick (right). Hans Memling, *The Annunciation* (detail), 1480–1489, oil on panel. New York, Metropolitan Museum of Art, inv. 1975.1.113.

Illuminating Intellectuals

Specific light sources were used for reading and writing, sometimes reflecting the gender of the user. The lamp is certainly the most present and most evocative of intellectual activities. Church Fathers such as Saint Jerome are typically depicted with a lamp beside them, seated at a desk with a lectern, large codex and various objects (e.g. inkwells and eyeglasses) symbolising their intellectual role.[15] Some objects for illumination only appear in Flemish iconography, such as the delicate 'waxed wicks', very long wicks coated in a few layers of wax and folded, like balls of wool, on themselves, depicted exclusively next to women (e.g. fig. 94).[16]

In Italian painting, reading women are usually depicted without lights, while most reading (and writing) men are depicted next to an (unlit) lamp.[17] In Flemish painting, however, this is not the case: women, like men, are equipped with lighting accessories. Jan van Eyck and Petrus Christus, for instance, give us Madonnas accompanied by books, lamps and candlesticks, in styles evidently widespread in that area.[18] The question arises as to whether this equal representation in Flemish painting in terms of gender is due to the greater diffusion of such accessories (given the reduced natural light and the particular reputation of local craftsmanship), or to a different and better consideration of women?

The range of objects available for lighting – together with government efforts to make wax, tallow and candles readily available at an affordable price – illustrates how indispensable artificial lights were in everyday life in the late Middle Ages.

1. For information about the variety of objects, see Del Bo, *L'età del lume*, 217–62; Heidbüchel, Poulain, De Clercq, *Shedding Some Light*, 384.
2. Another example of the prominence of lights in processions is the Procession of the Vow of Bruges (Brugse Belofte), attested since the year 1304, in which a huge candle of 36 Flemish pounds (15.5 kg) is carried; see Meulemeester, *De Brugse Belofte*, 145–50, 145–46. On candles in Italian processions, see Del Bo, *L'età del lume*, 170–81.
3. For information about individual terms, see the glossary in Del Bo, *L'età del lume*, 217–62.
4. Pinelli, *'E s'egli regha'*, [accessed online 21/01/25] https://journals.openedition.org/mefrm/2644.
5. Del Bo, *L'età del lume*, 91–92; see also Heidbüchel, Poulain, De Clercq, *Shedding Some Light*, 397.
6. Bruges, City Archives, Oud Archief, 384, for instance f. 5r, 6 May 1454–6 May 1455.
7. For examples from France, see Vincent, *'Fiat lux'*, 115; from Italy, see Del Bo, *L'età del lume*, 81.
8. Dumolyn, *et al.*, 'The Urban Landscape', 170–71.
9. Van de Velde, *Het ambacht der stoeldraaiers*, 47–56.
10. Gerits, 'De kaars in het volksleven', *Ons Heem*, 45 (1991), 120–36, 125.
11. Dumolyn, *et al.*, 'The Urban Landscape', 170.
12. An ornate example hangs above the heads of the so-called 'Arnolfini couple', portrayed by Van Eyck in 1434 (London, National Gallery, NG 186).
13. Respectively: Madrid, Museo Nacional Thyssen-Bornemisza, Inv. 252.a-c.; London, National Gallery, NG1045; Tournai, Musée des Beaux-Arts de Tournai, 284.
14. When the cathedral was destroyed in 1799, the relics were moved to the Cathedral of Saint Saviour in Bruges.
15. Plebani, *Il 'genere' dei libri*, 15–140; Plebani, *Le scritture delle donne*, 14–80.
16. Such artefacts are certainly used for evening reading, as the light they produce radiates into a very circumscribed area. See for instance *The Nativity with the Donors Peter von Clapis and Bela Bonenberg*, painted by Barthel Bruyn the Elder (1516, Frankfurt a.M., Städel Museum).
17. Del Bo, *L'età del lume*, 195–99.
18. National Gallery of Victoria, Melbourne, 1275-3; The Nelson-Atkins Museum of Arts, Kansas City, 56-51. For more examples, see Del Bo, *L'età del lume*, 199–203.

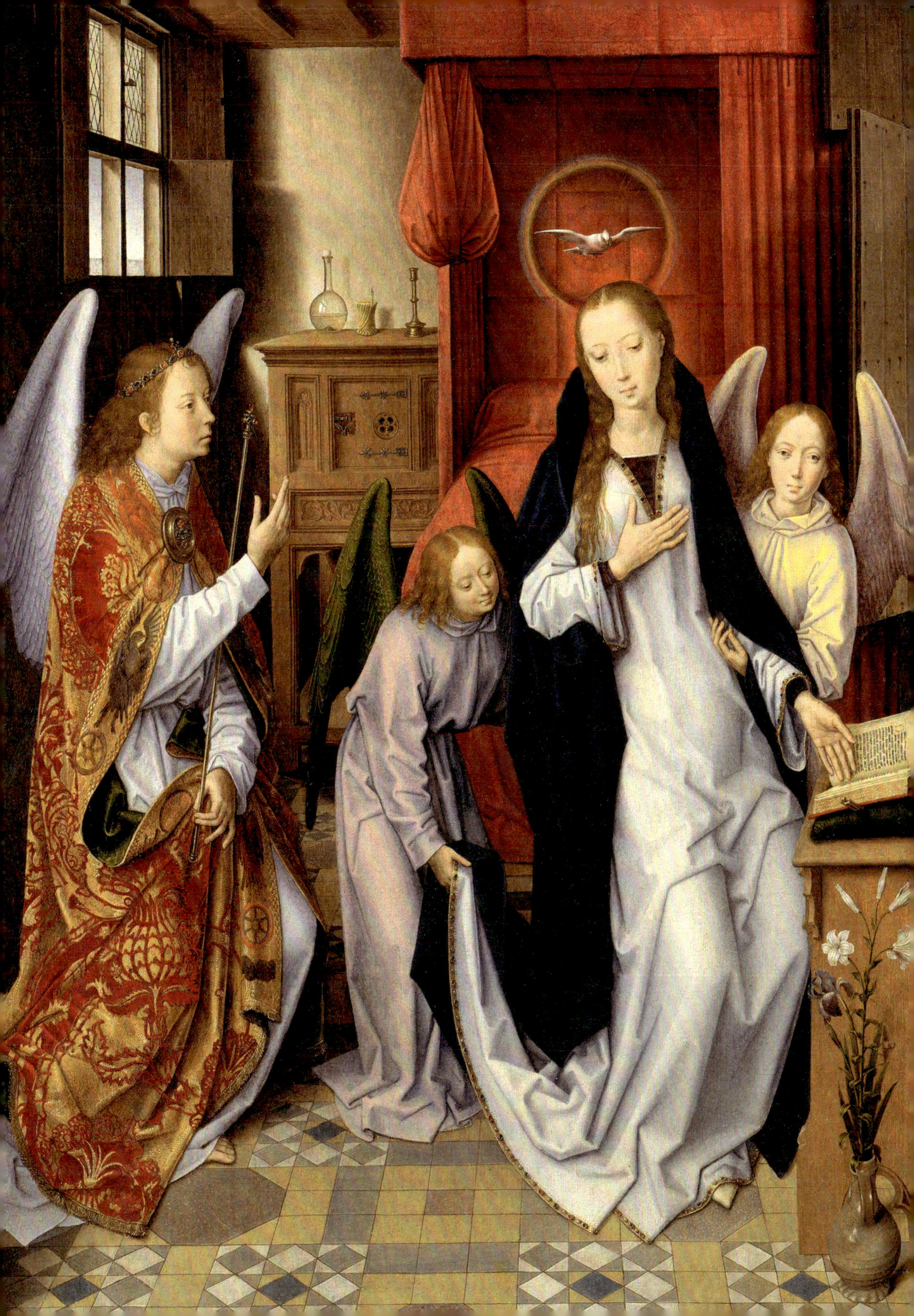

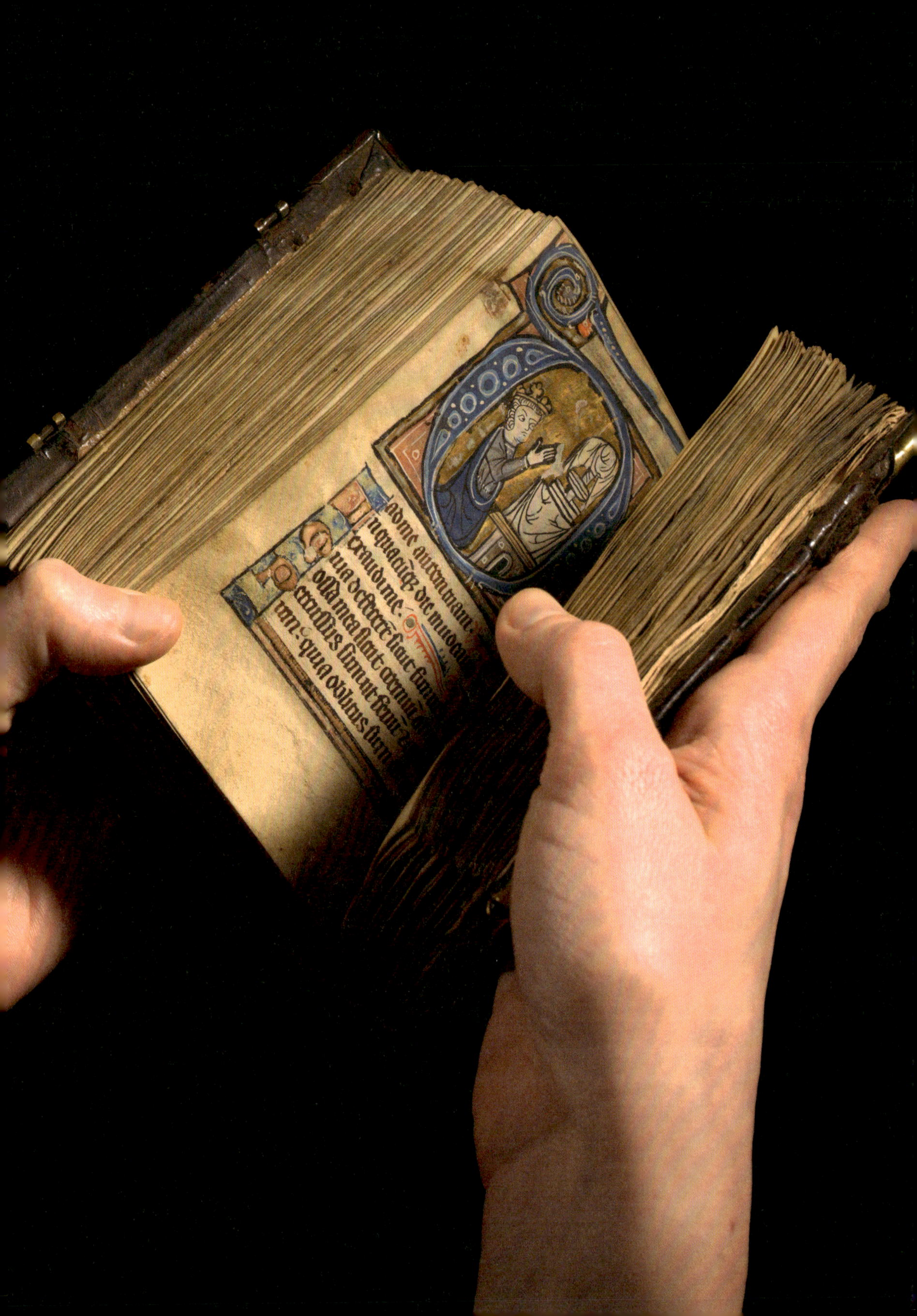

9. LIVING THE HOURS

My car recently spun out on the road in a quickly advancing storm. I skidded into a snow bank, flipped upside down, and rolled down a hill. Once the car landed in a grove of saplings, I stepped away badly rattled but unscathed. Pieces of the car were collected and towed away, and an officer returned me to my monastery, Saint Meinrad Archabbey in southern Indiana in the United States. I was hebdomadarian (prayer leader) that week. Although my mind was still racing, my heart palpitating and my hands lightly trembling, I returned to my seat in choir and inhaled deeply enough to intone the invocation for Vespers, 'O God, come to my assistance.' The monks then responded, as they do multiple times every day, 'O Lord, make haste to help me.' We then chanted Psalm 143/144 assigned to that day's Office.[1] 'Lord, what is man that you care for him, mortal man, that you keep him in mind; man, who is merely a breath, whose life fades like a shadow?' I had the same question as the Psalmist.

Br. John Glasenapp o.s.b.

fig. 95 Psalter, Ghent (?), c.1270–c.1280. Bruges, Public Library, Jean van Caloen Foundation Collection, Ms. 11, ff. 109v–110r.

Every night at Compline, we pray for a peaceful death should morning not come for us; and if it does, we praise God at Lauds for the great and undeserved blessing of that day. Books of Hours foster the spiritual discipline to remember that each hour of our lives is a gift. They are manuals for those seeking to understand their own lives and experiences within a greater whole. The saintly figures commemorated in their calendars, litanies, suffrages and in any additional *vitae* are models and personal intercessors whom the owner can relate to and converse with about their needs and intentions. Biblical events recalled in the liturgical calendar, the Hours of the Cross, and illuminations, such as the life and passion of Christ, prompt meditation on God's providential action in the world and the history of salvation. The Penitential Psalms and Office of the Dead acknowledge one's failings and brokenness and call upon God's mercy for oneself, those who are dear, and those who have passed. Though Books of Hours are composed of standard texts and traditional devotions, they are intimate possessions intended to guide their owners through the most personal joys and challenges of life in their most introspective and hidden moments.

A modern viewer of a medieval Book of Hours may regard such an object in radically different terms compared with its original owner. These are books of private prayer, but almost no one today would handle these books for that purpose. Instead, scholars scour them for historical information, curators display their visually splendid pages, and collectors admire them as a tangible link to a distant and evocative past. These books satisfy those interests well, but those pursuits obscure the function, meaning and spiritual *mentalité* their owners knew. To exhibit a Book of Hours as an art object in a museum, for example, detaches it from the pains and circumstances of daily life. Yet it was precisely those pains and concerns that would have occupied their users in the act of prayer as they cradled its pages.

The Office that forms the heart of a Book of Hours is among the richest and most complex forms of prayer. It contrasts markedly with the most basic mode, known as mental prayer, which consists of spontaneous and unstructured private conversation with God. Mental prayer addresses God (or an intercessor, such as the Blessed Virgin Mary) in a vertical second-person (I–you) singular relationship. It is direct and often affective. Other styles of prayer, for example, the rosary, combine pre-existing prayers with pre-determined subjects for meditation. When praying the rosary, an individual recites the same prayers, including ten 'Hail Marys' each decade (meaning section or division), while simultaneously meditating on an episode of the life of Christ and his mother, known as a 'mystery'. For the supplicant, the rosary may simply constitute a time of reflection on Christ or Mary, or she or he may offer that time to God for the sake of a particular intention.

Prayer in the canonical hours is more intricate. The texts are mostly taken from Scripture, especially the Psalms, and their arrangement is precomposed and prescriptive. The numerous individual components may seem incongruous. Psalms are flanked by antiphons, and the scriptural reading is paired with a responsory. What these texts mean in isolation and how they relate together is the additional interpretive work of the one praying. Though some components of each Office are associated with the time of day and the feast, the Office presents the supplicant with a wide and varied range of themes, Biblical references, and moods, including successive calls for revenge, lament, contrition, desperation, gratitude, fidelity, indignation and exuberance. The grouping of Psalms at each Office combines

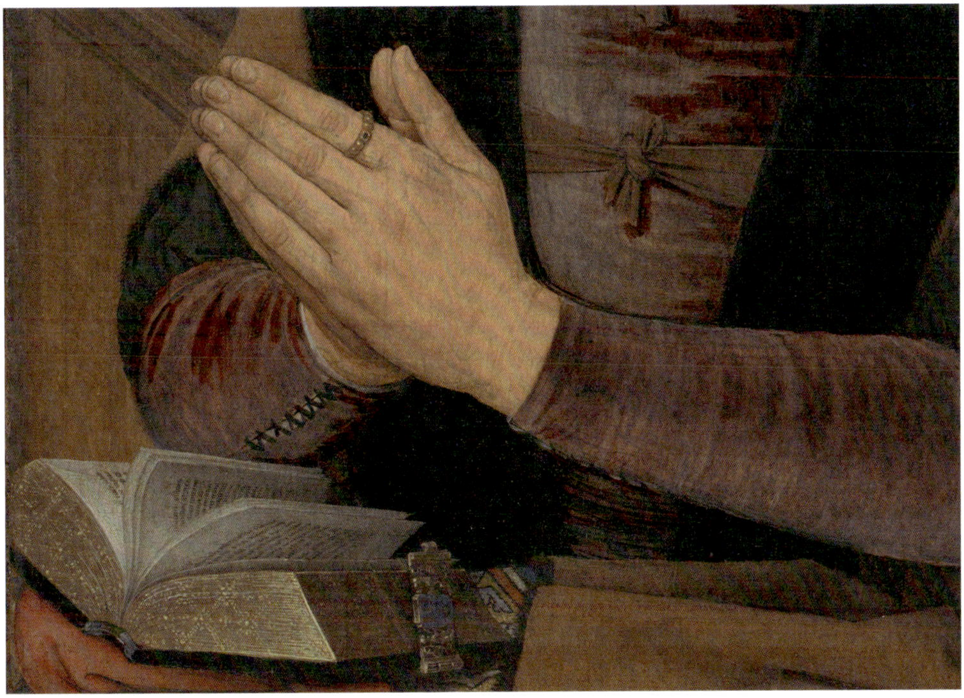

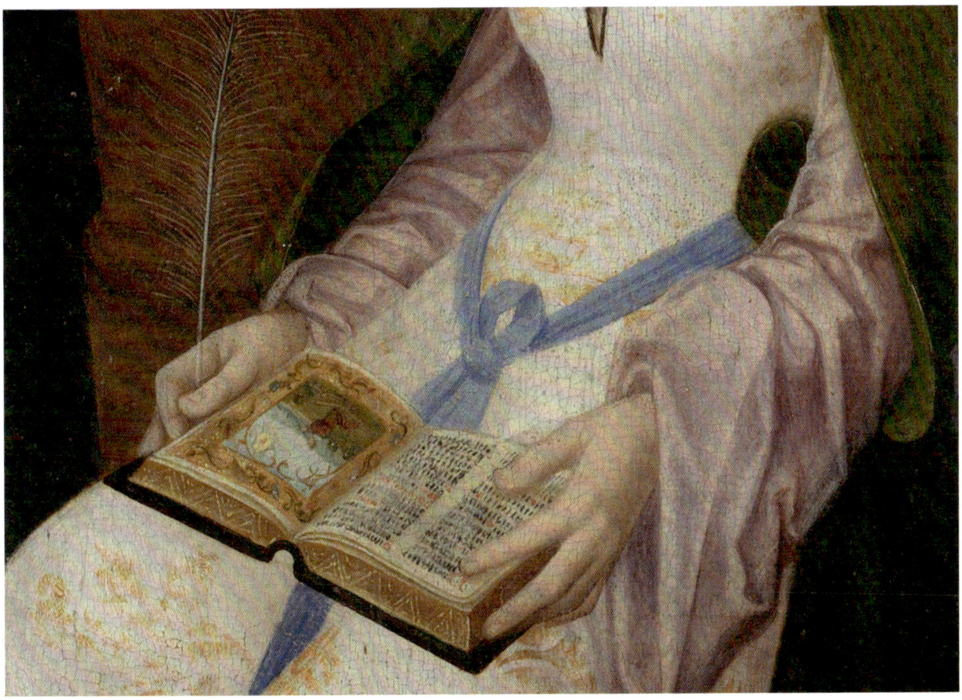

fig. 96 Hans Memling, *Diptych of Maarten van Nieuwenhove* (detail), 1487, oil on panel. Bruges, Musea Brugge, O.SJ0178.I.

fig. 97 Saint Barbara in prayer. Master of the Holy Blood, *Madonna with the Saints Catherine and Barbara* (detail), c.1509–c.1529, oil on panel. Bruges, Musea Brugge, 1991.GRO0008.I.

both vertical (I/we–God) and horizontal (I/we–we/you/he/she/they) address that encompass all types of relationships. The supplicant may address God, other faithful (e.g. the text 'come, let us adore him' in an invitatory for Matins), or even oneself. Such breadth, contrast, and rapid and unprepared transition may challenge and potentially disorient the one praying.

The thought and focus required highlight the first key feature of prayer in the Divine Office. To pray the Hours is to pray someone else's prayers. It is also to pray them in the established order that they have been handed down in the liturgy, regardless of the circumstances or concerns of one's own life. Consequently, what one reads or recites at any of the canonical hours may or may not be exactly how the individual would have phrased the same sentiment. The poetic voice of a given Psalm may be that of a different gender, social status or life circumstance from our own. The context, emotion or perspective may also be quite unfamiliar. For example, Psalm 136/137 narrates an episode set during the Babylonian exile that is unrelatable in a literal sense: *Super flumina Babylonis illic sedimus et flevimus, cum recordaremur Sion* (By the rivers of Babylon, there we sat and wept, remembering Zion). The Psalmist then recounts how a foreign captor approached his group of Israelites and asked them to sing a song from their homeland. They refused.

The Psalm then abruptly pivots into a soliloquy. The Psalmist swears fidelity to God by placing a curse on himself that he never be able to sing again if he loses faith in the God of Israel or assimilates in that foreign land. *Si oblitus fuero tui, Jerusalem, oblivioni detur dextera mea* (If I forget you, Jerusalem, let my right hand wither!) and *adhaereat lingua mea faucibus meis, si non meminero tui* (O let my tongue cleave to my mouth if I remember you not).

It is possible to recite this Psalm with little understanding and offer the action as a pious sacrifice of praise to God. That is still prayer at a rudimentary level. Indeed, many often read, speak or chant the text as a routine devotional exercise with little intellectual or affective engagement. For the Psalm to become their own prayer, however, they must adopt the Psalmist's voice as their own. To do so necessitates simultaneous application to their own life and intentions while they speak, read or chant the Psalm. The modern reader of Psalm 136/137 is imaginatively set weeping beside the river of Babylon. Since a straightforward interpretation is nonsensical, each person must decide what place or state 'Babylon' represents for them allegorically and spiritually. The reader then unites his or her voice and will with that of the Psalmist in pledging their steadfast commitment to God despite life's trials and temptations.

A difficulty emerges, however, in the closing verse of this Psalm. The text ends by cursing the Babylonian captors in violent and vengeful language whose literal meaning is incompatible with Christian theology. *Beatus qui tenebit, et allidet parvulos tuos ad petram* (Happy shall he be who takes your little ones and dashes them against the rock).

In the prologue of the *Rule of Saint Benedict*, the saintly abbot paraphrases an allegorical interpretation of this verse common among the Desert Fathers and Mothers when he urges one seeking God to reject evil thoughts immediately as they come to mind. 'While these temptations were still young, [the committed disciple] caught hold of them and dashed them against Christ.'[2] Thus, for Saint Benedict, the 'little ones' in this Psalm symbolise negative promptings or destructive urges (Gk, *logismoi*) rather than innocent children, and the 'rock' represents Christ, faith and truth rather than a violent weapon.

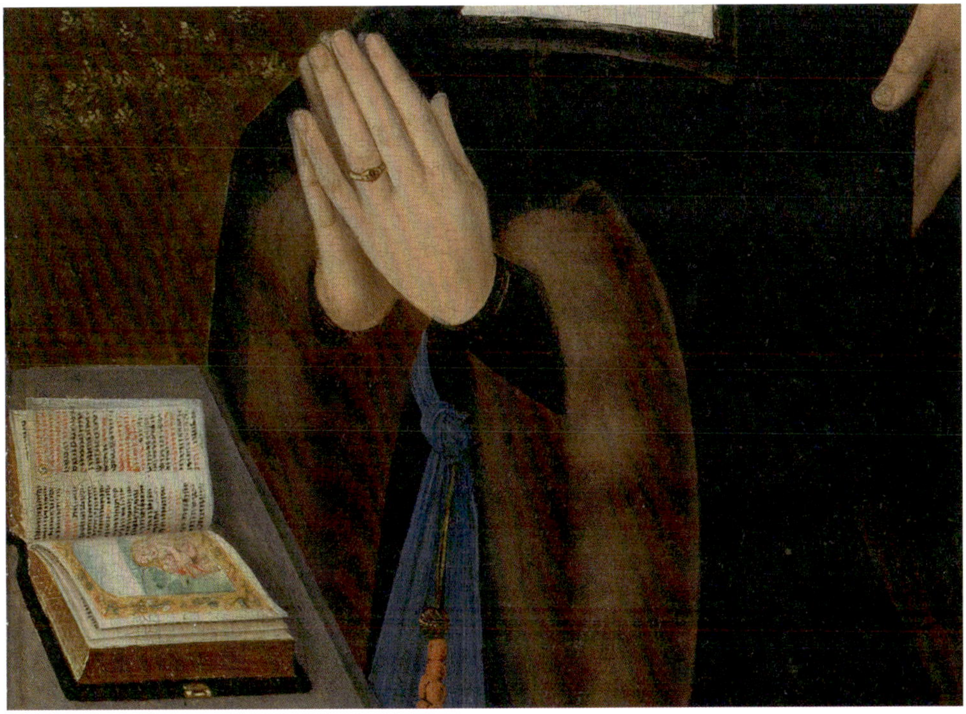

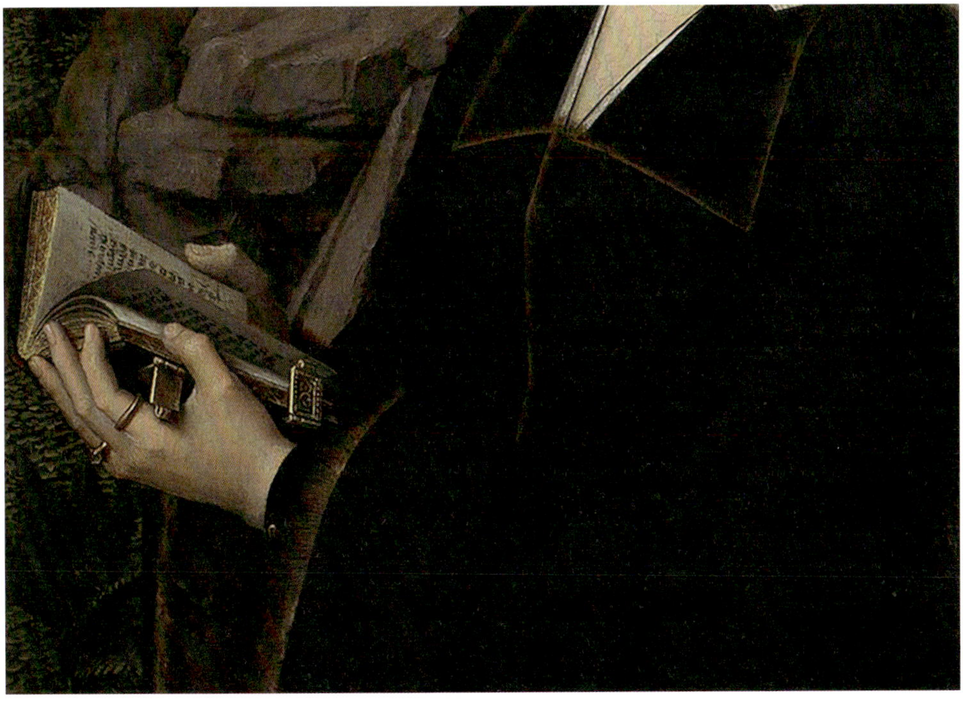

fig. 98 Jossine Lamsins in prayer. Master of the Holy Blood, *Madonna with the Saints Catherine and Barbara* (detail), c.1509–c.1529, oil on panel. Bruges, Musea Brugge, 1991.GRO0008.I.

fig. 99 Elisabeth van der Meersch in prayer. Gerard David, *Baptism of Christ* (detail), c.1502–c.1508, oil on panel. Bruges, Musea Brugge, 0000.GRO0035.I-0039.I.

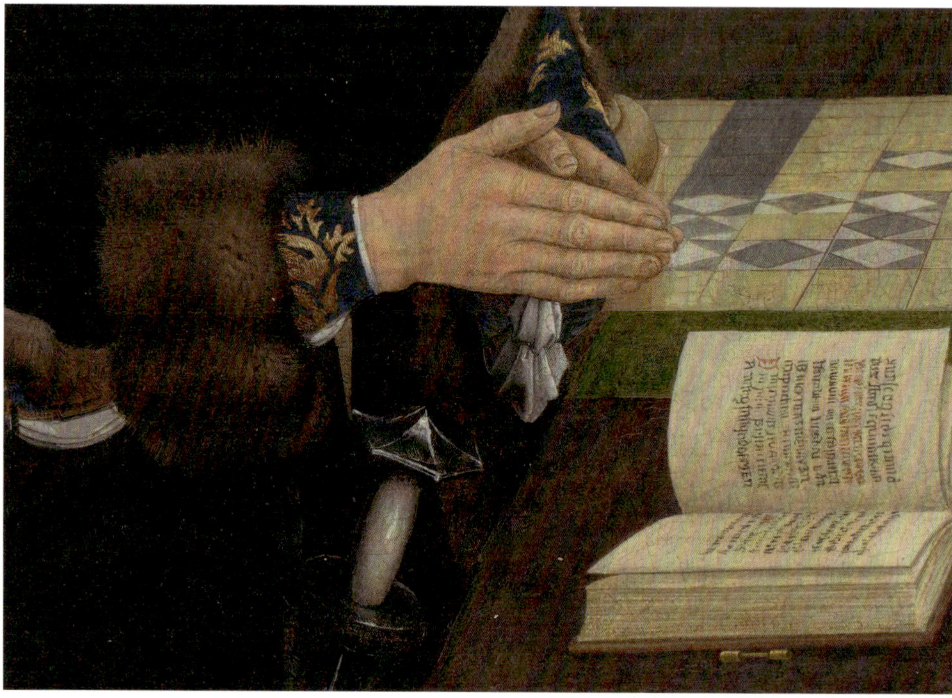

fig. 100 Hans Memling, *Portrait of a Member of the De Rojas Family* (detail), 1460–1470, oil on panel. Bruges, Musea Brugge, 2020.GRO0012.I.

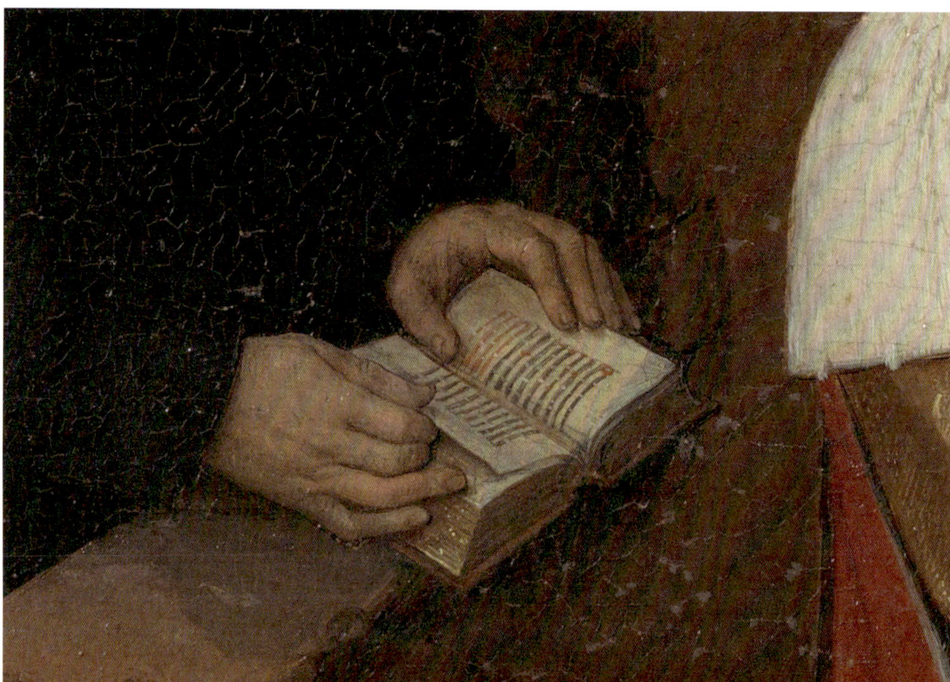

fig. 101 Jan Floreins in prayer. Hans Memling, *Adoration of the Magi* (detail), 1479, oil on panel. Bruges, Musea Brugge, O.SJ0173.I.

The faithful who pray the Hours inherited them from a spiritual tradition to which they presumably also belong, and which may influence how they hear and interpret scriptural texts, symbols and images. The reception and interpretation of the same texts may differ based on one's religious and cultural tradition. Because I am a Benedictine monk and am so familiar with the prologue to the *Rule*, for example, I am predisposed to think of *logismoi* whenever I recite this Psalm verse and often forget its literal meaning. While one person might pray that verse as damning their internal voice that continuously urges them to drink or abuse drugs, another casual visitor to the monastery may be shocked or confused by that same language.

It must be noted that the interpretation of Scripture as literal and historical as well as simultaneously allegorical and personal is not unique to Roman Catholics, medieval readers or the Divine Office. The African-American spiritual is a familiar contemporary example. Many song texts describe the captivity, exodus and redemption of Moses and the Israelites. The parallels to the struggles, hopes and joys of Black Americans are so strong and obvious that the connection never needs to be drawn explicitly. Other spirituals, such as 'Wade in the Water', are multivalent and concurrently suggest the parting of the Red Sea, the healing pool of Bethesda, Christian baptism, and the Underground Railroad through creeks to thwart slavecatchers' dogs. The ambiguous symbolism draws connections between all these watery avenues of liberation and restoration at the same time.

The second notable feature of the Liturgy of the Hours prayed specifically from a Book of Hours or breviary is that it is an adaptation for private use of an essentially public and choral celebration. The Divine Office spoken quietly and alone allows for greater introspection because the supplicant controls the pace and is not concerned with comportment or gestures associated with the liturgy (e.g. processing, bowing, standing, sitting, kneeling, genuflecting and striking the breastbone in time). Greater freedom and relative informality allow more opportunity to reflect on the meaning of the texts for one's own life. Conversely, the lack of peer observation may also permit rushed and thoughtless reading when prayer has become routine or desiccated and performed simply to fulfil a sense of personal obligation.

Books of Hours offered the laity a means of participating in a version of the liturgy observed by life-long professed monastic, religious and clerical communities – in other words, the so-called first estate of medieval society. This form of prayer, once readily available to the laity, must have been spiritually and socially ennobling, empowering and unifying. It must also have contributed to a feeling of community, universality and joint enterprise. (Lay affiliates of our monastery are given copies of our exact Office to pray individually while connected with us spiritually. Others join our monastic choir virtually through livestream for daily Mass and Vespers, which offers a twenty-first century analogue to this aspect of a medieval Book of Hours.)

While the Psalms, hymns and other texts may resonate differently with each individual whenever they are repeated, the simple fact that they are shared across time and cultures foregrounds our common humanity in a way that more individualistic mental prayer does not. That conviction poses obstacles, however. Many Psalms may not be relatable when they call for bloodshed, express notions of gender, or condone other forms of social inequality that we may find objectionable. We may deem the raw emotion of the Psalmist of Ps. 77/78:65 too intense and discomforting when he indicts God for behaving like a drunk and belligerent warrior, too inebriated or hungover to respond and right the injustices of the world. To adopt these texts as our prayers we must find our fundamental similarities even across such a significant chronological, geographical and cultural gulf. Many in our secular age might object to that effort and claim it is misguided to perpetuate ideas and values from the past that thwart the march of progress. They hold that it is better to free ourselves from antiquated and problematic sentiments and worldviews than to preserve and enshrine these ancient texts as timeless and still relevant. Medieval people struggled less than we typically do with inserting themselves in Biblical narratives and with drawing parallels between past and present. Christians believe that we are all bound up in the same overarching economy of salvation. A Book of Hours, therefore, links an individual to a greater community and an identity, and positions that person in a tradition that affirms their unique role in a larger cosmic story.

The third essential characteristic of the Liturgy of the Hours is that the Offices are prayed throughout the day at set times. The practice of punctuating each day with regular periods for prayer is not medieval, nor is it originally Christian. Morning and evening sacrifices were daily events at the Second Temple in Jerusalem, and diverse Jewish communities in the post-exilic period prayed at fixed times throughout the day, including the Shema every morning and evening. As the Psalmist declared, 'evening and morning and at noon, I utter my complaint and moan',[3] but the practice is far more ancient than the Second Temple. Scholars have traced the practice of routine cultic observance across the ancient Near East to the late Stone Age. Indo-Iranian pastoralists marked each morning, noon and evening with regular worship and ritual offering to maintain the hearth fire.[4] Zoroastrians later increased these times to five. The priestly class of the major temples throughout ancient Mesopotamia tended to the gods every morning and evening through propitiatory food offerings.[5]

While the exact relationship between the Second Temple and Christian daily liturgy is speculative, Robert Taft noted, 'more relevant, perhaps, than any direct relationship between Jewish or early Christian *forms* of public prayer and the later office, is the Jewish custom of praying *at set times*'.[6] Likewise, the *adhan* calls Muslims to prayer five times every day. Even though scholars disagree on whether the *adhan* was initially influenced by Jewish or Christian practice, the established rounds of daily prayer continue to unite the Abrahamic faiths above differences of content and belief.

People in the Middle Ages had many motivations for acquiring Books of Hours. Each person used and conceived of them differently. But, in general, they were exceptionally personal objects. As books of prayer and inspiration, they were tools to reflect on one's life through introspection and contemplation even while they anchored their individual readers in a spiritual community and grand plan of salvation.

The stunning decoration and illustration of so many Books of Hours is understandably a focal point and attraction, now as undoubtedly then. The decorative page may be likened to the interior of a church that draws in and captivates the supplicant's attention and wards off outside distraction while she or he communicates with God. That visual richness serves a greater purpose than simply to impress, fend off routine or boredom, or even to instruct or highlight. The acanthus leaves and other artistic features that surround the liturgical texts envelop, by extension, whatever personal thoughts and prayers

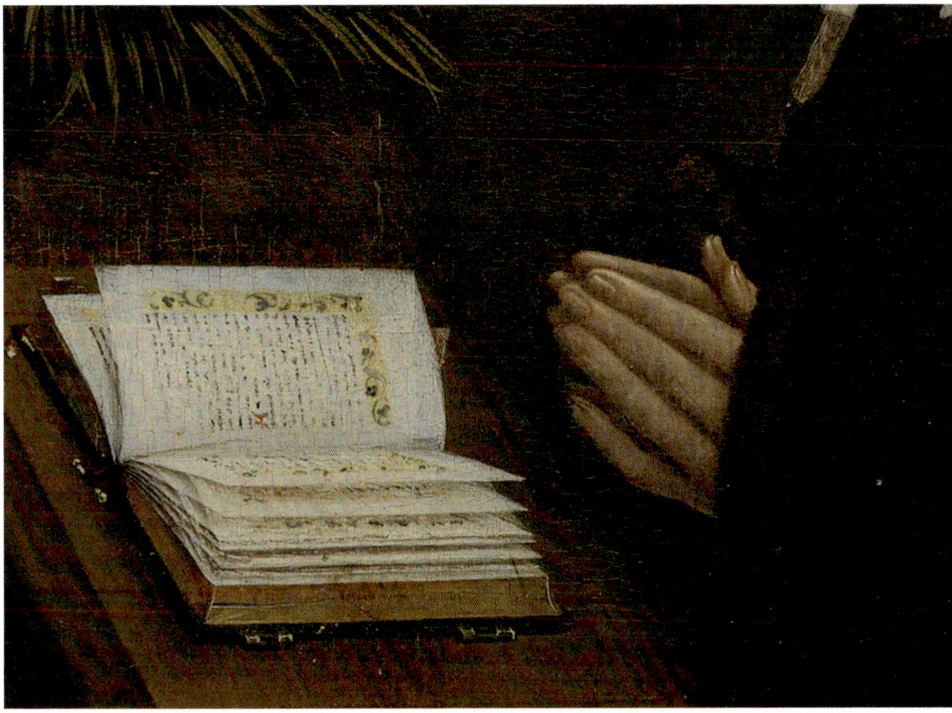

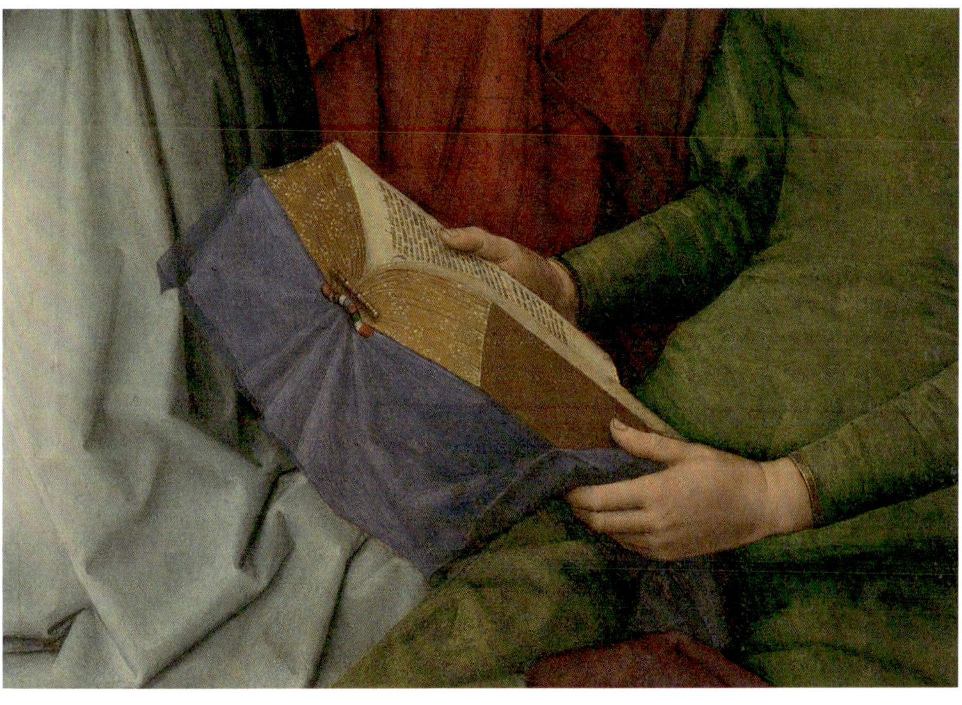

fig. 102 Anonymous sitter in prayer. Jan Provoost, *Portrait of a Donor and Saint Gudula* (detail), 1515, oil on panel. Bruges, Musea Brugge, 0000.GRO0217.I.

fig. 103 Saint Barbara in prayer. Hans Memling, *Triptych of John the Baptist and John the Evangelist* (detail), 1479, oil on panel. Brugge, Musea Brugge, O.SJ0175.I.

the reader applies to those same words. Their splendour affirms the dignity and worthiness of all that this person brings to prayer. Despite the pain, suffering and loss that each of us endures in this life, the sheer magnificence of so many of these books proposes an answer to that question raised earlier in Psalm 143/144, 'Lord, what is man that you care for him, mortal man, that you keep him in mind?' Books of Hours urge their readers: God seeks a relationship with us through prayer.

1. Psalm references include both the Vulgate and modern numbering. The English translations are taken from the Grail Psalms published as *The Psalms: A New Translation from the Hebrew* unless otherwise stated.
2. Fry, *RB 1980*, 162–63.
3. Ps. 55: 17 (New Revised Standard Version Updated Edition).
4. Boyce, *Zoroastrians*, 4, 32.
5. Von Soden, *Ancient Orient*, 188; Lambert, 'Donations of Food and Drink', 194.
6. Taft, *Liturgy of the* Hours, 5.

Suffrage for St Martin (detail, see p. 39)

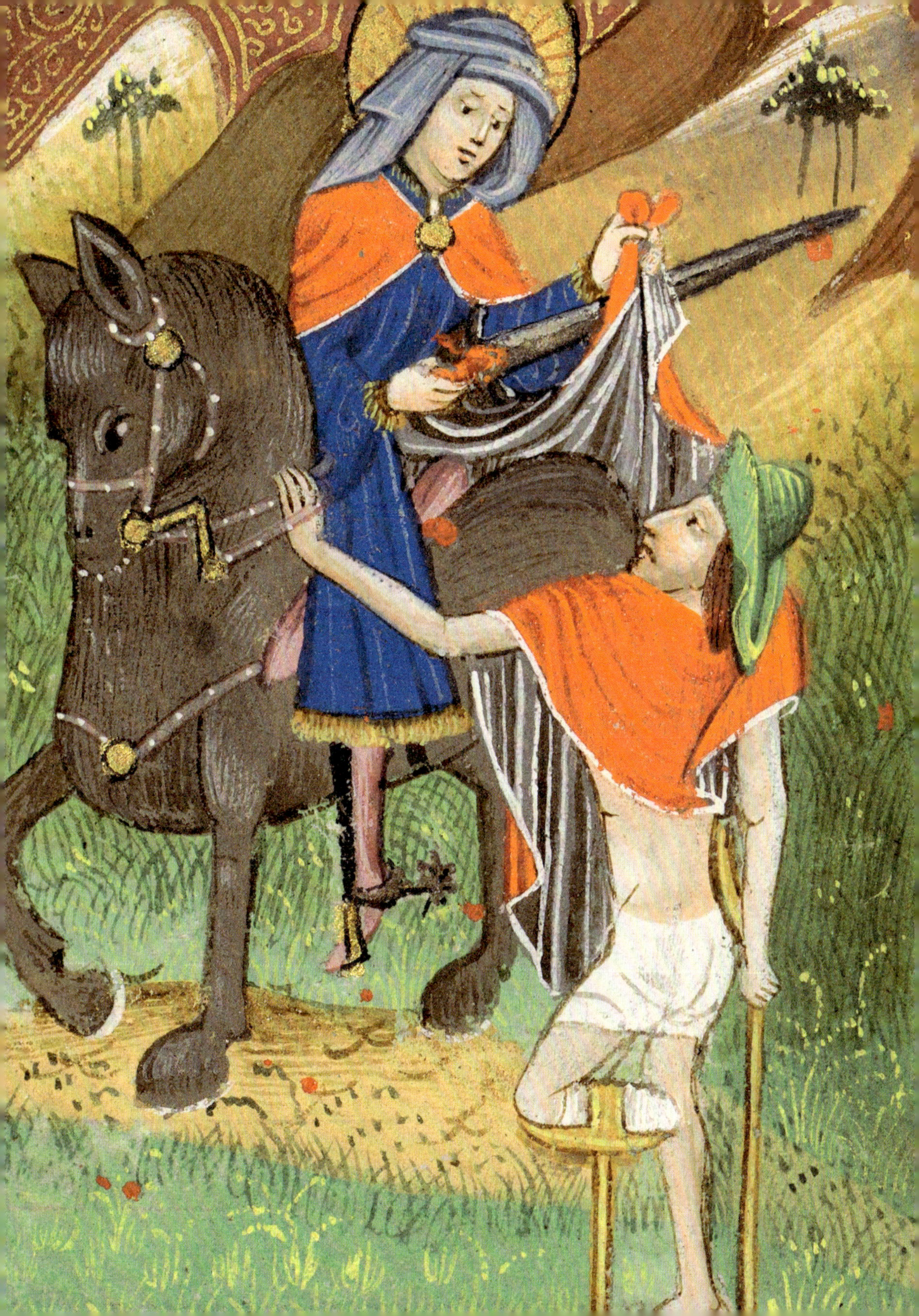

Bibliography

EDITED AND/OR TRANSLATED PRIMARY SOURCES

Ci nous dit: recueil d'exemples moraux, ed. G. Blangez, (2 vols). Paris: Société des anciens textes français, 1979.

Jean Gobi. La Scala coeli, ed. M. Polo de Beaulieu. Paris: Éditions du CNRS, 1991.

Jacobus de Voragine, *Sermones aurei in omnes quadragesimae dominicas et ferias*, ed. R. Cluyt, (2 vols). Augsburg: Bartl, 1760.

Eustache Deschamps, *Le miroir de mariage*, ed. M. Dufournaud-Engel. Unpublished dissertation, McGill University, 1975.

Peter of Limoges, *The Moral Treatise on the Eye*, ed. R. Newhauser. Toronto: PIMS, 2012.

Stephanus de Borbone, *Tractatus de diversis materiis predicabilibus. Prologus. Prima pars: de dono timoris*, eds. J. Berlioz and J.-L. Eichenlaub. Turnhout: Brepols, 2002.

The Exempla, or Illustrative stories from the sermones vulgares of Jacques de Vitry, ed. T. Crane. London: D. Nutt, 1890.

SECONDARY LITERATURE

Acres, A. 'Rogier van Der Weyden's Painted Texts', *Artibus et Historiae*, 21, no. 41 (2000), 75–109.

Adam, R. 'Printing Books in Bruges in the Fifteenth Century', in: *Colard Mansion: Incunabula, Prints and Manuscripts in Medieval Bruges*, (eds) E. Hauwaerts, E. de Wilde and L. Vandamme. Ghent: Snoeck, 2018, 53–57.

Alexander, J. *Medieval Illuminators and Their Methods of Work.* New Haven: Yale University Press, 1992.

Alexandre-Bidon, D. 'La lettre volée: Apprendre à lire à l'enfant au Moyen Age', *Annales. Histoire, Sciences Sociales*, 44, no. 4 (1989), 953–92.

Anderson, M. *Music and Performance in the Book of Hours*. New York: Routledge, 2024.

As-Vijvers, A.M. 'Manuscript Production in a Carmelite Convent: The Case of Cornelia von Wulfschkercke', in: *Books of Hours Reconsidered*, (eds) S. Hindman and J. Marrow. Turnhout: Harvey Miller, 2013, 279–96.

Aurell, M. *The Lettered Knight. Knowledge and Aristocratic Behaviour in the Twelfth and Thirteenth Centuries.* Budapest: CEU Press, 2017.

Bakhtin, M. *Rabelais and His World*, (transl.) Helene Iswolsky. Cambridge: MIT Press, 1968.

Bertrand, P. *Documenting the Everyday in Medieval Europe. The Social Dimensions of a Writing Revolution, 1250–1350.* Turnhout: Brepols, 2019.

Binski, P. *Gothic Wonder: Art, Artifice, and Decorated Style 1290-1350.* New Haven: Yale University Press, 2014.

Blockmans, W. 'The Creative Environment: Incentives to and Functions of Bruges Art Production', in: *Petrus Christus in Renaissance Bruges: An Interdisciplinary Approach,* (ed.) M. Ainsworth. Turnhout: Brepols, 1995, 11–20.

Bollmann, S. *Women Who Read Are Dangerous*, (transl.) C. Shuttleworth. New York: Abbeville Press, 2016.

Bousmanne, B. *'Item a Guillaume Wyelant aussi enlumineur' : Willem Vrelant, un aspect de l'enluminure dans les Pays-Bas méridonaux sous le mécénat des ducs de Bourgogne Philippe le Bon et Charles le Téméraire.* Turnhout: Brepols, 1997.

Boyce, Mary. *Zoroastrians: Their Religious Beliefs and Practices.* London: Routledge and Kegan Paul, 1979.

Brandi, C. *Spazio italiano, ambiente fiammingo.* Milano: La Nave di Teseo, 2020

Brown, A. and H. Callewier. 'Religious Practices, c. 1200-1500', in: *Medieval Bruges: c. 850–1550,* (eds) A. Brown and J. Dumolyn. Cambridge: Cambridge University Press, 2018, 329–88.

Busine, L., *et al.*, *Le vaste monde à livres ouverts: manuscrits médiévaux en dialogue avec l'art contemporain.* Brugge: Lannoo, 2002.

Camille, M. *Image on the Edge: The Margins of Medieval Art.* London: Reaktion Books, 1992.

Camille, M. *Mirror in Parchment: The Luttrell Psalter and the Making of Medieval England.* London: Reaktion Books, 1998.

Cardon, B. 'The Illustrations and the Gold Scrolls Group', in: *Typologische taferelen uit het leven van Jezus: A Manuscript from the Gold Scrolls Group (Bruges, ca. 1440) in the Pierpont Morgan Library, New York, Ms. Morgan 649,* (eds) B. Cardon and M. Smeyers. Leuven: Peeters, 1985, 119–66.

Carns, P. 'Making and Unmaking Love in the Macclesfield Psalter', *Gesta* 62, 1 (2023), 1–21.

Carruthers, M. *The Book of Memory: A Study of Memory in Medieval Culture.* Cambridge: Cambridge University Press, 2008.

Caviness, M. 'Patron or Matron? A Capetian Bride and a Vade Mecum for Her Marriage Bed', *Speculum* 68, 2 (1993), 333–62.

Clanchy, M. 'Images of Ladies with Prayer Books: What Do They Signify?', *Studies in Church History*, 38 (Jan. 2004), 106–22.

d'Allemagne, H. *Histoire du luminaire depuis l'époque romaine jusq'au XIX*[e] *siècle.* Paris, 1891.

De Hamel, C. *A History of Illuminated Manuscripts.* London: Phaidon, 1994.

de Hemptinne, T. 'Des femmes copistes dans les Pays-Bas au bas moyen âge (14e–15e siècle). Approche d'une activité féminine mal connue', in: *Secretum scriptorum. Liber alumnorum Walter Prevenier*, (eds) W. Blockmans, M. Boone and T. de Hemptinne. Leuven: Acco, 1999, 129–43.

de Jong, S. '"Read Some Good Dutch Books". Laypeople, Books, and Religious Reading in the Late Medieval Domestic Setting', *Queeste*, 25 (2018), 32–54.

De Munck, B. and H. De Ridder-Symoens. 'Education and Knowledge: Theory and Practice in an Urban Context', in: *City and Society in the Low Countries, 1100–1600*, (eds) A.-L. Van Bruaene, B. Blondé and M. Boone. Cambridge: Cambridge University Press, 2018, 220–54.

De Poorter, A. *Catalogue des manuscrits de la bibliothèque publique de la ville de Bruges.* Gembloux: J. Duculot, 1934.

De Ridder-Symoens, H. 'Education and Literacy in the Burgundian-Habsburg Netherlands', *Canadian Journal of Netherlands Studies*, 15 (1995), 6–21.

Del Bo, B. *L'età del lume. Una storia della luce nel Medioevo*. Bologna: il Mulino, 2023.

Demets, L. 'French Literature in Mono- and Multilingual Social Contexts', *Queeste* 28, 1 (2021), 30–60.

Demets, L. 'Bruges as a Multilingual Contact Zone: Book Production and Multilingual Literary Networks in Fifteenth-Century Bruges', *Urban History* 51 (2024), 313–32.

Desneux, J. *Rigueur de Jean Van Eyck. À propos d'un diagnostic médical sur un tableau de 1436*. S.l.: Édition des Artistes, 1951.

Dewitte, A. 'Boek- en bibliotheekwezen in de Brugse Sint-Donaaskerk XIIIe-XVe eeuw', in: *Sint Donaas en de voormalige Brugse kathedraal*. Brugge: Jong Kristen Onthaal voor Toerisme, 1978, 61–95.

Dewitte, A. 'Het Brugse St.-Jans en St.-Lucasgilde der librariërs 1457–1469', *Biekorf*, (1996), 334–40.

Dlabačová, A. and R. Hofman. *De Moderne Devotie: Spiritualiteit en Cultuur vanaf de Late Middeleeuwen*. Zwolle: WBOOKS, 2018.

Duffy, E. *The Stripping of the Altars: Traditional Religion in England c. 1400–c. 1580*. New Haven: Yale University Press, 1992.

Duffy, E. *Marking the Hours: English People & Their Prayers, 1240–1570*. New Haven: Yale University Press, 2006.

Dumolyn, J. *et al.*, 'The Urban Landscape II: c.1275–c.1500', in: *Medieval Bruges c. 850–1550*, (eds.) A. Brown and J. Dumolyn. Cambridge: Cambridge University Press, 2018, 152–95

Falque, I. *Devotional Portraiture and Spiritual Experience in Early Netherlandish Painting*. Leiden: Brill, 2019.

Gelineau, J. *The Psalms: A New Translation from the Hebrew Arranged for Singing to the Psalmody of Joseph Gelineau*. Mahwah, NJ: Paulist Press, 1983.

Gerits, J. 'De kaars in het volksleven', *Ons Heem*, 45 (1991), 120–36.

Gil, M. 'Les femmes dans les métiers d'art des Pays-Bas bourguignons au XVe siècle', *Clio: Femmes, Genre, Histoire*, 34 (2011), 231–54.

Gilliodts-Van Severen, L. 'L'Œuvre de Jean Brito, prototypographe Brugeois', *Annales de la Société d'Émulation de Bruges*, 47 (1897), 1–515.

Hanley, S. 'Optical Symbolism as Optical Description: A Case Study of Canon van der Paele's Spectacles'. *Journal of Historians of Netherlandish Art*, 1, 1 (2009), 1–21.

Hardwick, P. *Discovering Horn*. Guildford: Lutterworth Press, 1981.

Hauwaerts, E., E. de Wilde and L. Vandamme (eds). *Colard Mansion: Incunabula, Prints and Manuscripts in Medieval Bruges*. Ghent: Snoeck, 2018.

Hauwaerts, E. 'Middeleeuwse vrouwen in het boekenbedrijf', in: *Een geschiedenis van België in 100 voorwerpen: Van de prehistorie tot nu*, (eds) P. Scholliers, *et al.* Tielt: Lannoo, 2024, 275–79.

Hauwaerts, E. 'The Psalter of Countess Margaret II of Flanders: New Observations on a Hitherto Hidden Manuscript', in *Preserving Fragile Wisdom. Essays in Honour of Lieve Watteeuw*, (eds.) W. François, H. Hameeuw and M. Bassens, (Documenta Libraria Illustrata / Leuven Studies on Book Culture, 45). Leuven: Peeters, 2025.

Heidbüchel, N., M. Poulain and W. De Clercq. 'Shedding Some Light on Indoor Lighting in 15th-Century Flemish Urban Houses: An Experimental Archaeological Approach', *Medieval Archaeology*, 68, 2 (2024), 382–405.

Helsinger, H. 'Images on the Beatus Page of Some Medieval Psalters', *The Art Bulletin*, 53, 2 (1971), 161–76.

Herwaarden, J. van. 'Geert Groote's Tract on Meditation: *De Quattuor Generibus Meditabilium*', in: *Between Saint James and Erasmus: Studies in Late-Medieval Religious Life: Devotion and Pilgrimage in the Netherlands*, (transl.) W. Shaffer and D. Gardner. Leiden: Brill, 2003, 3–14.

Hindman, S. 'Gothic traveling coffers revisited', in: *Le livre, la photographie, l'image & la lettre: Essays in Honor of André Jammes*, (eds) S. Hindman, *et al.* Paris: Aux Éditions des Cendres, 2015.

Hindman, S. and J. Marrow (eds). *Books of Hours Reconsidered*. Turnhout: Harvey Miller, 2013.

Horowitz, J. and S. Menache. *L'humour en chaire: le rire dans l'Église médiévale*. Genève: Labor et Fides, 1994.

Hugen, J. 'Van lesboek naar leesboek. Taalonderwijs voor kinderen in laatmiddeleeuws Vlaanderen', *Madoc*, 36 (2022), 174–83.

Hunt, E. *Illuminating the Borders of Northern French and Flemish Manuscripts, 1270-1310*. New York: Routledge, 2007.

Ilardi, V. 'Eyeglasses and Concave Lenses in Fifteenth Century Florence and Milan: New Documents'. *Renaissance Quarterly*, 29, 3 (1976), 341–60.

Ilardi, V. *Renaissance Vision: From Spectacles to Telescopes*. Philadelphia: American Philosophical Society, 2007.

Janson, H. *Apes and Ape Lore in the Middle Ages and the Renaissance*. London: Warburg Institute, University of London, 1952.

Jones, P. 'Preaching Laughter in the Thirteenth Century: The Exempla of Arnold of Liège (d. c.1308) and His Dominican Milieu', *Journal of Medieval History* 41, 2 (2015), 169–83.

Jordan, E. *Women, Power, and Religious Patronage in the Middle Ages*. New York: Palgrave Macmillan, 2006.

Korteweg, A. '"Dit boeck hoert toe..." Een onderzoek naar eigendomskenmerken in Noord-Nederlandse getijdenboeken uit de vijftiende en begin zestiende eeuw', in: *Schriftgeheimen: opstellen over schrift en schriftcultuur. Verzamelde opstellen van Nederlandse boekhistorici ter ere van Jos Biemans*. Amsterdam, 2017, 335–59.

Kren, T. and S. McKendrick. *Illuminating the Renaissance: The Triumph of Flemish Manuscript Painting In Europe*. Los Angeles: J. Paul Getty Museum, 2003.

Lambert, W. 'Donations of Food and Drink to the Gods in Ancient Mesopotamia', in *Ritual and Sacrifice in the Ancient Near East: Proceedings*

of the International Conference organized by the Katholieke Universiteit Leuven from the 17th to the 20th of April 1991, (ed.) J. Quaegebeur. Leuven: Peeters and Departement Oriëntalistiek, 1993.
Landes, D. *L'heure qu'il est. Les horloges, la mesure du temps et la formation du monde moderne*. Paris: Gallimard, 1987.
Le Goff, J. 'Au Moyen Âge: temps de l'Église et temps du marchand', in: *Annales. Economies, sociétés, civilisations*, 15, 3 (1960), 417–33.
Linton, D. 'Reading the Virgin Reader', in: *The Book and the Magic of Reading in the Middle Ages*, (ed.) A. Classen. New York: Routledge, 1998, 253–76.
Lynch, S. 'Marking Time, Making Community in Medieval Schools', *History of Education Quarterly*, 61 (2021), 158–80.
Marnef, G. and A.-L. Van Bruaene. 'Civic Religion: Community, Identity and Religious Transformation', in: *City and Society in the Low Countries, 1100–1600*, (eds) A.-L. Van Bruaene, B. Blondé and M. Boone Cambridge: Cambridge University Press, 2018, 128–61.
Marrow, J. *Passion Iconography in Northern European Art of the Late Middle Ages and Early Renaissance: A Study of the Transformation of Sacred Metaphor into Descriptive Narrative*. Kortrijk: Van Ghemmert, 1979.
Martens, M., *et al.* 'Texts, Images and Sounds in the Urban Environment, c.1100-c.1500', in: *Medieval Bruges, c. 850–1550*, (eds) A. Brown and J. Dumolyn. Cambridge: Cambridge University Press, 2018, 389–444.
Martin, R. and T. Ford. *The Psychology of Humor: An Integrative Approach.* Chantilly: Elsevier Science & Technology, 2018.
Melinkoff, R. *Outcasts: Signs of Otherness in Northern European Art of the Late Middle Ages,* (2 vols). Berkeley: University of California Press, 1993.
Menestò, E. *Il fuoco nell'Alto Medioevo*, Spoleto, 2013.
Mentasti, R., L. Borrelli and C. Tonini. 'Venetian Conical Goblets of the Renaissance'. *Journal of Glass Studies*, 61 (2019), 157–95.
Meulemeester, J.L., 'De Brugse Belofte, een eeuwenoude processie met offerkaars', *Ons Heem*, 45 (1991), 145–50.
Miles, L. 'The Origins and Development of the Virgin Mary's Book at the Annunciation', *Speculum*, 89 (2014), 632–69.
Murray, J. 'Family, Marriage and Moneychanging in Medieval Bruges', *Journal of Medieval History*, 14 (1988), 115–25.
Naber, A. 'Bourgondische edelen en hun opvoeding', in: *Scholing in de Middeleeuwen*, (eds) R. Stuip and C. Vellekoop. Hilversum: Verloren, 1995, 239–53.
Neaman, J. 'The Mystery of the Ghent Bird and the Invention of Spectacles'. *Viator,* 24 (1993), 189–214.
Ottosen, K. *The Responsories and Versicles of the Latin Office of the Dead*. Aarhus: Aarhus University Press, 1993.
Pfaender, H. *Schott Guide to Glass*. Dordrecht: Springer, 2012.
Pietrini, S. 'Performing Alterities: Apes as Jesters in Medieval Imagery and the Triumph of the Body', *eHumanistica*, 56 (2023), 75–93.
Pinelli, P. '"E s'egli regha arienti o cera": prime indagini sul commercio della cera a Ragusa (Dubrovnik) fra XV e XVI secolo', *Mélanges de l'École française de Rome*, 172 (2), 2015, https://journals.openedition.org/mefrm/2644.
Plebani, T. *Il 'genere' dei libri. Storie e rappresentazioni della lettura al femminile e al maschile tra Medioevo e età moderna*, Milano: FrancoAngeli, 2001, 15–140.
Plebani, T. *Le scritture delle donne in Europa. Pratiche quotidiane e ambizioni letterarie (secoli XIII-XX)*, Roma: Carocci, 2019, 14–80.
Poulet, W. *Atlas on the History of Spectacles 2, The Arts and Spectacles over Five Centuries*. Ostend: Wayenborgh, 1980.
Prims, F. *Geschiedenis van Antwerpen IV, Onder Hertog Jan den Derde (1312–1355).* Brussels: Kultuur en Beschaving, 1977.
Randall, L. 'Exempla as a Source of Gothic Marginal Illumination', *The Art Bulletin* 39, 2 (1957), 97–107.
Randall, L. 'The Snail in Gothic Marginal Warfare', *Speculum* 37, 3 (1961), 358–67.
Randall, L. *Images in the Margins of Gothic Manuscripts*. Berkeley: University of California Press, 1966.
Ravenhill, J. 'The Earliest Recorded Spectacle Makers in Late Medieval England: Immigration and Foreign Expertise'. *Notes and Queries*, 65, 1 (2018), 11–13.
RB 1980: The Rule of St. Benedict in English and Latin with Notes, (ed.) Timothy Fry, OSB. Liturgical Press, 1981.
Reynolds, C. 'Illuminators and the Painters' Guilds', in: *Illuminating the Renaissance: The Triumph of Flemish Manuscript Painting in Europe*, (eds) T. Kren and S. McKendrick. Los Angeles: J. Paul Getty Museum, 2003, 15–33.
Rhodes, M. 'A Pair of Late Medieval Spectacles from The Trig Lane Site'. *London Archaeologist*, 4, 1 (2008), 23–25.
Rogers, N. 'Patrons and Purchasers: Evidence for the Original Owners of Books of Hours Produced in the Low Countries for the English Market', in: *Als Ich Can: Liber Amicorum in Memory of Professor Dr. Maurits Smeyers*, (eds) B. Cardon, J. Van der Stock and D. Vanwijnsberghe. Leuven: Peeters, 2002, 1165–81.
Rosen, E. 'The Invention of Eyeglasses'. *Journal of the History of Medicine and Allied Sciences,* 11, 1 (1956), 13–46.
Rosenthal, J. *Spectacles and Other Vision Aids: A History and Guide to Collecting*. San Francisco: Norman Publishing, 1996.
Rosenthal, J. 'Wooden Eyeglass Cases'. *Doc Ophthalmol*, 94, (1997), 19–23.
Rudy, K. 'Dirty Books: Quantifying Patterns of Use in Medieval Manuscripts Using a Densitometer', *Journal of Historians of Netherlandish Art*, 2, no. 1–2 (Summer 2010).
Rudy, K. *Piety in Pieces. How Medieval Readers Customized their Manuscripts.* Cambridge: Open Book Publishers, 2016. (https://doi.org/10.11647/OBP.0094)

Rudy, K. *Rubrics, Images and Indulgences in Late Medieval Netherlandish Manuscripts*. Leiden: Brill, 2017.

Sandler, L. *Studies in Manuscript Illumination, 1200–1400*. London: Pindar Press, 2008.

Scheepsma, W. *Medieval Religious Women in the Low Countries: The Modern Devotion, the Canonesses of Windesheim, and their Writings*. Woodbridge: Boydell, 2004.

Schouteet, A. 'Inventaris van het archief van het voormalige gilde van de Librariërs en van de vereniging van schoolmeesters te Brugge', *Handelingen van het Genootschap voor geschiedenis*, 100 (1963), 228–69.

Sheingorn, P. '"The Wise Mother": The Image of St. Anne Teaching the Virgin Mary', *Gesta*, 32, no. 1 (1993), 69–80.

Smeyers, M. 'Een getijden- en gebedenboek van Jacoba van Beieren?', in: *Miscellanea Martin Wittek: album de codicologie et de paléographie offert à Martin Wittek*, (eds) A. Raman and E. Manning. Leuven: Peeters, 1993, 295–313.

Smeyers, M. *Flemish Miniatures from the 8th to the mid-16th Century*. Leuven: Davidsfonds, 1999.

Smith, K. *Art, Identity and Devotion in Fourteenth-Century England: Three Women and Their Books of Hours*. London: British Library, 2003.

Soden, W. von. *The Ancient Orient: An Introduction to the Study of the Ancient Near East*, (transl.) D. Schley, W. Eerdmans, 1994. Originally published as *Einführung in die Altorientalistik*. Wissenschaftliche Buchgesellschaft, 1985.

Stabel, P., *et al.* 'Production, Markets and Socio-economic Structures II: c.1320-c.1500', in: *Medieval Bruges, c.850–1550*, (eds) A. Brown and J. Dumolyn. Cambridge: Cambridge University Press, 2018, 196–267.

Stanton, A. *The Queen Mary Psalter: A Study of Affect and Audience*. Philadelphia: American Philosophical Society, 2001.

Stasolla, F. 'Dal tramonto all'alba: strumenti e tecniche di illuminazione nell'alto medioevo', *Il fuoco nell'alto Medioevo*, 857–88.

Stock, B. *The Implications of Literacy: Written Language and Models of Interpretation in the Eleventh to Thirteenth Centuries*. Princeton: Princeton University Press, 1983.

Taft, R. *The Liturgy of the Hours in East and West: The Origins of the Divine Office and Its Meaning for Today*. Liturgical Press, 1986.

The Primer... in Latin and English, 1599, (English Recusant Literature, 1558–1640, Vol. 262), (select. and ed.) D. Rogers. London: The Scolar Press, 1975.

Treharne, E. *Perceptions of Medieval Manuscripts: The Phenomenal Book*. Oxford: Oxford University Press, 2021.

Van Buuren, A. '"Want ander konsten sijn my te hoghe". De stadsschool in de Nederlanden in de late Middeleeuwen', in: *Scholing in de Middeleeuwen*, (eds) R. Stuip and C. Vellekoop. Hilversum: Verloren, 1995, 221–38.

Van de Velde, A. *Het ambacht der stoeldraaiers, zeef- en waslichtmakers te Brugge*, Brugge, 1909.

Van Engen, J. *Sisters and Brothers of the Common Life: The Devotio Moderna and the World of the Later Middle Ages*. Philadelphia: University of Pennsylvania Press, 2009.

Vandamme, L. 'Colard Mansion et le monde du livre à Bruges', in: *Le berceau du livre imprimé, autour des incunables*, (eds) P. Aquilon and T. Claerr. Turnhout: Brepols, 2010, 177–186.

Vandewalle, A. 'Het librariërsgilde te Brugge in zijn vroege periode', in: *Vlaamse kunst op perkament: handschriften en miniaturen te Brugge van de 12de tot de 16de eeuw*, (ed.) W. Le Loup. Brugge: Gruuthusemuseum, 1981, 39–43.

Vauchez, A. 'Feu et lumière dans le haut Moyen-Âge', *Il fuoco nell'alto Medioevo*, 1–20.

Veeckman, J. and C. Dumortier, 'La production de verres à Anvers: Les données historiques', in: *Majolica and Glass from Italy to Antwerp and Beyond: The Transfer of Technology in the 16th–17th Century*, (eds) J. Veeckman and S. Jennings. Antwerp: Stad Antwerpen, 2002.

Vernimme, N. *Het librariërsgilde te Brugge. Een sociaal culturele studie*. Unpublished PhD thesis, KU Leuven, 1995.

Vincent, C. *'Fiat lux'. Lumière et luminaires dans la vie religieuse du XIII*^e^ *au XVI*^e^ *siècle*, Paris: Cerf, 2004.

Weale, W.H.J. 'Documents inédits sur les enlumineurs de Bruges', *Le Beffroi. Arts, Héraldique, Archéologie*, 4 (1872–73), 253–329.

Wieck, R., *et al. Time Sanctified: The Book of Hours in Medieval Art and Life*. New York: Braziller, 1988.

Wieck, R. *Painted Prayers. The Book of Hours in Medieval and Renaissance Art*. New York: Braziller, 1997.

Wieck, R. 'The Primer of Claude de France and the Education of the Renaissance Child', in: *The Cambridge Illuminations: The Conference Papers*, (eds) S. Panayotova, J. Marrow and G. Henderson. London: Harvey Miller, 2007, 267–77.

Wijsman, H. *Handschriften voor het hertogdom. De mooiste verluchte manuscripten van Brabantse hertogen, edellieden, kloosterlingen en stedelingen*. Alphen aan de Maas: Veerhuis, 2006.

Willemsen, A. *Back to the Schoolyard: The Daily Practice of Medieval and Renaissance Education*. Turnhout: Brepols, 2008.

Wirth, J. 'Les singes dans les marges à drôleries des manuscrits gothiques', *Micrologus* 8 (2000), 429–44.

Wirth, J. 'Problèmes de méthode', in *Les marges à drôleries dans les manuscrits gothiques (1250-1350)*, (ed.) J. Wirth. Genève: Droz, 2008, 11–43.

Woodall, J. '*De wisselaer*: Quentin Matsys's "Man Weighing Gold Coins and His Wife", 1514', *Nederlands Kunsthistorisch Jaarboek*, 64 (2014), 38–75.

Zwart, C. *Religious Book Owners and Their Networks. Lay Religious Practices and Social Connectivity in the Urbanized Low Countries (c. 1370–c. 1550)*. Unpublished PhD thesis, University of Groningen, 2024.

Person Index

Object Index

Photo Credits

Unless otherwise stated, all photos of objects from the Public Library of Bruges, the City Archives of Bruges, and Musea Brugge were taken by the photographic services of these institutions.

The photos of manuscripts and hands were made by Dominique Provost for © Openbare Bibliotheek Brugge: figs 1, 6, 30, 40, 50, 65, 75, 83, 95

Paintings by Hans Memling: © Musea Brugge / Royal Institute for Cultural Heritage (KIK-IRPA, Brussels) / http://closertovaneyck.kikirpa.be: figs 55, 56, 58, 60, 85, 94, 96, 100, 101, 103

BnF © Bibliothèque nationale de France: fig. 45

British Museum © The Trustees of the British Museum: fig. 43

Grootseminarie Ten Duinen © Openbare Bibliotheek Brugge: figs 46, 81

Jean van Caloen Foundation: fig. 8

Louvre © 2014 GrandPalaisRmn (Louvre Museum) / Tony Querrec: fig. 41

Nicholas Herman: fig. 51

Oostende, Atlantikwall Raversyde: fig. 80

Raakvlak Brugge: figs 10, 91

Royal Library of Belgium © KBR: fig. 79

The Metropolitan Museum of Art © Photo Scala, Florence: figs 77, 94

The Morgan Library & Museum: fig. 26

About the Authors

Evelien Hauwaerts is the curator of manuscripts at the Public Library of Bruges. She has a PhD in Medieval Languages and Literature (University of Poitiers), a Master's degree in Romance Languages (KU Leuven), and two advanced Master's degrees in Medieval History (KU Leuven and University of Poitiers). She is affiliated with the Henri Pirenne Institute for Medieval Studies (Ghent University). Her research focuses on reading culture and reception history, with a particular emphasis on monastic manuscripts and those from the Burgundian Netherlands. She was the curator of the exhibition *Pride & Solace – Medieval Books of Hours and Their Readers* (Groeningemuseum, 2025).

Caroline Van Cauwenberge is a PhD candidate in Art History at Rutgers University (New Brunswick, NJ), specialising in late-medieval art from northern Europe, with a particular focus on illuminated manuscripts and hybrid books. She earned her MA in Art History from the Courtauld Institute of Art in London in 2017. In addition to her doctoral research, she is the digital content coordinator at The Leiden Collection, a major private collection of seventeenth-century Dutch paintings in New York.

Hanno Wijsman is scientific collaborator at the Institut de recherche et d'histoire des textes (IRHT-CNRS) in Paris, where he coordinates the *Bibale* Database (https://bibale.irht.cnrs.fr). He has a PhD from Leiden University (2003), which was published in 2010 by Brepols as *Luxury Bound. Illustrated Manuscript Production and Noble and Princely Book Ownership in the Burgundian Netherlands (1400–1550)*. His research and publications focus on illuminated manuscripts (especially Flemish ones), book culture, library history and the transmission and provenance of medieval manuscripts, particularly in later medieval France and the Low Countries.

Jeroen Deploige is a professor of medieval history at Ghent University and a member of the Royal Historical Commission of Belgium. He specialises in the cultural history and historical anthropology of the High and Late Middle Ages. His research focuses on processes of group formation in religious, noble and urban environments, and he has also published on religious history.

Nicholas Herman is the Lawrence J. Schoenberg Curator at the Schoenberg Institute for Manuscript Studies, University of Pennsylvania. His research explores manuscript illumination and its relationship with other media in fifteenth- and early sixteenth-century Europe. He received his doctorate from NYU's Institute of Fine Arts in 2014. He has held fellowships at the Université de Montreal, the Courtauld Institute of Art, the Metropolitan Museum of Art, and Harvard University's Villa I Tatti. From 2007 to 2010, he worked in the Medieval and Renaissance Manuscripts department at the Morgan Library & Museum in New York. His books include *Le livre enluminé, entre représentation et illusion* (2018), *Making the Renaissance Manuscript: Discoveries from Philadelphia Libraries* (2020) and, co-written with Anne-Marie Eze, *Bourdichon's Boston Hours* (2021).

Elena Lichmanova is a PhD student at Merton College, University of Oxford, where she studies the rise of Gothic marginal images in English psalters (c.1230–1270). Her research interests include late-medieval manuscript illumination, book aesthetics and artistic invention. She recently undertook a PhD placement at the British Library working on the exhibition *Medieval Women: In Their Own Words* and has published several highlight studies on medieval female writers and artists.

Larissa van Vianen is a book historian and librarian at the Noord-Hollands Archief in Haarlem. She obtained her Master's degree in Book History from the University of Amsterdam and was awarded the 2023 Tiele Thesis Prize for her research on Pierre Lyonet (1706–1789) and his entomological publications. In 2024, she received a grant from the Stichting Art, Books and Collections for her research at the Huygens Institute on an annotated author's copy of the botanist and physician Rembert Dodoens (1517–1585) in the Librije of Enkhuizen, used in preparation for the second edition of his *Stirpium historiae pemptades sex* (Antwerp, 1583).

Beatrice Del Bo is a professor of Medieval History at the University of Milan and a member of several prestigious journal committees. She directs *I cetrangoli. Nuovi studi di storia medievale* and co-directs the Saluzzo Medieval and Ancient Book Festival. Her research focuses on material culture, court societies, banking and gender history in the late Middle Ages. Recent publications include *Arsenico e altri veleni* (Il Mulino, 2024) and *L'età del lume* (Il Mulino, 2023), which won the *Italia Medievale 2024* prize.

Br. John Glasenapp OSB is a monk and Assistant Professor of Liturgical Music and Medieval Studies at Saint Meinrad Archabbey, as well as the founding director of the Institute for Sacred Music at Saint Meinrad Seminary and School of Theology. His work on Cistercian chant and Observant reform appeared in the volume *Women and Monastic Reform in the Medieval West, c. 1000–1500: Debating Identities, Creating Communities* published by Boydell & Brewer in 2023. His research has been supported by the Alliance-Council for European Studies and the US Fulbright Program for Belgium. Br. John is a Senior Editor for the CANTUS Index.

Acknowledgements

This book would not exist without the support of the following people: Sara Colson, Natacha Hofman, Stephanie Van den bosch and Gautier Platteau at Hannibal Books, Isabelle van Caloen, Benoit Kervyn de Volkaersbeke, Lieve Watteeuw, Hans Feys, Marthe Lemmens, Jef Cuypers, Jan Vangansbeke, Derek Scoins, Hilde Pauwels, Dominique Provost, Koen Calis, Katelijne Vercaemer, Anne Van Oosterwijk, Heidi Keereman, Emilie Bollens, Sarah Verplancke, Dominique Van Eynde, Marie Vandeghinste, An Desmedt, Jana Vastiau, Alexander Soetaert, Kristin Van Damme, Cam Young, Bert Verpoest, July Van Malderen, Liesbeth Maene, Inge Geysen, Hilde Van Parys, Collyn Verlinde, Els Depuydt, Elviera Velghe, Ludo Vandamme, Noël Geirnaert, Jan D'Hondt, Joyce Klein Koerkamp, Jan Huyghe, Steven Hauwaerts, Imelda Geeraerts, the Van Lancker family, Max Merlot, Kris Baert, Marcus de Schepper, Christopher de Hamel, Guido Hauwaerts, Lieve De Kesel and James Marrow.

With special thanks to Emma De Nil and Caroline Van Cauwenberge, two exceptionally intelligent, pragmatic and creative individuals.

This work is dedicated to all young bookworms, especially Maarten and Elias, who are at the beginning of what will hopefully become a lifelong love affair with books.

Colophon

Concept and content editing
Evelien Hauwaerts
Emma De Nil
Caroline Van Cauwenberge

Texts
Evelien Hauwaerts
Caroline Van Cauwenberge
Hanno Wijsman
Jeroen Deploige
Nicholas Herman
Elena Lichmanova
Larissa van Vianen
Beatrice Del Bo
John Glasenapp

Text editing
Derek Scoins

Translation cover text
Lisa de Haan-Page

Project management
Sara Colson
Stephanie Van den bosch

Image research
Emma De Nil

Lithography
Séverine Lacante
die Keure, Bruges

Design
Jef Cuypers

Art Direction
Natacha Hofman

Printing
die Keure, Bruges

Binding
Abbringh, Groningen

Publisher
Gautier Platteau

ISBN 978 94 6494 195 1
D/2025/11922/21
NUR 654

HANNIBAL
BOOKS

First printing: April 2025
Second printing: July 2025

COVER
Master of the Holy Blood, *Madonna with the Saints Catherine and Barbara* (detail), c.1509–c.1529. Bruges, Musea Brugge.

TITLE PAGE
Saint Barbara in prayer. Hans Memling, *Triptych of John the Baptist and John the Evangelist* (detail), 1479. Bruges, Musea Brugge.